U0153643

國家圖書館出版品預行編目(CIP)資料

檔案中的中國遠征軍 / 王文隆, 鄺智文, 應俊豪, 周惠民
著;周惠民主編. -- 初版. -- 臺北市：國立政治大學政大
出版社, 國立政治大學人文中心出版：國立政治大學發
行, 2022.01
　　面；　公分. -- （中國遠征軍系列叢書）
　　ISBN　978-626-95670-0-3（平裝）

1.CST: 第二次世界大戰　2.CST: 中日戰爭　3.CST: 戰史

628.58　　　　　　　　　　　　　　　111001219

中國遠征軍系列叢書

檔案中的中國遠征軍

主　　編｜周惠民
著　　者｜王文隆、鄺智文、應俊豪、周惠民

發 行 人　郭明政
發 行 所　國立政治大學
出 版 者　國立政治大學政大出版社
合作出版　國立政治大學人文中心
執行編輯　朱星芸、蕭淑慧、吳信慧
封面設計　蘇海、談明軒
地　　址　116011臺北市文山區指南路二段64號
電　　話　886-2-82375671
傳　　真　886-2-82375663
網　　址　http://nccupress.nccu.edu.tw

經　　銷　元照出版公司
地　　址　100007臺北市中正區館前路28號7樓
網　　址　http://www.angle.com.tw
電　　話　886-2-23756688
傳　　真　886-2-23318496
戶　　名　元照出版有限公司
郵撥帳號　19246890

法律顧問　黃旭田律師
電　　話　886-2-23913808

排　　版　弘道實業有限公司
印　　製　鴻柏印刷事業股份有限公司

初版一刷　2022年1月
定　　價　680元
I S B N　9786269567003
G P N　1011100181

政府出版品展售處
• 國家書店松江門市：104472臺北市松江路209號1樓
　電話：886-2-25180207
• 五南文化廣場臺中總店：400002臺中市中山路6號
　電話：886-4-22260330

目　次

叢書序 i

序 iii
周惠民

從國際法的視角看中國遠征軍 001
王文隆

　　一、國際法慣例的限制 001

　　二、中央軍入滇 003

　　三、中英美聯席軍事會議 005

　　四、中國遠征軍入緬及駐印 016

　　五、中國駐印軍的法律地位 018

　　六、跨境作戰的法律常識 020

　　七、結語 022

　　檔案原件 024

中英軍事合作與「中緬印戰區」（1940-1945）：
英國檔案中的觀察 117
鄺智文

　　一、前言：英國在亞洲與太平洋戰場的角色 117

　　二、英國國家檔案局藏中緬印戰區相關檔案簡介 119

　　三、從英國國家檔案局資料看英國與中緬印戰區 122

　　四、結語 216

　　檔案原件 218

從英國檔案探究中國遠征軍與中緬印補給路線 229

應俊豪

　　一、前言 229

　　二、關於中國遠征軍的籌組及其爭議 230

　　三、關於中緬印補給路線的早期規劃及其爭議 241

　　四、結語 248

　　檔案原件 250

德軍太平洋戰爭情報地圖分析 273

周惠民

　　一、前言 273

　　二、說明 276

　　三、系列地圖 277

叢書序

　　2017 年開始，國立政治大學人文中心便推動中國遠征軍的研究，執行「中國遠征軍與第二次世界大戰研究計畫」。近代以來，中國軍事技術發展滯後，抵禦外侮時經常力不從心。雖然在自強新政時期，李鴻章（1823-1901）等謀國之士不斷主張富國強兵，但積重難返。民國成立之後，政府也力求強化國力，聘用外國軍事顧問與採購武器，但多消耗於內鬥，面對強敵環伺，頗有力不從心之嘆。從 1931 年起，日本即不斷蠶食鯨吞，由東北而華北，半壁河山，都在日本陰影之下。1937 年，國人已忍無可忍，讓無可讓，盧溝橋事變與淞滬會戰向日本宣示抗戰的決心。

　　1941 年底，中國已經獨立抗戰四年，戰火燃燒中國，並無外援可恃，局勢相當緊急。就在此時，太平洋戰爭爆發，日軍揮兵東南亞，壓迫長期盤據當地的大英帝國與尼德蘭。大英帝國日漸窘迫，只得求助於中、美。政府乃決定派遣國軍，出境作戰，這也是近代以來，第一次有中國軍隊在異域與盟邦並肩作戰。幾場重要作戰中，遠征軍英勇表現，改變列強對中國軍隊的刻板印象，中國更成為第二次世界大戰後的五強之一，實至名歸。

　　政府遷臺之後，不斷整理出版第二次世界大戰的文獻檔案，提倡戰史研究，數十年來，成果非凡。但遠征軍的研究相對較為缺乏，原因不一而足：許多將領滯留大陸，評價不易；英、美等國檔案資料解讀困難。七十餘年後，幾番代謝，人事具成古今，而歷史勝跡，且待我輩復臨。

　　政治大學人文中心乃邀請學界俊彥，重新檢視遠征軍相關課題，並從太平洋戰爭乃至第二次世界大戰的角度，微觀與宏觀並進，檢討遠征軍的意義與影響。其微觀者如仁安羌作戰研究，將 1942 年 4 月 18、19 兩日仁安羌作戰的實況，重新梳理。宏觀者如從英、美、德等國的檔案，觀察中途島海戰以後，太平洋戰區與第二次世界大戰各地戰區的關聯。

「中國遠征軍與第二次世界大戰研究計畫」分年依不同進程及步驟實施。第一年，由專家組建團隊，邀請青年學子參與，定期討論，舉辦期初論文研討會，凝聚共識，形成課題，包括：「遠征軍組織與編制」、「兩次入緬作戰行動」、「遠征軍與國際關係」、「緬北反攻影像實錄」等。第二年的期中論文研討，再廣邀學者，博訪周諮。第三年結案研討會之後，才將論文彙整出版。參與研究計畫的青年學者經過長期討論薰陶，也分別從外交、宣傳等角度，發表論文，頗有可採。

另一方面，人文中心多方蒐整國內外檔案，包含國史館、國家發展委員會檔案管理局、中央研究院近代史研究所檔案館、中央研究院臺灣史研究所檔案館、中國國民黨文化傳播委員會黨史館、中國第二歷史檔案館、日本國立公文書館亞洲歷史資料中心（国立公文書館アジア歷史資料センター）、英國國家檔案局（The National Archives）、美國國家檔案暨文件署（National Archives and Records Administration）、德國聯邦檔案館（Das Bundesarchiv）等重要檔案館所藏文書。自二次世界大戰結束以來的專刊、論文、報章等也在蒐集之列。此外，許多遠征軍官兵及其家屬也紛紛將所藏相片、文件等提供人文中心以為研究之用，一併統整建置成數位聯合目錄，裨益檢索之便。

三年多以來，研究團隊經過數十次的學術討論、三次大型研討會，將研究成果出版成書，分享讀者。計有專書 9 冊、檔案史料彙編 2 冊，集結為「中國遠征軍系列叢書」。付梓之際，特說明本叢書緣起，並祈高明不吝賜教，以補罅漏。

序

周惠民
國立政治大學歷史學系教授兼人文中心主任

　　文獻是歷史研究的重要基礎，孔子已經有「夏禮，吾能言之，杞不足徵也；殷禮，吾能言之，宋不足徵也。文獻不足故也，足則吾能徵之矣」之嘆。孔子去夏商的時間久遠，當時文字傳播工具又不發達，有文獻不足的困擾也不足為奇。現代人歷史「不足徵」的困擾倒不是因為文獻不足，反是因記錄工具發達、音像、文字、實物皆有，但是各執一詞。正如漢代相國曹參盡召長老諸生，請教所以安集百姓時，齊故諸儒以百數，言人人殊，使得曹參「未知所定」。

　　現代歷史研究中，不同地區的學者因所見檔案不同，正是言人人殊，莫衷一是。開羅會議原為協調中、美、英三國在亞洲戰場作戰而召開的「軍事會議」，會中有關處理戰後世界的原則以公報形式發布，並再度於波茨坦會議中確認當時列強領袖的共識，強調《開羅宣言》之條件必將實施。但至今仍有許多學者對開羅會議的性質存有異議。皆因各執片面之詞，蠡測管窺，未能參考他國文獻，得其全豹。

　　國立政治大學人文中心蒐集各國史料，重新討論中國遠征軍在第二次世界大戰的意義與貢獻，並就各國檔案中的相關論述，互相參照。經館藏單位授權後，爰將使用的原始文獻整理出版兩本史料彙編：一為仁安羌作戰檔案，一為各國檔案中的遠征軍。雖說是「所窺者大，所見者小，所刺者巨，所中者少」，但總是朝著一個正確的方向前進。

　　政治大學人文中心蒐集各國文書檔案時，特別注意各國對同一事件的敘述角度。天津南開大學歷史學院副教授王文隆曾任中國國民黨文化傳播委員會黨史館主任，對現代史的檔案資料極為熟悉，他利用 1930 年代到 1945

年間的中國及日本的各種文書檔案，從國際法的角度，討論中國遠征軍的國際地位，實為「於主權範圍外延展中國之國家武裝」。說明遠征軍境外作戰為國家主權的實施，並非美國少數人以「傭兵」視之。更足以說明蔣中正（1887-1975）對遠征軍指揮權的堅持，並非個人意氣，而是堅持國家地位。誠如王文隆教授在文末所說：「過往對於中國遠征軍課題的討論，以及蔣中正與史迪威之間的爭執，多從國家利益、感情糾葛等視角，然如以國際法為切入點，或許能看到另一個暗藏法理爭議與不同見解的面向。」

香港浸會大學歷史系副教授鄺智文曾負笈英倫，他檢視英國國家檔案局所藏的中緬印戰區相關檔案，選出 26 件，討論英國對中緬印戰區的態度。從太平洋戰爭爆發前英國政府對中國的政策、戰爭初期中英合作及戰爭末期邱吉爾（Winston Churchill, 1874-1965）的各種言行，看出兩國對中緬印戰區的不同理解與反應。鄺教授認為邱吉爾對軍事困難不感興趣，僅關心英國如何繼續其在東南亞的影響力。鄺教授也指出：「英國與中國在中緬印戰區的合作，實為合而兩利，分則俱傷的關係。」若能從這一角度了解，可以更清楚解釋英國的各種政策。

國立臺灣海洋大學海洋文化研究所教授應俊豪也從英國檔案中整理英國政府的中國政策，尤其是討論中國計劃派遣遠征軍援助英國駐印部隊的時機與兩國對於滇緬印運補路線的攻防戰。英國政府為維護其在印度的優先利益，對蔣中正提議派遣遠征軍的計畫頗多疑慮，也拒絕中國的運補路線規劃。如果單從中國檔案文獻考察，不容易理解英國政府的態度。誠如應教授指出：「如果從英國軍方與外交部門的檔案，去研究中國遠征軍，倒是可以對其有更為清楚的了解。」鄺智文與應俊豪兩位教授的大作，正是檔案交互參照重要性的最好範例。

國立政治大學歷史學系教授周惠民則利用德國聯邦檔案館的軍事檔案館所藏「國防軍最高統帥部」（Oberkommando der Wehrmacht, OKW）檔案，從太平洋戰爭爆發後日軍兵力配置看中緬印戰區的發展。1939 年以後，希特勒（Adolf Hitler, 1889-1945）主導的德意志帝國已經在歐洲地區點燃戰火，原本與亞洲無涉，但因為三國共同防共協定之故，對亞洲戰事也頗關心。1938 年，希特勒下令撤出在華軍事顧問，1941 年底，中國又宣布對德斷交。但德國在中國境內及亞洲許多地區仍有各種外交與軍事人員，定時將亞洲戰事通報柏林國防部。從德國檔案中，可以看出各種戰事的發展與評析。作者特別挑選多幅德國軍方繪製的東亞戰爭形勢圖，可以從第三者的立場觀察亞洲戰事的發展。1942 年 6 月，日軍與美軍為爭奪太平洋中部的控制權，先後爆發中途島海戰（Battle of Midway）、聖克魯斯群島作戰（Battle of the Santa Cruz Islands）和瓜達康納爾島戰役（Guadalcanal campaign），迫使日軍增援，從而減輕了中緬印戰區的壓力。到 1943 年底的塔拉瓦作戰（Battle of Tarawa）之後，日本損失大量飛機與飛行員，戰力消耗甚鉅。在東南亞地區的空中優勢完全喪失。從德意志最高指揮部所藏的作戰地圖中，可以明顯看出日軍在太平洋兩岸勢力的消長對中緬印戰區的影響。

　　為利讀者圖文對照，僅擷取檔案局部；原件則另附於文末，以昭公信。為呈現檔案文字，將大幅圖檔以夾頁編排，以利檢視。英國國家檔案局原始數位檔空白頁亦予保留，未加刪減。地圖以彩色拉頁收錄，並祈儘量呈現檔案完整原貌，或可使讀者認識歷史檔案之用。

　　政治大學人文中心推動中國遠征軍相關史料、文獻徵集工作，並邀集國內現代史重要學者專家，利用新史料，以宏觀角度從新探討中國遠征軍在中國現代史上的意義。許多人雖對歷史有極大興趣，但未必理解史料的性質與的或如何利用文獻檔案以研究歷史。政治大學人文中心特別邀集學者，利用檔案說明史事，以推廣歷史，讓讀者更了解史料，或有助於歷史學習。

從國際法的視角看中國遠征軍

王文隆
南開大學歷史學院副教授

　　民國之後,中國軍隊出境作戰,僅得兩次。第一次是 1918 年由北洋政府偕同列強出兵干涉西伯利亞,第二次是抗日戰爭時期的中國遠征軍。1942 年因應日軍侵略,被派往英屬緬甸的中國遠征軍,並非民國之後中國第一次派兵出境,但卻是最為國人所熟知的一段經歷。

　　以往關於中國遠征軍的討論,大多圍繞著戰爭的經過,包括部隊派遣、戰場變化、指揮權爭奪、中國駐印軍與中國遠征軍的訓練等等,兼及中英美三方角力,以及相關的國際背景,然而關乎於中國遠征軍出境作戰的法律規制,與國際法相關的認識卻不是太多。本文從這個視角切入,討論中國遠征軍出擊的國際法問題,希望藉此將幾個爭議與爭點作出解釋。

一、國際法慣例的限制

　　國際公法分為平時與戰時兩種,適用的區隔在於宣戰與媾和。凡宣戰為戰時之始,媾和為戰爭之終,這是法律行為,通常並不符節於實際戰爭的始終。比如,1931 年九一八事變爆發,中日之間已經處於部分區域陷入戰爭的狀態,但由於雙方並未宣戰,因此國交仍舊持續,甚至中日關係還在 1935 年 5 月自公使級升格為大使級。

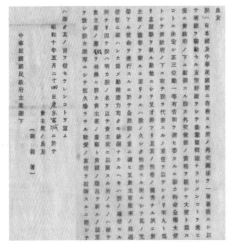

檔案1：日本天皇致中華民國國民政府主席函（1935年5月24日）
資料來源：〈日本駐華使節呈遞國書暨使館升格〉，《外交部》，國史館藏，數位典藏號：020-100400-0026。

　　即使1937年發生盧溝橋事變，中日兩國爆發全面戰爭的情況下也沒有宣戰，僅由中日兩國撤回使領，中斷實質往來，就法理上來說，並未絕交。待國民政府西遷重慶，才在珍珠港事變後，於1941年12月9日對日宣戰。

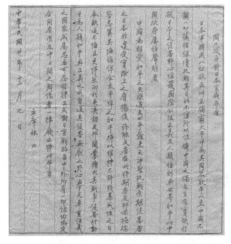

檔案2：「國民政府對日本宣戰布告」（1941年12月9日）
資料來源：〈革命文獻—抗戰方略：重要指示〉，《蔣中正總統文物》，國史館藏，數位典藏號：002-020300-00004-077。

　　中日間的武裝衝突，大多發生在中國境內，原本的情況相對單純，僅有日軍在中國境內違犯中國主權，以及戰罪問題。然而，隨著太平洋戰爭的爆發，日軍在東亞的活動跨入東南亞，改變了整個東亞的平衡，也使得戰局不再僅限於中國境內，促成中英美三國結為同盟，也讓在東亞保有充足兵力的中國，有了再度派遣國軍出境助戰的可能。

　　出境到他國宣示主權範圍內，進行作戰，依國際法相關規範，必須取得該主權宣示國的同意方可為之。這是基於國家主權受限於國界，而軍隊為國家力量之延伸，且僅聽命於其所屬國家之指揮使然，因此軍隊在境外得享治外法權。即使不在戰時，而在平時，未經許可，外國軍隊都不得駐在或經過他國領土。即便是中立國，也可強制要求入境之外國軍隊卸除武裝，一則以此維護其中立地位，避免其他參戰國錯認該國放棄中立立場，一則解除武裝後的軍隊才能保有治外法權。

檔案 3：現行國際法關於陸軍的規定
資料來源：甯協萬，《現行國際法》（北平：國立北平大學俄文法政學院，1931年），頁 145。

二、中央軍入滇

　　雲南為中南半島諸多河川的發源地，與法屬印度支那、英屬緬甸接壤，地理位置重要。位居盟軍物資自英屬緬甸的仰光（Rangoon）透過滇緬公路，以及自法屬印度支那的海防（Hải Phòng）透過滇越鐵路轉運的接點，可謂重慶大後方的命脈。然該地長年為滇系把持，中央的力量相對薄弱。

　　中央軍的第 5 軍及第 6 軍開往雲南的規劃，早於珍珠港事變之前，在 1941 年 7 月間便已著手進行，期間為了與控制雲南的地方實力派龍雲

（1884-1962）協商，才延至同年 11 月開拔。一開始的設定，僅在防禦雲南，避免日軍由法屬印度支那撲往昆明，襲擊大後方的後背。軍事委員會參謀團團長林蔚（1889-1955）在 1941 年 11 月間的日記中，所提到的滇防計畫，在第一階段著重的是雲南開遠及南盤江，第二階段著重於宜良、陸良、瀘西、霑益，幾處地方都在滇越間的要道上，對於滇西的防禦尚無規劃。

　　這樣的規劃著眼於境內防禦，沒有出境作戰的問題，著重的方向也在雲南的東部。即使如第 6 軍第 93 師派往雲南最南端的西雙版納，也是基於該地和法屬印度支那接壤的緣故，所側重的是法屬印度支那。

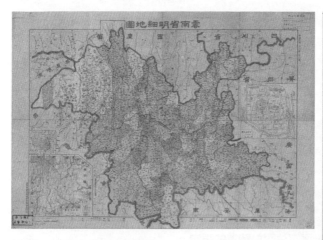

檔案 4：《雲南省明細地圖》
資料來源：亞新地學社，《雲南省明細地圖》（武昌：亞新地學社，1939 年）。

檔案 5：林蔚抗戰日記（1941 年 11 月 18 日）
資料來源：〈林蔚文抗戰日記節錄〉，《陳誠副總統文物》，國史館藏，數位典藏號：008-010701-00001-011。

　　法國在 1940 年 6 月中旬巴黎淪陷後，另建維琪政府與納粹德國合作，成為軸心陣營的一員，法屬印度支那也歸於維琪法國管治。在此局面之下，法屬印度支那總督德古（Jean Decoux, 1884-1963）為了謀求當地不被日軍直接占領，乃與日本於 1940 年 9 月 22 日簽署協議，同意日軍為配合桂南會戰的進行，能夠利用法屬印度支那治下的三處空軍基地（富壽〔Phú Thọ〕、嘉林〔Gia Lâm〕、老街〔Lào Cai〕），得以自海防登岸，並且准許為數 6 千以下的日本軍隊過境。日軍進駐法屬印度支那，讓該地成為日軍可能突破中國後方的缺口，使得滇東暴露於敵軍威脅之下。這正是林蔚規劃滇東防禦的背景。

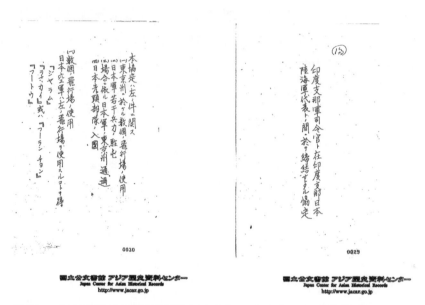

檔案 6：法屬印度支那總督與駐印度支那日本陸海軍代表簽署之協議（1940 年 9 月 22 日）

資料來源：「印度支那軍司令官と在印度支那日本陸海軍代表との間に於て締結されたる協定」（1940 年 9 月 22 日），〈昭和 15・6 ～ 16・6　仏印進駐関係記録（1）〉，《海軍一般史料》，防衛省防衛研究所藏，JACAR（アジア歴史資料センター），Ref. C14121105400。

　　日軍進駐法屬印度支那，是進到另一個國家所主張的主權範圍，因此必得先經過合法的國際法程序，在雙邊事先溝通與協商完備後，才能進行。與此相類，中國遠征軍出國境，也必須處理相關的程序。

三、中英美聯席軍事會議

　　太平洋戰爭爆發後，日本同時策動數個戰線，分別進擊英屬香港、美屬菲律賓與英屬新加坡。英國在遠東的兵力不敷，當香港與新加坡陷於困局時，急尋其他盟國協助防禦英屬緬甸及印度。自歐美派兵過來，或許鞭長莫及，而距離最近的援兵，就屬重慶，從而開啟了中、英、美三方在英屬緬甸協同作戰的可能。

　　蔣中正（1887-1975）早就希望重慶國民政府能在遠東戰局中扮演一個比較重要的角色，只是在太平洋戰爭前，這個期待未能實現。直到太平洋戰爭爆發，蔣中正有了機會，先於 1941 年 12 月 14 日致電美國總統羅斯福（Franklin D. Roosevelt, 1882-1945），盼由美國出面組織在東亞的軍事聯繫合作機構，藉著推促美國領銜的機會參加，以加重重慶當局在盟軍中的分量。然而羅斯福似乎沒有出面的打算，便致電美國駐華軍事代表團團長馬格魯德（John L. Magruder, 1887-1958）代轉其意，要蔣中正於 12 月 17 日前自行籌開，並建議找來英、美、蘇、荷四國共同參加。羅斯福為使會議能順利進行，發給馬格魯德的電文中，順便指派了勃蘭德（George H. Brett, 1886-1963）將軍為正式代表，另分電英、蘇，請彼等在新加坡與莫斯科召開同樣會議。羅斯福在電文中還提到，「召集聯合軍事會議，交換情報，並討論在東亞戰區最有效之陸海軍行動，以擊敗日本及其同盟國。」這給了蔣中正一個廣闊的想像空間與期待。

檔案 7：「羅斯福電蔣中正建議在重慶召集聯合軍事會議交換情報」（1941 年 12 月 16 日）

資料來源：〈革命文獻─同盟國聯合作戰：重要協商（一）〉，《蔣中正總統文物》，國史館藏，數位典藏號：002-020300-00016-016。

　　要在重慶、新加坡與莫斯科三地召開軍事聯繫會議的規劃，就使得在重慶的會議不那麼突兀，蔣中正依羅斯福所訂時間，在 12 月 17 日晚上以晚宴的形式集會。他的心急，或許能從英、蘇兩國都還沒指派代表，便要約時間碰面見得。而英、蘇兩國在重慶的軍事代表團此時同意派員出席，或也是看在羅斯福拍電的面子上應允的。惟因英、蘇出席的代表並未獲得該政府的授權，因此著急的蔣中正只能先開一場非正式的談話會。

　　蔣中正向英、美、蘇等軍事代表團發表初步構想的綱領，這包括了四個要項：

（一）以軍事代表會議或參謀團為名，設立聯合作戰機構

（二）在重慶集會

（三）由美國總代表主持

（四）討論的軍事任務

　　這部分的內容繁多，主要是國軍與英、美、蘇、荷在中國境外之作戰、運輸與溝通，另也涉及租借法案物資的調撥、跨境空運的規劃，以及對東南亞之軸心國陣營成員（法屬印度支那、泰國）之因應。

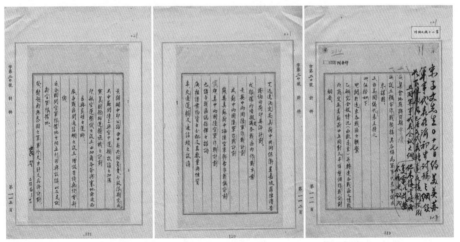

檔案 8：「蔣中正召集美英蘇軍事代表等就召集聯合軍事會議交換意見」（1941 年 12 月 17 日）

資料來源：〈革命文獻—同盟國聯合作戰：重要協商（一）〉，《蔣中正總統文物》，國史館藏，數位典藏號：002-020300-00016-021。

很顯然地，蔣中正所盼望的，不僅是要成為英美盟國在亞洲緊密的夥伴，也希望更深入地參與東亞戰爭，除了參酌作戰規劃，在中印公路的鋪設、租借法案物資的分配都能夠涉足。獲取資源之餘，也寄望有所「貢獻」。

對蔣中正來說，蘇聯代表崔闊夫的出席，或許滿足了他另一個深沉的期待。自中日全面戰爭爆發後，蔣中正一直盼望日蘇衝突發生。實力遠遠強於中國的蘇聯，如能投入對日作戰，不僅能壓迫日方，也能使中國能從中日衝突的泥淖中掙脫。然而，蘇聯因為《日蘇互不侵犯條約》的限制，加上不願意造成兩面作戰的態勢，即使日蘇在滿蒙邊界上經常爆發衝突，但實際上沒有和日本全面戰爭的打算。英國則並不信任重慶當局和蔣中正，這不僅表現在情報共享的疑慮上，對於重慶方面能提供怎樣的支持，也抱持懷疑態度，甚至認為蔣中正只是要將其他盟國拖下水，並在戰後強占一個角色，參與國際社會。這嚴重影響到英國對於重慶當局參與東亞戰局的支持，也不樂見蔣中正所提的大計畫可以如願以償。

蔣中正的企圖或許很外顯，他的興奮也藏不住。1941年12月20日的日記中寫道，除了軍事之外，關於政治與經濟問題，也希望使各國在尊重中國主權及領土完整的前提下，一併解決不平等條約，從列強手中，取回治外法權、租借地與租界等特權。他的期許承載著中國人自鴉片戰爭以來，希冀擺脫三等國家命運擺布的盼望，也肩負起國父遺言中，要同志們廢除不平等條約的囑託。彷彿中日戰爭擴大為世界大戰之後，不僅中國長久以來所引頸期盼的平等地位終於有了實現的一天，甚至還能一舉成為舉足輕重的東亞強國，在歷史定位上，蔣中正也必將永載史冊。

十二月二十日　星期六　氣候晴

雪恥　本黨之不振，實由於一般老者事事把持而不放，事事包攬而不為，所以不能有絲毫進步與起色，可痛之至。應澈底諷刺，使若輩覺悟也。

預定　一、各國同盟條約必須附帶政治與經濟條件在內　甲、對英要求其承認西藏、九龍為中國領土之一部。乙、對俄要求其外蒙、新疆為中國領土之一部。丙、東四省、旅大、南滿,要求各國承認為中國領土之一部。丁、凡各租借地及治外法權與各種特權及東交民港等,皆須一律交還中國與取消一切不平等條約。二、對印度軍總司令魏非爾〔魏菲爾〕及美國空軍勃來特〔勃蘭德〕談話稿之準備。三、先開三國軍事會議。四、全會之要務決定。

檔案9:「蔣中正日記」,1941年12月20日,史丹福大學胡佛研究所藏。[1]

即使檯面下各國立場迥異,甚至看似同床異夢,但在日本這一大敵當前的局面下,也不能不維持表面上的協作關係。然而,跨境合作,要使國軍踏入他國宣示主權範圍內,就必須先嘗試取得該主權所屬國的同意,尤其需要英、美兩國的支持,這不是會議開完就能處理的問題。這是國際法原則運作下,首要解決的前提。

面對日軍的凌厲攻勢,英國指派駐印英軍司令魏菲爾(Archibald P. Wavell, 1883-1950)兼管緬甸防務,也因此,當羅斯福提請英國派員參加在重慶召開的軍事聯席會議時,魏菲爾便被英國受任為代表。就在魏菲爾抵達重慶不久,蔣中正急切地於1941年12月22日晚上9點,召來魏菲爾與勃蘭德,要商議隔天正式會議的議題。

蔣中正期盼重慶當局能在戰局中扮演重要角色的試探,能在他向魏菲爾與勃蘭德提及:希望討論盟軍全盤戰略綱要,也建議在美國首都華盛頓設置軍事聯繫的永久中心想見。然而,魏菲爾與勃蘭德給了蔣中正軟釘子,直說他們層級不夠,沒能對此建議加以回應。而蔣中正期與英美共同擬定東亞戰略的盼望,也在魏菲爾以時間倉促,不及策劃的託辭中落空。魏菲爾甚至挑

1　「蔣中正日記」(Chiang Kai-shek diaries, 1917-1972)暫存於美國史丹福大學胡佛研究所圖書檔案館(Hoover Institution Library and Archives, Stanford University),檔案館將日記原件拍成微卷,再以微卷複印為紙本,自2006年起開放供研究者到館參閱、抄錄,數位檔未上線。因此文後檔案原件,未包含「蔣中正日記」。

（委座）予擬先提重要問題數項備作明晨初步談話之資料第一討論反侵略集團之戰畧綱要第二討論子所提組織聯軍之資料切聯絡之永久中心機構其地點應為華盛頓令卲吉爾首相已扰早盛頓即行討論此項問題此外中英中美軍事合作問題中美陸空軍合作問題以及在南太平洋中美軍事合作問題當堅持商定願衛佛爾將軍之物蘭德將軍表高見（衛）本人以為我等悉尚未解決第一點之能力甚為高見各國政府當局如能知彼知己者實由政府決定之開此項談列已念在遠行中目前本人所最関切者為保衛緬甸問題解決如何興青國及銷屋部隊緊切合作集中作戰器材及空軍力量以完成此舉事為本之職責（勢）本人同意衛佛爾將軍之言決定戰畧綱要似非沙太廣非此間所能討論

檔案 10：「蔣中正與魏菲爾談話紀錄：磋商軍事合作問題」（1941 年 12 月 22 日）

資料來源：〈革命文獻—同盟國聯合作戰：重要協商（一）〉，《蔣中正總統文物》，國史館藏，數位典藏號：002-020300-00016-027。

明了說，他所關切為防衛緬甸的事情，期許國軍支援陸軍與空軍，共同完成此項任務，不願多說其他。雖說防禦緬甸直接關乎滇緬公路輸運的安全，然而蔣中正也明白，租借物資抵華後，撥付給國軍的可說是少之又少，大部分其實都交付給美國人了，維持這條通路，或許更重要的是象徵意義。

　　顯然地，蔣中正希望扮演的角色並不僅止於協助盟軍防衛緬甸、維持滇緬公路運輸的安全，這跟他在 17 日所提的大計畫、大戰略落差太大。因而他繼續問道泰國在英國所劃防區歸屬，以及中印軍是否能合擊泰國，進一步

（附註衛佛爾將軍在其言談中透露其此行目的有三（一）來渝要求我國允予之協助（二）獲取我國儲存在仰先租借法案器材之一部份（三）要求委座准許計畫諸德部下美國志願空軍留緬參加保衛緬甸作戰彼並未言及奉英國政府命令代表出席

檔案 11：「蔣中正與魏菲爾談話紀錄：磋商軍事合作問題」（1941 年 12 月 22 日）

資料來源：〈革命文獻—同盟國聯合作戰：重要協商（一）〉，《蔣中正總統文物》，國史館藏，數位典藏號：002-020300-00016-027。

攻擊泰境日軍。眼見蔣中正對於合擊泰國的殷切，勃蘭德出來打了圓場，他以地緣關係為慮，告訴蔣中正經緬攻泰為佳，欲說服蔣中正同意先分撥軍力，協助英國守住緬甸。魏菲爾此行想達成的目的有三：（一）要求中國兵力的協助；（二）獲取部分儲存於緬甸的中國租借法案物資；（三）爭取美國志願空軍駐守緬甸。這三點都與防衛緬甸有關，而且都需要挪用中國戰場上有限的資源。

　　蔣中正對於這次的會談，有些失望。一則蔣中正期待的是一個中國能參與大局的契機，但英國只在乎緬甸；二則美國竟然也跟著附和英國，沒有給予蔣中正預期中的支持。這讓蔣中正在當晚日記中，狠狠把魏菲爾與勃蘭德罵了一頓，說勃蘭德之於魏菲爾，猶如雞之於伏狼，罵了他倆心理怪異，還罵了他倆形體怪異，可見心中相當不快。不僅如此，蔣中正還把所有英國人、美國人都罵了一頓，說美國人膚淺、英國人陰沉，美國處處表現落在英國之後，還要接受英國領導不可，指的大概就是勃蘭德出來打圓場，附和魏菲爾只守緬甸的觀點。

> 　　注意　一、印度軍英總司令魏非爾〔魏菲爾〕與美國軍事總代表勃蘭達〔勃蘭德〕二人，昨夜初次來見，甚感覺美國人之浮淺與英國人之陰沉，所以美國人處處表現其落在英國之後，而非事事受英領導不可。觀乎勃之於魏，如雞之伏狼，其形狀與心理，殊可怪也，甚矣。英人外交手段之毒竦〔辣〕與靈敏，亦可佩也。

檔案 12：「蔣中正日記」，1941 年 12 月 22 日，史丹福大學胡佛研究所藏。

　　前一晚談得不快，可以想見 23 日當天的會議大概也沒甚麼好期待的。

　　經過了一晚的休息，23 日上午 9 時，由軍事委員會參謀總長何應欽（1890-1987）代表中方，與魏菲爾與勃蘭德舉行會前會。會中僅就國軍協防緬甸、調撥租借物資，以及美國志願空軍進入緬甸等項做討論，可說是由英方完全主導了該次會議。

檔案 13：「蔣中正召集美英澳等國代表舉行第一次聯席軍事會議」（1941 年 12 月 23 日）

資料來源：〈革命文獻—同盟國聯合作戰：重要協商（一）〉,《蔣中正總統文物》,國史館藏,數位典藏號：002-020300-00016-029。

　　當天下午 4 時召開的正式會議，中、英、美、澳四方參與，地點在蔣委員長官舍，由蔣中正主持。從魏菲爾做的匯報看來，英國已然徵得美國同意，撥派一支在中國駐紮的空軍 P-40 前往緬甸助拳，除了在緬租借物資的徵用與調撥外，還點名希望入滇的國軍第 93 師與第 49 師開入緬甸，若國軍開入緬甸的增援部隊能增加更好。這般匯報，似乎沒有給予蔣中正商量的餘地，蔣中正便想起了羅斯福曾在 16 日電報中提過的：「召集聯合軍事會議，交換情報，並討論在東亞戰區最有效之陸海軍行動，以擊敗日本及其同盟國。」又再提了成立盟軍永久聯絡機構以及擘劃太平洋整體戰略的事情。在蔣中正的構想中，由華盛頓成立總會，各地成立分會，而重慶所在是東亞分會之所在，並嘗要求隨扈將他與羅斯福的往來電文內容讀出，希冀藉著羅斯福之口，反制全場，進而申明緬甸戰場僅為全般戰局的一部分。然而，幾乎掌握全場的魏菲爾，不僅取得中美兩方支援緬甸的許諾，對於蔣中正所盼，成立永久聯絡機構的提議也未有直接回應，將整個討論侷限在英屬緬甸一處，甚至不包括泰國、印度。沒有了長期的戰略規劃，有的僅是一個「滾動式」的隨機調整。

十二月二十三日　星期二　氣候陰

　　雪恥　上午到全會主席，行閉會禮，發表各院部更調人員，外交郭泰祺部長免職，是為生平用人不可操切之一大教訓，此人真是小人之尤者，永不能有改變氣質之望，於此免職之令，實為余生平最自得安心之一事。正午宴全會委員。下午對全會委員深切訓誡，黨務與革命之前途可危也。四時召集英、美軍事代表第一次會議，中、英、美三國之軍事代表會議至此乃正式成立，會議至下午七時餘休息。晚餐後繼續開會，至深夜丑時方畢。英人之貪詐自私、毫無協同作戰之誠意、對我國之輕視侮蔑，尤為可痛，余不得已，乃正色厲聲向之責問，彼等方轉變態度，勉強決議休會，從此更可知英人之陰狠奸猾，不禁為亞洲前途危也。

檔案 14：「蔣中正日記」，1941 年 12 月 23 日，史丹福大學胡佛研究所藏。

　　最終，做成的遠東聯合軍事行動準則六條當中，除了關乎作戰跟緬甸的事項之外，僅在永久聯繫機構一點得到一個「早日實現」的空言。雖說這與蔣中正一開始對於羅斯福來電的解讀不同，也與他自身期待有相當距離的落差，但在中國長年遭到不平等待遇情狀下來看，已經有所突破，堪稱中國外交史上的大事了。

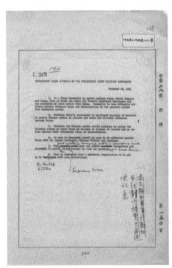

檔案 15：「蔣中正召集美英澳等國代表舉行第一次聯席軍事會議」（1941 年 12 月 23 日）
資料來源：〈革命文獻—同盟國聯合作戰：重要協商（一）〉，《蔣中正總統文物》，國史館藏，數位典藏號：002-020300-00016-029。

　　這樣的結果對蔣中正以及重慶當局來說都不盡滿意，但如果套上國際法的基本概念，整個畫面就會有不同的解讀。緬甸是英國殖民地，英國在緬甸具有主權，對英國來說，她能夠許諾在英屬緬甸境內的事情，出了英國主權範圍之外，其實她也無能為力。關於蔣中正寄望中英合擊泰國，進而弭平泰境日軍的提議，會遭到英美忽視，或許並非英美無視蔣中正的建議，而是基於當時國際關係的整體背景。首先，此時中泰之間並沒有外交關係，國軍出兵襲擊泰國，沒有破壞兩國關係的問題，但英、美與泰國的關係與中泰關係不同，雖說日本以武力壓迫泰國參加日泰同盟，但英泰、美泰之間的外交關係尚未中斷，況且英泰之間才在 1940 年 6 月簽署了《英泰互不侵犯條約》。基於外交關係依舊維持，且有互不侵犯條約許諾的外在環境下，英國自無答應蔣中正所提，要由國軍與英軍分自雲南與印度出兵攻擊泰國的可能，而美國也沒有參與這場攪和的道理。荷蘭與蘇聯沒有參加正式會談的理由，從國際法的角度來看也能理解。日軍進犯荷屬東印度群島的時間是 1942 年 1 月 11 日，在此之前荷日關係依舊維持，而同樣地，蘇聯與日本也簽署了互不侵犯條約，這都使得蘇聯與荷蘭沒有立場參加在重慶召開的軍事聯絡會議。

　　一、對倭與對德、意〔義〕軸心各國同時宣戰，在重慶成立中
　　　　英美軍事委員會，是為我國外交史之一大事，惜俄國未能如
　　　　期參加，不無缺憾。而英、俄侮華之傳統政策始終不變，亦
　　　　無覺悟之象，俄態更為可痛，美則較優，然其下級者未能以
　　　　英、俄為戒，殊可惜耳。然而人不自立而欲人之不侮者，難
　　　　矣，國亦如之。要在反求諸身，只要求其在我，則於人無與
　　　　也。

檔案 16：「蔣中正日記」，1941 年 12 月反省錄，史丹福大學胡佛研究所藏。

　　一、外交。本年國際變化甚大，故我外交勝利亦達空前之境。其
　　　　一為十一月二十六日對美之嚴正表示，使美、倭妥協不成，
　　　　終至倭寇對美、英不得不冒險進攻，使其對英、美傳統妥協

政策根本，為之粉碎無遺；其次為德國攻俄，而使俄國不能坐大，此對於我立國成敗之前途為尤大也。卒至英、美在重慶成立中、美、英、荷之軍事會議。兩年以來受盡俄國對我之侮辱，史大林〔史達林〕對我之函電概置不覆；而英國魏佛爾〔魏菲爾〕在會議席上，又明言為搶奪唐人襪子之在緬甸者，其汙衊可謂異甚。而美國政府對我態度較優，然而其一般中級人員輕侮華人之觀念，仍不能根本改變。惟自本年二月以來，每於內政、外交、軍事、經濟危急之際，幸有美國不斷的援助之表示，而其租借法案適用於中國，派軍事代表來華合作，英、美、荷、澳在太平洋上之聯防會議，以及其菲列濱〔菲律賓〕、關島等各地之設防，皆對敵倭施以壓力，使敵不能專心對華，是其精神上之作用發生極大之影響，然而實際上對我物資之接濟則無幾，若與其援英之數相比，實不及百分之一耳。八月間，羅〔斯福〕、邱〔吉爾〕會議宣言實與軸心侵暑者一大打擊，而予我國民精神上之奮興振作亦非尠也。至於上海、天津租界被敵佔踞，香港、菲列濱失陷，以同盟國形勢而論，當有不利，然而於我國民之心理與民族之精神，實開創歷史未有之奇觀，至少將一般賣〔買〕辦富商、官僚政客、叛逆盜匪、托庇於外國勢力保護之下，以為安全之觀念，與百年來依賴外國，重外輕內之奴隸惡劣根性，可說一掃而光，滌蕩無餘。此實為我總理革命主義五十年來惟一之政策，而今日完全實現矣，能不自勉自強，期其澈底完成乎。

檔案 17：「蔣中正日記」，1941 年反省錄，史丹福大學胡佛研究所藏。

在此情狀之下，蔣中正當然只能失望。更糟糕的是，國軍出境協防緬甸，連一張白紙黑字的協議都沒有，能憑藉的只是遠東聯合軍事行動準則六條的結論。

四、中國遠征軍入緬及駐印

　　蔣中正回復羅斯福，同意接任中國戰區最高統帥的時間是 1942 年 1 月 2 日，然而必須留意這個中國戰區的範圍，僅包括中國本土、法屬印度支那及泰國。除了中國本土之外，其他兩處不僅沒有國軍進駐，也沒有盟軍進駐。值得注意的是，英屬緬甸、馬來亞、美屬菲律賓、荷屬印尼都不在中國戰區的範圍之中。這是盟軍的劃分法，美軍所劃的中緬印戰區（China Burma India Theater, CBI），主要是為了管轄這個區域內的美軍，其實跟盟軍、國軍都無關。對英國來說，印緬是同一戰區。就此來看，國軍出境緬甸協助盟軍作戰，不僅是跨越國界，也是跨越盟軍劃給蔣中正的責任範圍。

　　依據國際法之原則，軍隊跨境，無論目的是過路或是作戰，都必須取得該主權國之同意。這一點，在 1941 年 12 月 23 日的會議中，基本已經有了共識，英國同意國軍與美軍赴緬作戰，接著要處理的是指揮權的問題。中國軍隊出境，仍應由中國政府指揮，而在重慶當局控制下的國軍，就得由軍事委員會委員長下指示，這也就是第一次遠征軍先由衛立煌（1897-1960），後由羅卓英（1896-1961）擔任司令長官，第二次遠征軍由陳誠（1898-1965）

檔案 18：「賀耀組電蔣中正馬歇爾轉史汀生稱與宋子文商得諒解以史迪威將軍任中國戰區參謀長將儘速來華報到已函復表示歡迎」（1942 年 2 月 13 日）

資料來源：〈遠征入緬（一）〉，《蔣中正總統文物》，國史館藏，數位典藏號：002-090105-00006-035。

接任的原因。但這僅解決了國軍必得由國軍將領指揮的問題，但沒能解決國軍跨境後，作為盟軍之一分子的中國遠征軍，如何與其他盟軍配合的問題。

這時，派往重慶就任中國戰區參謀長的史迪威（Joseph W. Stilwell, 1883-1946），就成了能加以運用的特殊身分與關鍵人物。史迪威所受的命令，一方面是作為中國戰區參謀長，輔佐最高統帥蔣中正，管理所有美國援華物資的分配，一方面作為指揮中國戰區內之美軍的最高指揮官，且為美軍中緬印戰區之最高指揮官。因而，將中國遠征軍調撥為史迪威指揮之部隊，能合於該支部隊隸屬中緬印戰區，且仍於中國戰區參謀長指揮之名義，順利越境作戰，突破中國戰區不及於英屬緬甸，而國軍卻又必須跨出中國戰區進入英屬緬甸作戰的困境。因而在 1942 年 3 月間，入緬的第 5 軍、第 6 軍在蔣中正的同意之下，全歸史迪威指揮。而史迪威也向蔣中正問道，如英國駐印總司令魏菲爾要求調度入緬國軍時應如何辦理，蔣中正明白地要求史迪威拒絕魏菲爾的命令。這一方面是基於國軍只能由中國戰區之官長調度，另一方面也基於英軍並非中國遠征軍之上級單位所致。因而，國軍與英軍之間的聯繫，仍是透過居間的聯絡官進行協同作戰，而沒有一個統整指揮的指揮部存在。

檔案 19：「蔣中正與史迪威談話紀錄：第五第六軍歸史指揮緬甸中英軍隊統一指揮」（1942 年 3 月 11 日）
資料來源：〈革命文獻—同盟國聯合作戰：遠征軍入緬（一）〉，《蔣中正總統文物》，國史館藏，數位典藏號：002-020300-00019-016。

　　蔣中正與史迪威會爆發衝突，大概也是緣於對於部隊指揮權跟區域劃分的認知不同。對蔣中正來說，入緬的中國遠征軍都是國軍，自當聽從他這個中國戰區最高統帥的指示，何況史迪威是中國戰區參謀長，是一個本該聽命於蔣中正的角色，卻在出境之後成了遠颺的風箏。而在史迪威在緬作戰不利時，蔣中正為了挽救危亡，直接指揮入緬部隊，這對蔣中正來說沒有甚麼不妥。然而，蔣中正可能沒有意識到，英屬緬甸並不在中國戰區範圍之內，當初為了指揮的便利，已經將指揮權託交美軍中緬印戰場指揮官史迪威。對史迪威來說，蔣中正作為中國戰區最高統帥，無權越區指揮，他自認自己才是指揮官，也因此無視許多蔣中正發出的作戰指示。

五、中國駐印軍的法律地位

　　第一次遠征軍的失敗，讓史迪威退往印度，也迫使入緬國軍後撤，一部分冒險穿越北方的野人山（Kachin Hills），一部分撤入英屬印度境內。撤入英屬印度的國軍，一度被要求必須繳械，這是基於中英美之間的協防區域，僅言定限縮於英屬緬甸的關係，在未經知會與同意的情況下，他國部隊不得任意越界。進入了英屬印度的國軍，就是越界的部隊，依照國際法的慣例，

檔案 20：「蔣中正電宋子文駐印軍新編二十二師第三十九師歸史迪威羅卓英整訓」（1942 年 7 月 7 日）

資料來源：〈革命文獻—同盟國聯合作戰：遠征軍入緬（二）〉，《蔣中正總統文物》，國史館藏，數位典藏號：002-020300-00020-072。

必須繳械以候差遣。然而在史迪威的調解下，使英國於 1942 年 10 月同意這批國軍，留在印度的蘭伽（Ramgarh）整訓。整訓期間，史迪威為指揮官，羅卓英則為副指揮官。另在 1942 年 10 月 26 日成立中國駐印軍總司令部，由史迪威任總指揮，柏德諾（Haydon L. Boatner, 1900-1977）為參謀長。

　　1942 年 10 月 26 日，就在中國駐印軍總司令部成立當日，為了使英印當局得以管理外國駐印軍牽涉英人及印人之民刑案件，英印政府立法部門特別頒布了一份名為〈1942 年第 LXI 號條例：為規定關於同盟國及外國軍隊在印軍隊辦法事〉（Ordinance No. LVI of 1942: An Ordinance to make certain provisions respecting the armed forces in British India of foreign Powers allied with His Majesty, and of certain foreign Authorities）的文件。[2] 這份文件雖然名義上得管理所有外國軍隊，且所有民刑案件一文件所示概交印度法庭管轄，然當時在印度的外國軍隊實際上僅有中美兩國，而美國因與英國曾於 1942 年 7 月簽署法律協議，議定英美互予所屬軍隊於彼國境內之治外法權，因而該份文件實際上僅對國軍適用。這樣的規範在落實上頗多困難，英印方面便透過口頭表示，中國法律得在中國軍營中適用，如牽涉中印之糾紛，則分別帶開，由中印雙方分別辦理後，將辦理結果相互知照，然這些都是口說無憑。

　　外交部也深知國際公法的相關規範，認為各國慣例多能接受因公外派之軍隊擁有治外法權，受其本國司令官或軍事法庭管轄，雖透過駐英大使館及英國駐華大使居間，但都沒有結果。之所以英印當局不願給予國軍等同美軍在英之地位，實源於在印華人身分的不確定，這有兩個問題。第一，有一些在阿薩密省犯罪的華人被捕後、起訴前，聲稱為請有長假之軍籍人士，或是透過管道加入軍籍，希望遞解中國駐印軍處置，想要規避英印法庭的審理。

2　惟查英屬印度出版的法律集，該條文編號為 LVI，中文資料（參見檔案 21）顯然抄錄錯誤，詳見：The Manager of Publication, *A Collection of the Acts of the Central Legislature Governor General for the Year, 1942* (New Delhi: The Manager, Government of India Press, 1943), pp. 247-252.

第二，有中國駐印軍的逃兵在印境犯罪，牽涉當地民刑事案件，然因逃兵掩飾身分，產生不知該如何移送的問題。

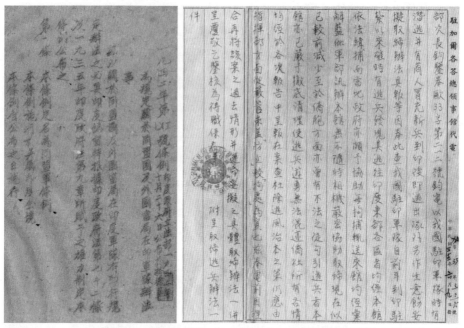

檔案 21：1942 年第 LXI 號條例：為規定關於同盟國及外國軍隊在印軍隊辦法事（1942 年 10 月 26 日）

資料來源：〈駐印度國軍法權管轄問題〉，《外交部》，國史館藏，數位典藏號：020-011903-0017。

檔案 22：駐加爾各答總領事館致外交部加字（33）第 336 號代電（1944 年 6 月 9 日）

檔案來源：〈駐印度國軍法權管轄問題〉，《外交部》，國史館藏，數位典藏號：020-011903-0017。

六、跨境作戰的法律常識

　　1943 年年底，由史迪威指揮的中國駐印軍向緬北挺進，搭配由國內出發的第二次中國遠征軍，發起反攻。作為第二次遠征軍總司令的陳誠，在他所遺存的檔案中，有一份《遠征手冊》，約莫 100 頁的內容中，有 13 頁是國際公法，內容節選自《海牙公約》的戰爭法規、陸戰法規、空戰法規等。

讓部隊的指揮官得以在跨境作戰期間，了解國際公法中針對戰爭行為作出的規範與定義，諸如何作戰、交戰期間如何對待俘虜、傷病人員、救援組織等，這能避免在戰時發生違犯國際公法相關規定的爭議，以免在戰後衍生賠償、審判等麻煩。

　　陸戰法規通常指的是 1899 年第一次海牙保和會中通過的《海牙第二公約》，以及 1907 年第二次海牙保和會通過的《海牙第四公約》。這是無法避免國家採用戰爭作為國際爭端解決手段的情況下，定義參與戰爭的人員、規範戰爭的細節、參加戰爭之各方的權利與義務，以及戰爭之結束與局外中立的要點。設下諸多的原則，使得戰爭可以規範化、文明化的國際公約，雖有因應時空的調整，但大多仍是及至今日依舊有效的國際慣例。相較之下，比較特別的是空戰法規。國際法中實際上並沒有完整的空戰法規，僅有 1899 年通過的《海牙第一公約》，禁止自氣球上投下投射物和爆炸物，隨著航空器的不斷進化，卻沒有跟上調整，僅能自陸戰與海戰法規中借用相關的概念與規範。

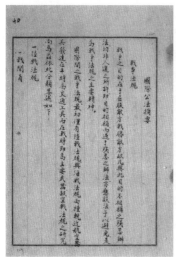

檔案 23：國際公法摘要
資料來源：「遠征手冊」，〈遠征軍司令長官任內資料（一）〉，《陳誠副總統文物》，國史館藏，數位典藏號：008-010701-00068-002。

　　這一份關乎交戰的國際法注意事項，節選戰爭法的相關規定，定義戰場上可能會遭遇的人員與情況。如收錄之陸戰法規中便定義何謂戰鬥人員，何謂間諜，何謂俘虜。所占篇幅頗多的是俘虜，詳載俘虜抓捕後的權利與義務、看管與救護等細節。此外，另著重於戰爭中會遭遇的情況，如對方來使時要如何處理，投降時應該怎麼做，休戰又應該怎麼做，軍事占領的做法如何等等。而中國遠征軍走的是山路，出發的也只有陸軍，因此相關規範中便沒有提及海軍，不過因為與中國遠征軍出擊搭配了空軍，因而在此也羅列了部分空戰法規，主要是有關於飛機轟炸的部分。

七、結語

　　國際社會的基礎與國際交往的依據是現代國際法。中國遠征軍要出境作戰，不僅要顧及友邦的感受，更重要的是必須依循國際規範與國際慣例行事。因此，如何詮釋、引用相關國際法規範，就成了自高層迄基層都必須了解的重要內容。無論是中國遠征軍出境作戰，中國駐印軍的訓練與管轄，其實都牽涉到國際法的運用。

　　從國際法的視角切入，或許更能理解中國遠征軍出境前，中英美三方有協調之必要，如此才能在英國的首肯下，於主權範圍外延展中國之國家武裝。此外，或也能從另一個側面了解蔣中正與史迪威之間，為了中國遠征軍與中國駐印軍之指揮權的爭議背後，隱含國軍出境後，還能否保有原指揮系統控制這些出境部隊的不同見解。蔣中正作為中國戰區最高指揮官，但中國戰區從未包括英屬緬甸，也是埋下此一爭論的主因，以上所述，在在都與國際法有關連。

　　過往對於中國遠征軍課題的討論，以及蔣中正與史迪威之間的爭執，多從國家利益、感情糾葛等視角，然如以國際法為切入點，或許能看到另一個暗藏法理爭議與不同見解的面向。

檔案原件

檔案 1：日本天皇致中華民國國民政府主席函（1935 年 5 月 24 日）

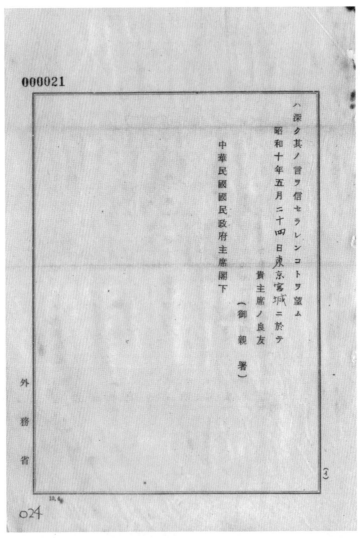

000021

中華民國國民政府主席閣下

外務省

八深ク其ノ言ヲ信セラレンコトヲ望ム

昭和十年五月二十四日東京宮城ニ於テ

貴主席ノ良友

（御親署）

資料來源：〈日本駐華使節呈遞國書暨使館升格〉（1935 年 5 月 24 日），《外交部》，國史館藏，數位典藏號：020-100400-0026。

寫

000020

良友

朕ハ日本國及中華民國間ニ存在スル所ノ外交關係ヲ一層親密ニシ以
テ兩國ヲ聯結セル友情好誼ヲシテ益鞏固輯睦ナラシメンコトヲ希ヒ
爰ニ貴政府ノ下ニ駐箚スル朕カ外交使節ノ資格ヲ隆シテ大使ト爲ス
コトニ決定シ正三位勳一等有吉明ヲ選ヒ委ヌルニ朕カ特命全權大使
トシテ貴政府ノ下ニ在テ朕ヲ代表スルノ重任ヲ以テシタリ明人ト爲
リ忠誠職ヲ執ル勤勉ニシテ又才幹アリ且其ノ性格ノ優秀ナル夙ニ貴
主席ノ寵眷ヲ蒙ルニ至リタルハ朕ノ久シク知悉スル所ニシテ其ノ光
榮アル使命ヲ遂行スルニ於テ全然朕ノ意ニ適ヒ又貴主席從來ノ殊遇
信任ニ因ハンカ爲メ勵精盡力苟クモ缺漏ナカルヘキハ朕ノ確信スル
所ナリ因テ朕ハ明カ朕ノ名ヲ以テ貴主席ニ以聞スル所ノモノハ總テ
貴主席ノ憑信ヲ得殊ニ朕カ貴主席ノ慶福ト貴國ノ隆昌ヲ祈ルノ誠意
ヲ致シ朕カ深厚ニシテ恒久渝ラサル敬愛ノ衷情ヲ披陳スルニ際シテ

外務省

10.4

023

檔案 2：「國民政府對日本宣戰布告」（1941 年 12 月 9 日）

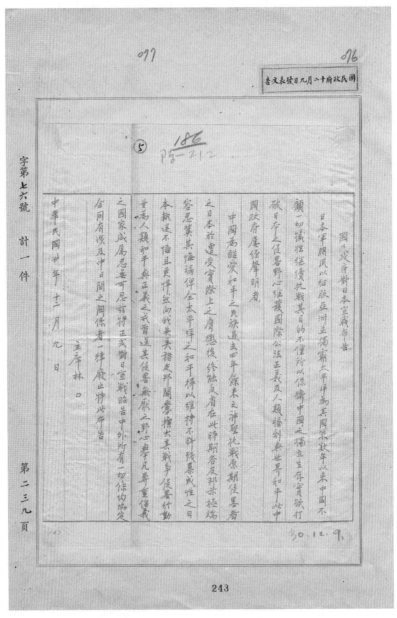

資料來源：「國民政府對日本宣戰布告」（1941 年 12 月 9 日），〈革命文獻—抗戰方略：重要指示〉，《蔣中正總統文物》，國史館藏，數位典藏號：002-020300-00004-077。

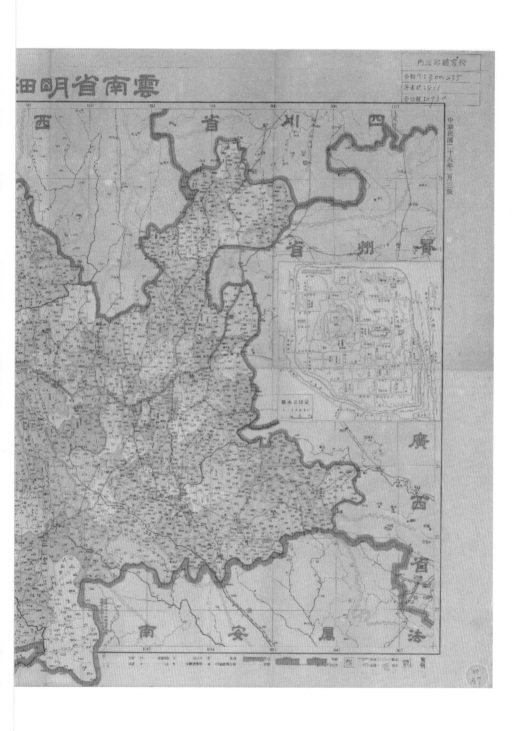

檔案 5：林蔚抗戰日記（1941 年 11 月 18 日）

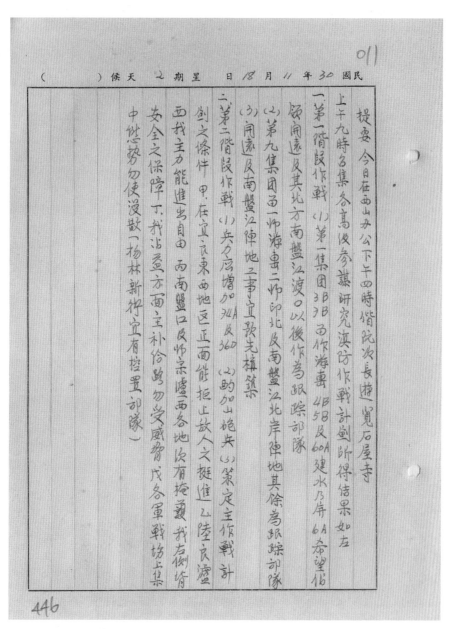

資料來源：〈林蔚文抗戰日記節錄〉，《陳誠副總統文物》，國史館藏，數位典藏號：008-010701-00001-011。

檔案6：法屬印度支那總督與駐印度支那日本陸海軍代表簽署之協議
　　　　　（1940年9月22日）

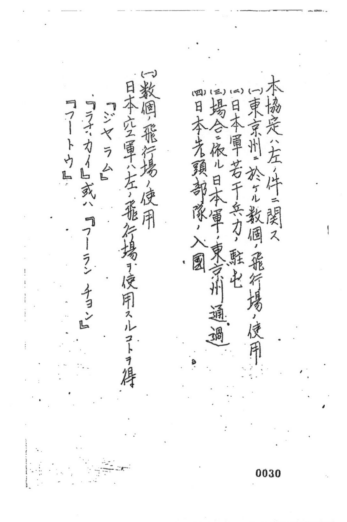

本協定ハ左ノ件ニ關ス
（一）東京州ニ於ケル數個ノ飛行場ノ使用
（二）日本軍若干兵力ノ數個ノ飛行場ノ使用
（三）場合ニ依ル日本軍ノ東京州通過
（四）日本先頭部隊ノ入國

（一）數個ノ飛行場ノ使用
日本空軍ハ左ノ飛行場ヲ使用スルコトヲ得
　『ジャラム』
　『ライ・カイ』或ハ『フーラン・チョン』
　『フートウ』

0030

〔圖章〕國立公文書館 アジア歴史資料センター
Japan Center for Asian Historical Records
http://www.jacar.go.jp

資料來源：「印度支那軍司令官と在印度支那日本陸海軍代表との間に於て締結されたる協定」
（1940年9月22日），〈昭和15・6～16・6　仏印進駐関係記録（1）〉,《海軍一般史料》，防
衛省防衛研究所藏，JACAR（アジア歴史資料センター），Ref. C14121105400。

(ハ)

印度支那軍司令官ト在印度支那日本
陸海軍代表トノ間ニ於テ締結セラレタル協定

人員及整正備人員）

(い)左ノモノニ對スル補給品、輸送及ヒ護衛ノ
笠二頃ニ記載、諸飛行基地及支那印支國境
附近ノ支那領土內ニ於テ目下作戰中ノ日本
部隊

(ニ)海防港ノ通過輸送及ヒ同地方ニ施設セラルヘ
病院ノ運營等

右ノ兵力ハ前記諸任務達成上必要限度ニ制限セラ
ルヽモノニシテ如何ナル場合ニ於テモ六千人ヲ超ヘザルモノトス
右ノ兵力ノ駐屯地區ハ日佛軍事當局者間ノ共同
合意ニヨリ決定セラルヽモノトス
日佛兩參謀部間ノ合意ニ依リ定メラレタル最小限

日本空軍ハ九月四日ノ協定ニ依リ定メラレタル諸條
件ニ從ヒ右諸飛行場ノ設備ヲ行フコトヲ得

右諸飛行場ノ警備ニ任スル兵力ハ日佛當司者
間ノ合意ニ依リ決定セラルベク　右兵力ハ其ニ任
務達成上ニ必要ナル最少限度ニ限定セラルルモノ
トス

(二) 日本軍若干兵力ノ駐屯
左ニ任務ヲ有スル日本諸部隊ノ兵力ハ日佛軍事
當局者間ニ於ケル共同合意ノ後決定セラルベキ
モノトス

(3) 第一項記載ノ諸飛行場ノ警備
(4) 右諸飛行場ノ使用 (日本飛行隊ニ屬スル飛行

0031

(三)日本軍ノ東京州通過

日本軍司令官ガ東京州北方國境ヨリ發足シテ
地上兵力ニヨリ攻擊作戰ヲ行ハントスル場合
(該司令官ハ目下ノ之ヲ考慮シアラズ)若クバ海防
港ヨリノ栗船ヲ必要トスベキ部隊ノ行動
ヲ爲シサントスル場合ニ佛軍司令官ノ決定セル
數條ノ交通路ハ作戰ノ必要ニ從ヒ日本軍ニ依リ
利用セラレ得ルモノトス

右ノ輸送ノ實施方法ハ千九百四十年九月四日
署名ノ協定基礎事項中ニ定メアル條件ニ
ヨリ規定セラレ、モノトス

日本通過ノ部隊ノ兵力ハ必要度ニ應ジ追テ
決定セラルベキモノトス

度ニ限定セラレタル　前記兵力中ノ一部ハ諸飛行場
ニ直接接スル部落ヲ利用スルコトヲ得
但シ『ハノイ』市ハ此ノ限リニ非ズ
日本軍ノ司令部又ハ部隊ハ『ハノイ』ニ定著シ又ハ同
市ヲ通過セザルモノトス但シ両参謀部間ノ連絡ヲ計
ル為ニ必要ナル将校ハ此ノ限リニ非ズ
諸飛行場内ニ於ケル日本飛行部隊及其ノ警備部隊ノ
施設ハ日本軍當局ニ於テ頁擔スルモノトス
海防市日佛両参謀部間ノ合意ニ依リ定メラルル條件
ニ依リ上陸地点トシテ利用セラルルモノトス
如何ナル場合ニ於テモ　軍艦ハ『ドーソン』―『アポワン』ヲ
連又ル線ヨリ六海里以内ニ近接セザルモノトス
水雷驅級ヲ超ヘザル　軍艦一隻ハ海防港内ニ碇泊スルコトヲ得

(五)日本軍ノ東京州通過輸送

目下支那印支國境附近ニ在ル日本部隊ハ日
本當局ノ要求ニ基キ海防港乗船ノ爲印度
支那領土ヲ通過シテ輸送セラレ得ルモノトス
此部隊ノ輸送ハ詳細ナル研究ヲ必要トスルヲ以テ
両參謀部間ニ於ケル特別協定ヲ要ス
此協定ガ成立セザル限リ何レノ日本部隊モ印
度支那國境ヲ超ヘザルモノトス

(六)一般事項
本協定ニ掲ケアル諸規定事項ヲ除キ千九百四
十一年九月四日署名ノ協定基礎事項ハ全部
効力ヲ有スルコト勿論ナリ

0036

然レドモ通過部隊及ビ第二項ニ記述ノ部隊ノ部隊ノ
全兵力ハ八千九百四十五年九月四日調印ノ協定ニ
基礎事項ニ依リ定メラレタル数ヲ超ユルヲ得
ザルモノトス。

(四)　日本先頭部隊ノ入國、
九月二十二日二十二時八日本當局ニ依リ嚴守セラルベ
キモノナルニ鑑ミ部隊搭載ノ第一船ハ右期日二
海防二入港スルコトヲ得
然レドモ上陸部隊ノ上陸條件及ビ駐屯地点へノ
移動條件ニ關スル特別協定が成立セザル限リ
部隊ハ其ノ船舶ヨリ下船セズ　又其他ノ輸送船
ハ港内ニ入ラザルモノトス

両参謀部ハ本協定ノ實施方法ヲ定ムル

爲ニ爾今常時相連絡スルモノトス

千九百四十年九月二十二日

於「ハノイ」

西原少將

「マルタン」將官

檔案 7：「羅斯福電蔣中正建議在重慶召集聯合軍事會議交換情報」
　　　　（1941 年 12 月 16 日）

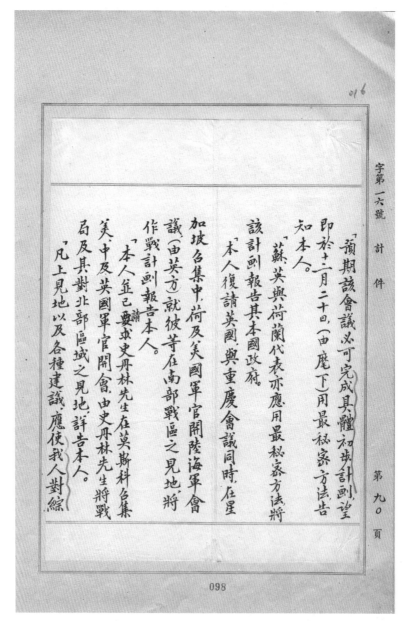

資料來源：〈革命文獻—同盟國聯合作戰：重要協商（一）〉，《蔣中正總統文物》，國史館藏，
數位典藏號：002-020300-00016-016。

016

⑫ 234

276 卅三件

馬格魯德將軍致　委座備忘錄

內容：羅斯福總統來電。

一、羅斯福總統囑駒將致　鈞座來電全文錄呈如下：

"立即發動步驟準備一致行動以禦共同敵人，應視為異常重要之舉。為達成此項目的起見，本人敬建議由麾下最遲於十二月十七日，在重慶召集聯合軍事會議，交換情報，並討論在東亞戰區最有效之陸海軍行動，以擊敗日本及其同盟國。

"本人並建議，參加該會者應為英中荷蘇及美國之代表，同時本人可立即派定勃蘭德將軍為美國代表，由馬格魯德將軍副之。

U. S. MILITARY MISSION TO CHINA
OFFICE OF THE COMMANDING GENERAL
CHUNGKING, CHINA.

CODE ADDRESS
"AMMISCA"

December 16, 1941

MEMORANDUM for: His Excellency, The Generalissimo.

Subject : Message from President Roosevelt.

　　　　1. President Roosevelt has directed me to transmit to you a message substantially as follows:

　　　　"It is of the greatest importance, in my judgment, that immediate steps be initiated to prepare for common action against the common enemy. With this end in mind, I respectfully suggest that you call a joint military conference in Chungking not later than December 17th to exchange information and consider the most effective military and naval action in eastern Asia to bring about the defeat of Japan and her allies.

　　　　"I suggest that the conferees consist of representatives of Great Britain, China, the Dutch, the U.S.S.R., and the United States, and can designate at once Major General George H. Brett as U. S. representative, assisted by Brigadier General John Magruder.

　　　　"I am of the opinion that this conference can arrive at a concrete preliminary plan which can be communicated to me in strictest confidence by December 20th.

　　　　"The Russian, British, and Dutch representatives should also communicate the plan by most secret means to their respective governments.

　　　　"Concurrently with the preliminary conference in Chungking, I am requesting the British to hold a military and naval meeting in Singapore with Chinese, Dutch and American officers, and for them to report plans of operation as they view it from the southern zone.

　　　　"I have also asked Mr. Stalin to call a conference with American, Chinese, and British officers in Moscow, and for him to inform me of the situation and his views from the northern point of view.

　　　　"These views and recommendations should give us all equally a clear picture of our combined problem. I hope too that the preliminary talks might lead to the creation of a permanent body for planning and directing our common effort. In the meantime I am using every means at my disposal to continue and to increase supplies to you."

　　　　2. The President sends you his warmest personal greetings.

JOHN MAGRUDER
Brigadier General, U. S. Army,
Chief, U. S. Military Mission to China.

美援統書二
字第一六號　計件

第九二頁

100

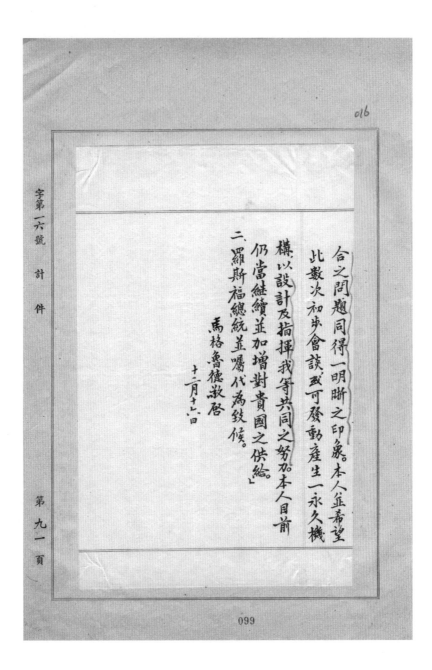

016

合之問題同得一明晰之印象。本人並希望
此數次初步會談或可發動產生一永久機

橫以設計及指揮我等共同之努加本人目前
仍當繼續並加增對貴國之供給。

二、羅斯福總統並囑代為致候。」

馬格魯德敬啟
十二月十六日

檔案 8：「蔣中正召集美英蘇軍事代表等就召集聯合軍事會議交換意見」
　　　　（1941 年 12 月 17 日）

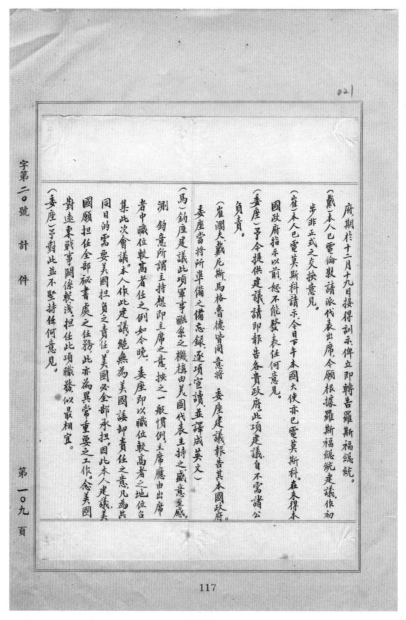

字第二○號　計件　第一○九頁

府期於十二月十九日接得訓示俾立即轉告羅斯福總統。

（戴）本人已電倫敦請派代表出席，令願根據羅斯福總統建議作初步非正式之交換意見。

（崔）本人已電莫斯科請示令日下午本國大使亦已電莫斯科。在未得本國政府指示以前恕不能發表任何意見。

（委座）予令提供建議請即飛告各貴政府此項建議自不需諸公負責。

（崔）關大戴尼斯馬格魯德皆同意將　委座建議報告其本國政府。

委座當將所準備之備忘錄逐項宣讀並譯成英文）

（馬）鈞座建議此項軍事聯系之機構由美國代表主持之盛意至感。

測　鈞意所謂主持想即主席之意，按之一般慣例主席應由出席者中職位較高者任之例如今晚：委座即以職位較高者之地位主集此次會議本人作此建議絕無為美國諉卸責任之共同目的需要美國担負之責任，美國必全部承担，因此本人建議美國願担任全部秘書處之任務，此亦為異常重要之工作。念美國勢遠東戰事關係較淺担任此項職務似最相宜。

（委座）予對此並不堅持任何意見。

117

資料來源：〈革命文獻—同盟國聯合作戰：重要協商（一）〉，《蔣中正總統文物》，國史館藏，數位典藏號：002-020300-00016-021。

275　附件

字第二○號　計七頁件

第一○八頁

三十年十二月十五日羅斯福總統來電建議由　委座召集聯合軍事會議因
於十二月十七日晚八時約宴崔潤夫、戴尼斯、馬格魯德及其高級參謀人
員，並約何總長應欽、徐部長永昌、商主任震、周主任至柔、劉次長為
章參加共同討論其談話紀錄如次：

（委座）十二月十四日予致電羅斯福總統，建議在美國領導之下成立軍事
聯繫合作之機構以禦太平洋上共同之敵人，昨日接羅斯福總統復電建
議由予召集英美蘇中荷五國軍事代表會議交換意見，並商定軍
事合作之計劃，來電並稱，彼已分電英政府及史丹林先生同時在星
加坡莫斯科召開同樣會議，因特約請諸公來此會商羅斯福總
統業已任命勃蘭德將軍為正代表，馬格魯德將軍副之，惟英蘇
兩國尚未選派代表，擬請崔潤夫將軍及戴尼斯將軍即電貴國
政府指派代表出席，令晚則開非正式會議，俾得彼此交換意見。予
接羅斯福總統電中，堅屬此項會議最遲應於十二月十七日召集，並共
十二月二十日前將會議決議告彼，予已準備應建議若干條為時無
多，希望崔潤夫與戴尼斯兩將軍立將此項建議電達各貴政

116

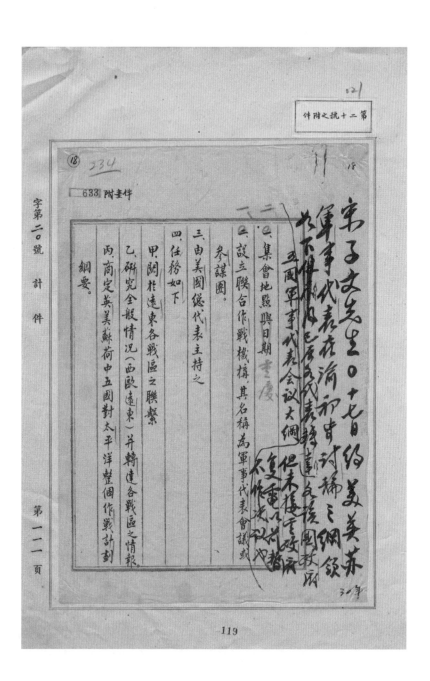

021

件附之抚十二第

⑱ 234

18

［633］附查件

字第二○號　計件

第一一二頁

第子文先生○十七日約美美蘇軍事代表在渝初步討論三綱領

五國軍事代表會議大綱

一、集會地點與日期　重慶。

二、設立聯合作戰機構，其名稱為軍事代表會議或參謀團。

三、由美國總代表主持之

四、任務如下

　甲、關於遠東各戰區之聯繫

　乙、研究全般情況（西歐遠東）并轉達各戰區之情報。

　丙、商定英美蘇荷中五國對太平洋整個作戰計劃綱要。

（談話自崔席開始而中斷。飯後復繼續討論。委座所提建議經署加修改後即分發蘇、英、美各武官收執。）

崔潤夫將軍建議為便利起見重慶、星加坡、莫斯科三處會議似可合併為一。戴尼斯與馬格魯德兩將軍亦以為戰區雖分成數處，然緊密合作至關重要故皆同意此言，惟念目前遠東局勢緊急，已非建議合併之時，蓋欲達成合併目的必信使往來，經過若干時間始可得有結果。

（委座）予今派定參謀總長何應欽為中國出席此項會議之總代表，由徐部長永昌商主任震副之。

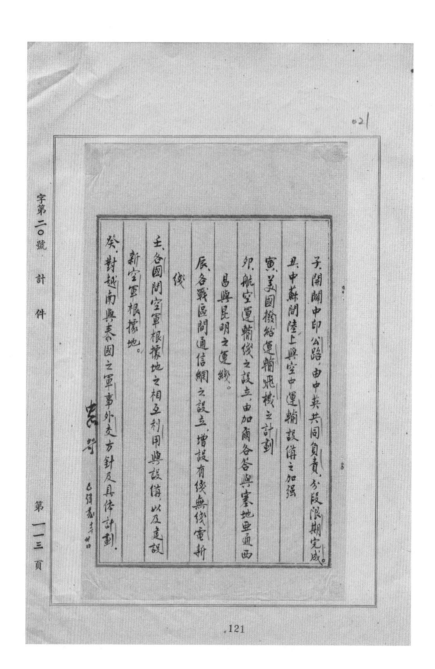

子、開闢中印公路，由中英共同負責，分段限期完成。

丑、中蘇間陸上與空中運輸設備之加強。

寅、美國撥給運輸飛機之計劃。

卯、航空運輸線之設立，由加爾各答與塞地亞西昌與昆明之運線。

辰、各戰區間通信網之設立，增設有後無線電新線。

壬、各國間空軍根據地之相互利用與設備，以及建設新空軍根據地。

癸、對越南與泰國之軍事外交方針及具體計劃。

計件

121

02

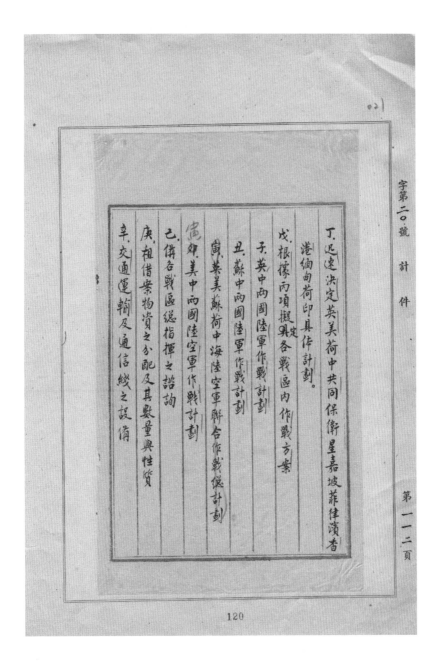

丁.迅速決定英美荷中共同保衛星嘉坡菲律濱香
港緬甸荷印具作計劃。

戊.根據兩項擬具各戰區內作戰方案

子.英中兩國陸軍作戰計劃

丑.蘇中兩國陸軍作戰計劃

寅.美蘇荷中海陸空軍聯合作戰總計劃

卯.美中兩國陸空軍作戰計劃

己.備各戰區總指揮之諮詢

庚.租借案物資之分配及其數量與性質

辛.交通運輸及通信線之設備

檔案 10、檔案 11：「蔣中正與魏菲爾談話紀錄：磋商軍事合作問題」
（1941 年 12 月 22 日）

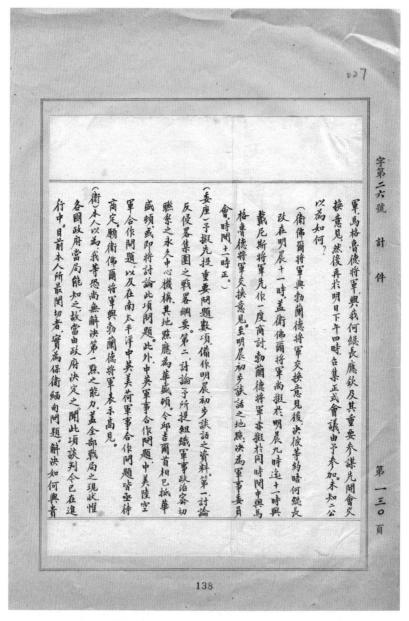

資料來源：〈革命文獻—同盟國聯合作戰：重要協商（一）〉，《蔣中正總統文物》，國史館藏，數位典藏號：002-020300-00016-027。

270

三十年十二月二十二日下午九時接見英美特派軍事專使談話紀錄

（英國軍事專使衛佛爾將軍由英大使卡爾及英國駐華軍事代表團團長戴尼斯將軍陪同先至，美國專使勃蘭德將軍則與美國駐華軍事代表團團長馬格魯德將軍及該團參謀長麥克莫倫上校，參謀霍德上校同來。何總長應欽，商主任震參加談話。）

（委座）今日得歡迎將軍業渝討論與兩國有密切關係之戰略戰術俾得早定計劃付諸實施實至感快慰。

（衛）本人亦有同感。本人此次離印，彼處局勢緊張，百端待理，亟盼一切問題能於明日一日中討論而解決之，俾得在星期三晨乘機經仰光返德里，鈞座倘能助成此忠感銘無已。

（委座）將軍早早返防，亦為我等共同之利益。深信星期三離渝當可做到。

（衛）印度總督凌力斯高囑携手函及禮物二件奉呈。

（委座）望代為致謝。

（談話至此，勃蘭德將軍由馬格魯德將軍及其部下陪同莊止。

委座與作寒暄後，即表示能得兩重要名將同來重慶研究作戰計劃，至感快慰）。

（委座）予建議明晨九時，衛佛爾與勃蘭德兩將軍偕同戴尼斯將

陸軍或用空軍襲擊日本在泰國之根據地，苟有發動此舉之必
要，本人自當承認泰國應在本人作戰區域之內。鈞座以玖為字之
主張本人完全同意惟準備尚需時間，作戰器材尚待補充。星加坡
受日軍奸詐襲擊之後，第一要圖為打退敵人在泰之根
據地發動空軍以打擊敵人在泰之根據地，換言之，緬甸境內之公路
與海港應先使獲得不受敵方侵襲之安全。

（委座）未識勃蘭德將軍之高見如何？

（勃）本人同意衛佛爾將軍之言，試披地圖觀之，玖泰最良之根據
地實在緬甸空軍活動距離既不遠，而軍事器材之補充此實為
集中之中心，他處根據地之就用甚不能及焉，緬境之根據地鞏固之後即
可發動空軍襲擊曼谷與西貢，毀壞敵方之交通線與飛機場以為
陸軍正面進攻之準備。

（委座）未識勃蘭德將軍對中美陸空軍之合作有何高見否？

（勃）美國將考量他處可以抽調之飛機與中國空軍合作以打擊我
等之敵人。本人尚未能熟諗此閒戰局，正與衛佛爾將軍相同適舉
羅斯福總統電令覆通，尚未有暇披閱，窮意各該電中必另有方針
指示此外，馬格魯德將軍亦必有其資料見示，俾得作為詳細討論之

027

國及　鈞座部隊密切合作，集中作戰器材及空軍力量以完成此
舉實為本人之職責。

（勃）本人同意衛佛爾將軍之言，決定戰畧綱要，似覺涉太廣，非此間
所能討論。

（委座）未識衛佛爾將軍能於明晨提出遠東作戰計劃否？

（衛）本人尚未有擬具此項提議之準備。蓋於日本突襲英美以前本
人職司印度總司令，防区範圍祇及東印，惟在英美對日宣戰之
後，始兼任保衛緬甸之責，數日前奉命來渝，親聆　鈞諭，擬
於明晨興戴尼斯將軍詳細討論，聆取各種情報，或即能擬具提
案矣。

（委座）未識將軍所負職責之範圍究竟如何？

（衛）保衛緬甸為本人之專責，此外另有東区總司令，其總部設於星
加坡，其防区某及香港並與澳洲荷印完成聯防。

（委座）未識泰國亦在將軍作戰区域內否？余意倘能發動中國興印度
軍隊進攻泰國藉以解星加坡一部份之圍，實為戰略上策。

（衛）倘　鈞座根據採取攻勢為保衛緬甸之上策為原則，主張或用

得聯絡來印稍留仍可返緬,敝部現在德里,俟閣興仰光交通至便,

飛機來往一日可達。

(委座)予願接受此項建議,當令該員除現有任務外,另任予與將

軍間之聯絡任務。

(附註、衛佛爾將軍在其言談中透露其此行目的有三(一)來渝要求

我國人力之協助;(二)獲取我國儲存在仰先租借法案器材之一部份;

三要求

委座准許奉諾德部下美國志願空軍留緬參加保衛緬甸作戰。

彼並未言及奉英國政府命令代表出席

委座根據羅斯福總統建議所召集之重慶聯席軍事會

議,故彼之地位與勃蘭德將軍似有不同。蓋美政府之任命勃蘭德

將軍代表出席該會議係由馬格魯德將軍正式通知

委座者也。擬請

委座於今日下午正式會議之時詢問衛佛爾將軍是否奉有英

國政府命令,代表其統帥部,出席此項會議。

根據。

（委座）兩將軍既皆認有進次泰國之必要，至感快慰。明晨會議之另

一重要議案即余適已提及之在華盛頓組織一總系軍事政治

之永久機構問題。余認此舉關係至大。羅斯福總統未來電，要求在

渝召集軍事聯席會議交換情報擬具依作戰計劃，並稱此項同樣

性質之會議在星加坡及莫斯科亦同時舉行。惟各項計劃若無

一中心機構指揮之，則實施之時，必將發生種種困難故云此舉

關係至大。我等職責固限於研究軍事實提出方案。至此方案之

應否實行，則由有關各國政府決定之。

（衛佛爾與勃蘭德兩將軍皆表示願考量擬具方案之建議惟

衛佛爾將軍表示，大部份時間應注重於討論及決定太平洋

最緊迫之防務問題尤以保衛緬甸為最要。）

（衛）閣　鈞座正擬派一高級軍官赴仰先，未知其任務如何？

（委座）予曾已派一高級軍官赴仰先，其任務係為英國當局與

中國派赴緬境之部隊及予本人間之聯絡員。目前予尚不擬另派

專員赴印，蓋一時尚無可調遣之人。

（衛擬請令派赴仰先之貴國軍官常赴印度與本人及敝部參謀取

檔案 13、檔案 15：「蔣中正召集美英澳等國代表舉行第一次聯席軍事會議」
　　　　　　　　　　（1941 年 12 月 23 日）

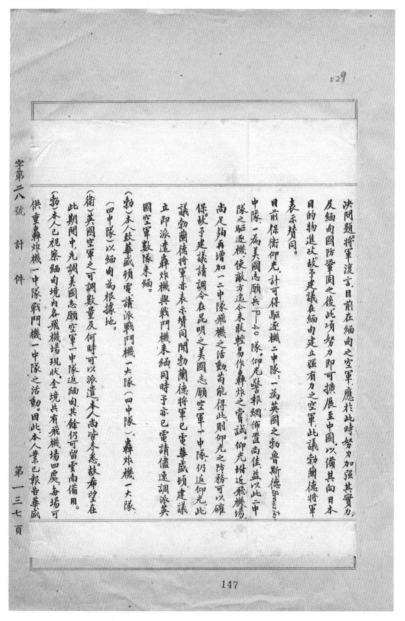

決問題將軍復言目前在緬甸之空軍應於此時努力加強其實力

及緬甸國防鞏固之後此項努力即可擴展至中國以備其向日本

目的物進攻故予建議在緬甸建立強有力之空軍此議勃蘭德將軍

表示贊同。

目前保衛仰光計可得驅逐機二中隊一為英國之勃魯斯德 Brewster

中隊一為美國志願兵 P-40 隊仰光警報網佈置尚佳益以二中

隊之驅逐機使敵方逸今不致輕易作轟炸之嘗試仰光坿近飛機場

尚足夠再增加二中隊飛機之活動苟能得此則仰光之防務可以確

保故予建議再議請令在昆明之美國志願空軍一中隊仍返仰光此

議勃蘭德將軍表示贊同。開勃蘭德將軍已電華盛頓建議

立即派遣轟炸機與戰鬥機來緬同時予示已電請儘速調派英

國空軍數隊來緬。

（勃）本人致華盛頓電請派戰鬥機一大隊（四中隊），轟炸機一大隊

（四中隊）以緬甸為根據地。

（衛）英國空軍之可調數量及何時可以派遣本人尚望未在

此期間中先調美國志願空軍一中隊返緬甸其餘仍可留雲南備用。

（勃）本人已視察緬甸境內各飛機場現狀全境共有飛機場四處每場可

供重轟炸機一中隊戰鬥機一中隊之活動目此本人業已報告華盛

頓

029

147

資料來源：〈革命文獻―同盟國聯合作戰：重要協商（一）〉，《蔣中正總統文物》，國史館藏，
數位典藏號：002-020300-00016-029。

029

字第二八號　計二頁件　第一三六頁

按照羅斯福總統建議召開聯席軍事會議紀錄

地點：委座長官舍

時間：三十年十二月廿二日下午四時

出席者：委座夫婦　何總長應欽　徐部長永昌　商主任震　劉次長斐章

周主任至柔　毛總指揮邦初　澳洲公使愛格斯登　衛佛爾將軍

勃蘭德將軍　馬格魯德將軍　戴尼斯將軍　沃勃登空軍參贊

霍克上校　麥克米倫上校　班林中校　司高脫蘭德副官（衛

佛爾將軍之副官）

飯後繼續開會增加出席者，英大使卡爾，美國志願空軍司

令希諾德上校，與特立克上尉及賴德穆顧問。

委座宣佈開會後，即請衛佛爾將軍令晨與何總長應欽、勃蘭德

將軍及英美駐華軍事代表團團員等開非正式預備會議時所討

論之建議案向本會報告。

（衛呈晨討論者計分三點：㈠空軍在緬甸最妥善之分配與行動㈡撥用一

部份中國在緬甸之租借法案器材為保衛緬甸之用。㈢中國軍隊協

助保衛緬甸。予意仰光與緬甸之防衛至關重要。仰光根據地與緬甸

境內之交通線實有確保其安全之必要。今晨開會時勃蘭德將軍

報告空軍現狀，亦云確保根據地之安全，為空軍活動最重要之先

146

字第二八號　計件　第一三九頁

擬作保衛緬甸之用。

本人第三建議為中國派部隊入緬之直接援助。本人在今晨會議中報告，

由泰國至緬甸邊境之道路為數既寡且甚崎嶇可以用者南北各二耳。

故在公路交通未改善前，不論為守為攻皆有不能出動大規模部隊

之困難。因之除自有交通路線聯接其本國國土之地區以外，欲使聯軍

部隊分別割定各自之防區實感困難，最近九十三師之一團派赴東

緬之孟揚佈局至當因其地位既可扼敵方由泰國進犯時之東側同時

又自有交通線聯接中國。本人視此一團為有價值之貢獻亟盼鈞座

能將其實力由一團增至一師，至第四十九師之一團今在北緬呃叮此

亦一有用之後備部隊。鈞座又稱可續增部隊至一軍或兩軍之數

盛意至感惟如何可以使其有隔別防區及交通路線則困難至難

解決。結果恐難免不與英國部隊混合作戰此又為亟應避免者。

今晨會議時本人偵報告已由印度調部隊增援緬甸不久當可到

達。宏意印度增援部隊到達之後，益以中國業已先派之部隊，

當可以之保衛緬甸，不需再請中國增援矣。

（奏座）印度援軍何時可以抵緬遵海道耶抑陸路耶，

（衛）印度增援部隊最近數星期中當可到達。印緬間公路甚為故彼

等不能遵陸路行令正等候運輸船隻及護航海軍出發深盼鈞

029

字第二八號　　計件　　第一三八頁

頻軍政部倘能得適當之警報網及高射砲本人可於目前緬境內已有之飛機外再調派轟炸機一大隊驅逐機一大隊至緬甸境內。

（衛）本人所要求者只為調派美國志願空軍一中隊其餘中國空軍仍可用以協助他處中國軍隊。

本人第二建議為撥用一部份令在緬甸境內之器材問題深信確保仰光與滇緬公路之安全實為中英二國之共同利益故必商定防衛緬甸之其體辦法緬甸方面器材之短缺甚多例如完成警報網必需之電話器材高射砲馬達運輸車輛以及修理飛機及卡車之工具及材料等皆所急需開租借法案項下之供給中適有此類器材故決向中國軍隊商請撥用今已擬具清單一紙擬請儘先將現已運到者撥一部份備用深知中國方面需用亦甚急迫此項請求或求惠過多惟念保衛緬甸之重要性中國亦有同感或不致斥為狂妄令自當借撥之後異日自當設法歸還也。

（馬）本國軍政部已授權本人取得中國方面同意之後得將中國租借案器材移轉他國換言之辦理移轉之時本人將管理簿記將此項器材轉入接受國家之下。

（衛）本人建議由馬格魯德將軍或其代表會同中國方面代表及余之代表組織一小組委員會考核該項清單決定存貨中若何種類及數量可以

148

029

議、電文可由董副部長宣讀之。今該會已正式在重慶成立矣、此實為
太平洋各國代表第一次之正式會議、除英美代表而外予復特約澳
洲公使愛格斯登亦來參加、並曾同時邀請蘇聯與荷蘭政府指派
代表興會、迄今尚未得復、此後該二國何時願來參加、自皆所歡迎。
就目前問題而言、蘇聯之關係高淺、蓋彼之注意集中此方也。對目前問
題最感關切者、為英為美為中、為荷、而此次集會之主題、則為「研究
在東亞最有效之陸海軍行動以擊敗日本及其同盟國」、此即為羅斯
福總統來電最後之一句。故除業已討論之三點而外、本會主要任務
為挨照羅斯福總統建議、擬定整個計劃及組織永久機構、換言之、應
研究太平洋興歐洲之戰畧、及在華盛頓成立一永久組織、邱吉爾首相
今在華盛頓、予希望其此行結果、能在華盛頓成立聯軍最高軍
事委員會以聯繫各方之戰事行動以訂定同盟國間有關戰畧之
各種問題、未識諸公意見如何？

（銜）鈞座主張應有一中心機構以研究整個戰略。本人完全同意此項中心機構
之所在地自以華盛頓為相宜、本人以為華盛頓方面應屬各戰區軍事
分會各將其本區之意見報告華盛頓、同時亦將其所擬方案由各國代表
報告其本國政府、倘經蘇聯主張、華盛頓成立一總會各戰區分別成立分會、
恐戰區之分佈既如是廣泛、問題發生之時、擬具方案轉輾商核、恐欲推

座,再派部隊入緬問題,當視該印度增接部隊能否及時對到而定之,倘
彼等能及時趕到則中國所派上送四十九師及九十三師部隊以外之軍隊儘
可調充中國他處軍事行動之用。

更有一點應請注意者,在各處牽制日軍,使之忙於應付,亦有其重要性,
不容忽視。竊意中國如準備未周絕無急於在各方面發動反攻之必要,
而日軍在中國之交通,則應以有計劃有步驟之破壞,俾其不能抽調
中國部隊派赴他處更重要之戰區,牽制在華日軍,不使分其餘力於
他處其價值之重要實不容輕易忽視之。

(委座)予識勃蘭德將軍對衛佛爾將軍之各項建議有何意見否?

(勃)本員意衛佛爾將軍之建議除關於空軍問題願備諮詢外,其他並無
意見補充。

(委座)茲可暫時休息。

休息時,進茶點。迄下午五時,復繼續開會。

(委座)予謹向參加各會員,衛佛爾將軍,勃蘭德將軍及愛格斯登公使
致歡迎之忱。適衛佛爾將軍報告令晨預備會所討論之三點,皆屬專
門技術問題,予茲同意其原則,詳細辦法,可由一小組委員會討論之。蓋
予主張集中器材與,集中人力為玖勝之必要條件,英美之戰爭即為
中國之戰爭,反之亦然。此次開會動機,係最近由羅斯福總統來電建

字第二八號　計　件　第一四〇頁

029

字第二八號　計件

（委座）予以為太平洋區應包括印度洋，惟究竟區域應如何劃定，余願由

華盛頓總會決定之。在重慶本會之重要任務為對日作戰。

（勛）決定整個戰略，主要任務為規定某一戰區人力與器材分配之優先權，

此當由華盛頓總會決定之，故本人主張，應先令華盛頓認識遠東局勢

之嚴重，俾能獲取支配人力與器材之優先權。

（委座）各戰區之軌急疏緩，應有適當理由與兄份事實以判斷之根據，

倘斷定亞洲戰區為某一時期最重要之區域，則自當決定戰畧予該戰

區以一切支配之優先權。屆時其他各戰區應本擁護民主陣綫利益之共

同目的而犧牲其本身之利益然絕不容許某一戰區並不危急惟為保

全其本身利益起見，排擠他戰區，反使落後。予今並不主張目前對整個

戰略有何決定惟不妨彼此交換意見而已，目前可暫置實際需要不加討論。

（勛）一切軍事行動皆以實際需要為基礎，而華盛頓決定整個戰畧，請

公恐無多人能知遠東戰區軍事行動之如何重要也。

（委座）重慶軍分會應自行決定其戰畧及擬定計劃，主器材供給之優

先權，則可另組小組委員會決定之，予意今應按照議程進行討論議

程第一項為遠東各戰區之聯繫問題。

（勛）此項問題恐已不在重慶軍分會職權範圍之內，不觀總統已將星加坡

劃出本區另立一軍分會乎？余人以為聯繫工作應由華盛頓總會住之。

第一四三頁

字第二八號　計　件　第一四二頁

029.

勁各戰區之行動度時多而效率反受影响。

(勃)本人測縱統所稱之戰略當祇限於東亞。

(衛)本人以為各戰區之戰略,實彼此互有關聯,例如北菲及地中海之戰略勢必影响及中國之戰局,就余本人言,中國與近東之戰局,一東一西,皆有重要之

關係,則本人注意勢不得不兼顧東西。換言之,本人負責印度之防務,亦同時負責西面在伊朗伊拉克之作戰,東被緬甸方面襲擊之虞,屆時本

本人防衛或有西面受伊朗方面進攻,東向在緬甸之作戰,將來局勢突變,

人所負責之後備軍究應派赴何方增援,惟本人能洪之。再申言之,如何在

西部防衛中東,巴勒斯丁,叙利亞等區在東部保衛緬甸與中國等區本

人皆應擬具體計劃,故本人主張,各區軍分會究應負責若何地區必

先明白規定,而重慶實非討論海軍戰署之適當地點,勢必於他處解決

之,究竟此次會議當前目的為何本會議所定計劃應規定如何範圍尚望

鈞座明教。

(委座)本柈十二月十五日向有關各國提出建議案,茲願當場宣讀之。(宣讀畢)

願諸公對此發表意見。

(衛)此項建議皆極合理,亟應付諸實施,惟所願知者,其所指之地區範圍如何

耳,是否本委員會所代表之區域為太平洋區,苟然者,此種規定似仍太嫌

含混。

項建議並決定計劃。

（上述辦法經全體一致同意通過。）

（委座）令請各統帥推舉代表，組織此永久軍分會，予派何總長應欽為代表。

（衛）本人派戴尼斯將軍為代表，此後或將再加一人。

（勃）本人代表麥克魯瑟將軍請馬格魯德將軍為代表。

（該會秘書處之秘書長一致同意應由美國代表所派者任之，並經決議一切專門問題，應由秘書處擬具計劃以備各代表執行，秘書處議為該處保存紀錄及檔案。）

（委座）按照議程次項應討論草擬電稿向羅斯福總統報告會議結果。

（勃）本人主張以將來軍行動之可能發展，向總統作概要之報告，令擬有電稿一份，請付公決。（即將電稿宣讀）

（衛）此電所建議之計劃為時似太遠，當知當前一二月實為異常重要關頭，益以此項計劃決非目前實刀所能辦到即發動空軍攻勢實有難能，抉樂觀態度作長時期之計劃固足嘉尚然使長官確知一月內之真相雖帶悲觀論調亦屬必要。

（勃）本人擬另加入華軍在中國各處擾亂日軍交通一節未知可否？

字第二八號　計件　　　　第一四五頁

155

字第二八號　計件　　第一四四頁

（委座）請勒蘭德將軍草擬本會對遠東各戰區聯繫辦法之決議案俾
得電告羅斯福總統。

委座當即按照其十二月十五日致各國政府備忘錄所列各項從第二項
起逐項說明並蒙加意見後,即宣告暫時休會。晚飯前將所擬列強
聯合行動計劃書當場分發。
晚飯後九時三十分重行開會,繼續討論。

（委座）本會討論範圍令將以下列二點為限:(一)飯前分發之各項建議,(二)
重慶軍分會之組織,對於第二點之最重要者為組織一秘書處,
俾得立即報告羅斯福總統。

（衛）成立此永久機構之最妥善方法,應任命各總司令之代表成立一委員會。
本人建議該委員會應由　釣座麥克愛瑟將軍、衛佛爾將軍及蘇聯
西伯利亞總司令各派代表組成之此四統帥所統轄之作戰區域即為
該委員會之區域範圍。

（委座）荷屬東印度應亦派代表參加。

（衛）荷屬東印度究屬何戰區高難確定恐將劃入新加坡區域中,

（委座）該委員會之一部份工作既為交換情報則請荷屬東印度及澳
洲參加自示合理。

（衛）倘此項組織辦法,經本會通過,即可進而討論　釣座備忘錄所提各

029

二三星期傳能得一實際計劃方案之為愈也。

(馬)我人當念早其計劃送去亦為促成給予優先權之刺激俾編統能明瞭此閒緊迫之需要。

(委座)予所擬建本會既無詳細討論之時閒當另行單獨送交總統。今請勃蘭德將軍宣讀其四點建議(勃宣讀後)予願雁知此後中國戰線究將如何支持,迄今為止討論忠心皆集中於保衛緬甸來閒一言及支持中國戰線者,中國單獨抗戰已四年有半,今令並取得新器材之可能亦將消失矣!

(勃)鈞座可向總統聲明繼續抗戰之決心此即為需要新增供給之表示惟緬甸如入敵人之手,美國供給亦無從置華此點亦應細察。本人所提建議擬如入「應考慮支持中國戰線」一節。

(委座)中國如不能支持其戰線全部保衛緬甸之計劃亦將瓦解,予確認保衛緬甸自有其價值惟租借法案器材中國自有其應享之權利亦望勿加忽視。

(衛)倘鈞座以為我方撥用租借法案器材對中國國防有不利之影响本人願竭自有物資以衛緬甸。

(委座)撥用租借法案器材以衛緬甸,予早作願以相助之表示,所願慮者惟以後之接濟耳。總之,致總統電中,應列入支持中國戰線一節。中國軍隊

字第二八號　計件

第一四七頁

157

（委座）予願對勃蘭德將軍之建議另作補充。

（衛）所擬計劃務必以一二個月時間限度為標準。

（委座）於報告羅斯福總統以前擬具全盤計劃實有必要。

（衛）予反對此說，報告羅斯福總統之計劃應注重當前緊要問題。

（委座）中英美三國余既並肩作戰自需一全盤整個之計劃，我人試檢討過去之行動大都頭痛醫頭腳痛醫腳待事件發生始倉卒應付以與我共同敵人週旋，此後我人計劃自應着眼於整個戰區之防衛，防衛緬甸亦包括在內，如是則不作六個月之計劃，必將犯目光短視之嫌，緬甸之防守固屬重要，香港呈加坡之「保衛亦當容忽視，此尝為本會所應兼籌並顧之處。余盼在兩將軍離渝之前必擬具計劃以答總統侍衛佛爾將軍堅持反對自不妨碍商修改之。

（美）委座之意本會應明自通如英美兩國不能希望中國不得援助而可無限繼續其抗戰凡致總統電文中峏應詳細說明中國目前之地位。

（委座）予可贊成勃蘭德將軍所提四點，無局部計劃，全盤計劃自亦失其擬訂之根據，然於實施局部計劃以前，亦應先知全盤計劃之概要。或者我人可將各項建議畫向總統報告之。

（衛）本人反對此舉，蓋目前根本尚無可以報告之資料，應組織小組委員會詳加研究決定之，就目前言，我人既無擬具六個月計劃之準備不如再候

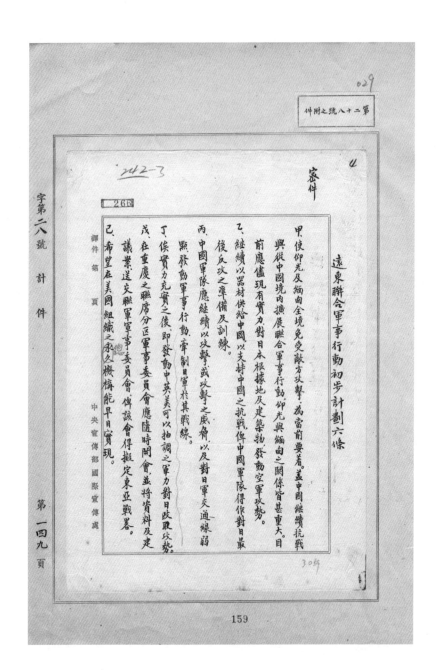

案件

242-3

266

遠東聯合軍事行動初步計劃六條

甲、使仰光及緬甸全境免受敵方攻擊，為當前要著。蓋中國繼續抗戰與從中國境內擴展聯合軍事行動，仰光與緬甸之關係皆甚重大。目前應儘現有實力對日本根據地及建築物，發動空軍攻勢。

乙、繼續以器材供給中國以支持中國之抗戰俾中國軍隊得作對日最後反攻之準備及訓練。

丙、中國軍隊應繼續以攻擊或攻擊之威脅，以及對日軍交通線弱點發動軍事行動，牽制日軍於其戰線。

丁、俟實力充實之後，即發動中英美可以抽調之軍力對日政取攻勢。在重慶之聯席分區軍事委員會俾該會得擬定東亞戰署。

戊、建議業送交聯軍軍事委員會應隨時開會，並將資料及建議業送交聯軍軍事委員會俾該會得擬定東亞戰署。

己、希望在美國組織之永久機構能早日實現。

029

可調赴任何地點，惟於事前應詳知作戰計劃。

（衛）承識　鈞座對借調希諾德上校部下志願空軍之請已有決定否，倘可借調，希立即實施。不然，則將向他處另行設法。

（委座）本人可同意此項計劃惟因與志願空軍訂有合同關係，尚須徵求希諾德上校之意見，再有聲明者，即令准予調用，待英國增援到達之後，該中隊即應返中國原防。

勃蘭德所建議之決議案最後改成六點，一同意將該案全文電告羅斯福總統。其六點如下：甲、使仰光及緬甸全境免受敵方攻擊，為當前要著。蓋中國繼續抗戰與從中國境內擴展聯合軍事行動，仰光興緬甸之關係實基重大。日前應儘現有實力，對日本根據地及建築物發動空軍攻勢。乙、繼續以器材供給中國以支持中國之抗戰俾中國軍隊得作對日最後反攻之準備及訓練。丙、中國軍隊應繼續以攻擊，或攻擊之威脅，以及對日軍火通線弱點發動軍事行動牽制日軍於其戰線。丁、俟實力充實之後，即發動中英美可以抽調之軍刀對日改取攻勢。戊、在重慶之聯席分區軍事委員會俾該會得擬定東亞戰略。己、希望在美國組織之聯軍軍事委員會，該會得應隨時間機構能早日實現。委座聲明所擬建議，擬單獨送致總統。

029

267

RECOMMENDED PLANS APPROVED BY THE PRELIMINARY JOINT MILITARY CONFERENCE

December 23, 1941

1. As a first essential to secure against enemy attack Rangoon and Burma, both of which are vital for China's continued resistance and any extension of joint action from China. Meanwhile to take offensive air action against Japanese bases and installations to the greatest extent that resources permit.

2. Maintain China's resistance by continued supplies of material to enable Chinese armies to prepare and train for ultimate offensive against Japan.

3. Meantime the Chinese armies should continue to occupy the Japanese forces on their front by attacks or threats of attacks and by action against their vulnerable lines of communication.

4. As soon as resources permit to pass to an offensive against Japan with all forces available, Chinese British and American.

5. This *Joint military council sitting in Chungking will* meet and submit information and proposals to enable Allied Council to work out strategy *for East Asia*.

6. Hope is expressed that a permanent organization to be set up in Washington will soon materialize.

the United States

Supreme War

遠東聯合軍事行動部
步計劃六條業已通過
凌改為

檔案 18：「賀耀組電蔣中正馬歇爾轉史汀生稱與宋子文商得諒解以史迪威將軍任中國戰區參謀長將儘速來華報到已函復表示歡迎」（1942 年 2 月 13 日）

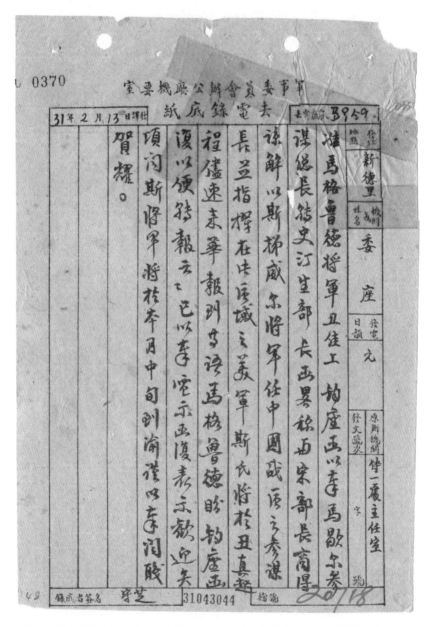

資料來源：〈遠征入緬（一）〉，《蔣中正總統文物》，國史館藏，數位典藏號：002-090105-00006-035。

檔案 19:「蔣中正與史迪威談話紀錄：第五第六軍歸史指揮緬甸中英軍隊統一指揮」（1942年3月11日）

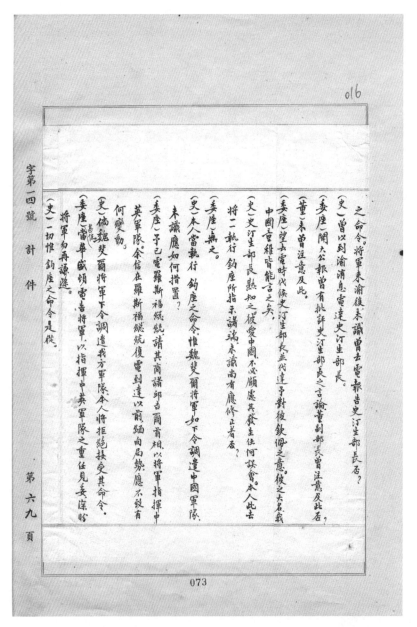

之。(蔣)命令。將軍來渝後未識曾去電報告史汀生部長否？

(史)曾以到渝消息電達史汀生部長。

(蔣)聞大公報曾有批評史汀生部長之言論董副部長曾注意及此否，

(董)來曾注意及此。

(蔣)望去電時代候史汀生部長正代達予對彼欽佩之意。彼之大名我中國童維皆能言之矣。

(史)史汀生部長熟知之彼愛中國不必顧慮其發生任何誤會本人此去將二執行 鈞座所指示講端末識尚有應修正者否？

(蔣)無之。

(史)本人當執行 鈞座之命令。惟魏斐爾將軍如下令調遣中國軍隊，末識應如何措置？

(蔣)予已電羅斯福總統。請其商諸邱吉爾首相以將軍指揮中英軍隊。余信在羅斯福總統復電到達以前緬甸局勢應不致有何變動，

(史)倘魏斐爾將軍下令調遣我方軍隊本人將拒絕接受其命令，

(蔣)當華盛頓電告將軍以指揮中英軍隊之重任見委深盼將軍勿再謙遜。

(史)一切惟 鈞座之命令是從。

字第一四號 計 件

第六九頁

073

資料來源：〈革命文獻－同盟國聯合作戰：遠征軍入緬（一）〉，《蔣中正總統文物》，國史館藏，數位典藏號：002-020300-00019-016。

016

36-29

字第一四號　計二頁件

三一年三月十一日上午十一時接見史蒂威爾將軍談話紀錄　第六八頁

（商主任在座）

（委座）余令晨業已下令「第五第六兩軍歸將軍指揮」。

（史）感甚。

（委座）我方在緬甸設有無線電台數處，據其三月八日及九日來電告英軍於三月七日退出仰光，惟目前日軍在城中縱大焚燬所餘卡車三、月八日晨十二時日軍三千人入仰光。昨晚何繼長接到英方軍事代表通告，魏斐爾將軍已負指揮緬甸全部作戰之責，予意魏斐爾將軍不能勝此重責，深恐我入緬部隊不願受彼指揮，余仍保持我原來主張緬甸中英軍隊皆應由將軍指揮之，未識將軍對緬甸總部之組織已有所規劃否？

（史）本人擬先派少數參謀人員赴第五軍軍部所在地，本人亦擬以大部時間駐留該處，蓋該處交通設備既甚完備而第六軍目前尚不致有何動作，正可以全部注意集中於第五軍也。

（委座）如此佈置甚佳，林參謀團長蔚文之總部令在臘戌將軍後方辦事即可利用彼之機構，予已令彼予將軍以一切便利，即可儘量利用彼之參謀協助工作將軍在後方林即可為將軍之參謀長，林參謀團長以下如第五軍第六軍軍長等皆已奉命絕對服從將軍

檔案 20：「蔣中正電宋子文駐印軍新編二十二師第三十九師歸史迪威羅卓英整訓」
　　　　（1942 年 7 月 7 日）

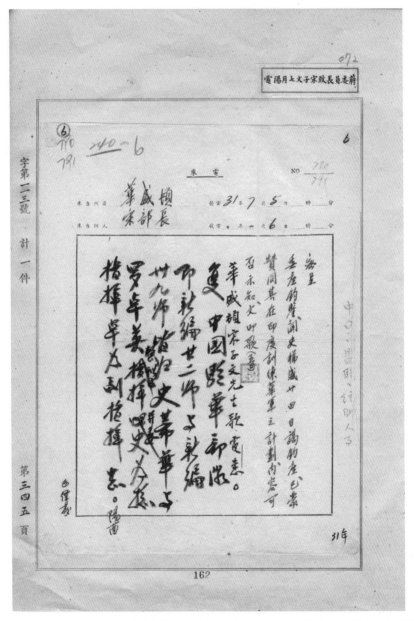

資料來源：〈革命文獻—同盟國聯合作戰：遠征軍入緬（二）〉，《蔣中正總統文物》，國史館
藏，數位典藏號：002-020300-00020-072。

檔案 21：1942 年第 LXI 號條例：為規定關於同盟國及外國軍隊在印軍隊辦法事
（1942 年 10 月 26 日）

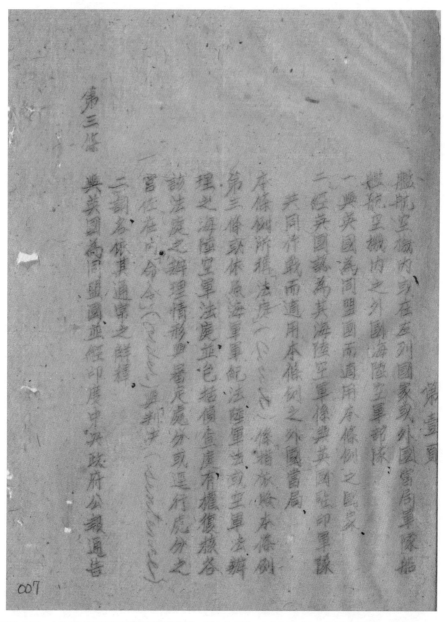

資料來源：〈駐印度國軍法權管轄問題〉，《外交部》，國史館藏，數位典藏號：020-011903-0017。

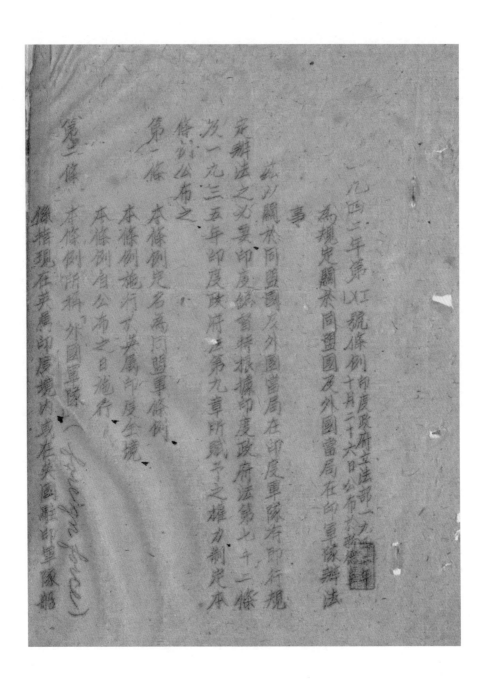

一九四二年第 LXI 號條例　印度政府立法部（一九⋯⋯十月二十六日公布⋯⋯號條例）

為規定關於同盟國友外國當局在印度軍隊辦法

事

兹以關於同盟國友外國當局在印度軍隊有即行規
定辦法之必要印度條督将根據印度政府法第七十二條
及一九三五年印度政府法第九章所賦予之權力制定本
條例並公布之

第一條　本條例定名為同盟軍條例
本條例施行于英屬印度全境
本條例自公布之日施行

第二條　本條例所稱「外國軍隊」（foreign force）
係指現在英屬印度境内或在英國屬印軍隊船

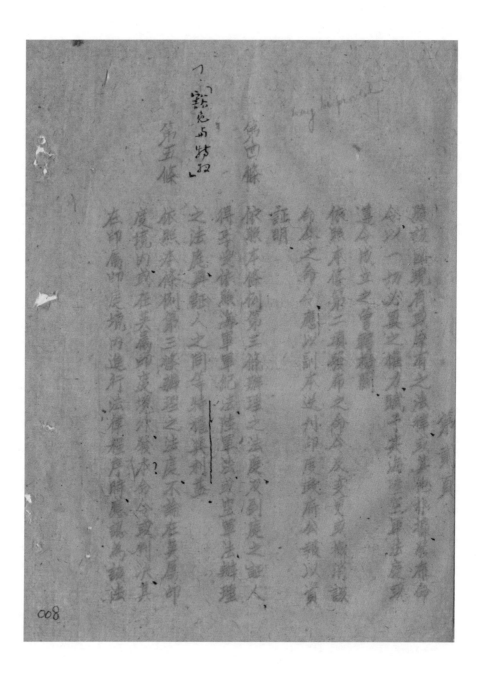

第十條

（略）

華軍被此間行預主之刑事罪行而已即處法律明文

視免誚如印度政府視為必要時所有在印華軍官兵、

犯此刑各罪者必科以極刑即處軍刑同時兵

注意所加重營之範圍僅限於該營本身之世界而已

並不另指給該匪徒即用加城在內

四

依所斯述是見在印華軍官兵為其本身利益計實應

與此事加以合作每一官兵均負有精練之責任無論

何地何時見有違法行為時即與印華合作之即醫已

賦有效定之權力對任何中國人有可疑狀態或妨

五

害秩序者均得制令制止並諭其往老階級其部屬

吾人於此復要求卷師長或其位長官之合作〔英軍

印警民吏間之糾紛此為〕何那謂印度民政用真誠合

013

備忘錄

一、指揮部高級參謀人員與哈查立寺加區域副長官之
會議方告完畢軍前加侖在該區域就現在之內該副長官
則負責處理該區域所有民眾警政事宜撤離於過去
數月來中印人士在該馬均之合作備向司令部各長
官表示謝忱並希望此員合作得能廣議

二、關於華軍在印法律地位實際情形似宜向司令部
長官加以說明

三、該副長官願司令部在宣長對於中國軍士在印加軍
營外之帆律與行動能採取一切必須之措施但須切
責說明若此與彼個人之責任無關在印華軍官兵均
應遵守印度之法律所能制外者僅為在朋加軍營內

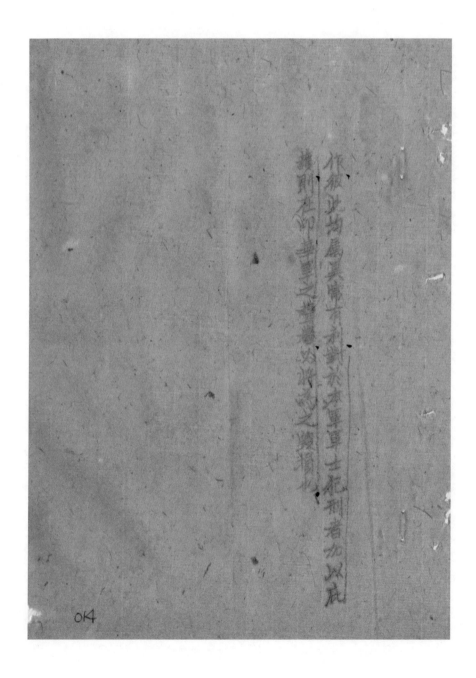

作敵此均應具報之不僅本軍軍士死刑者加以砲

誰則在師長重之責任如將校之瀆職

檔案 22：駐加爾各答總領事館致外交部加字（33）第 336 號代電（1944 年 6 月 9 日）

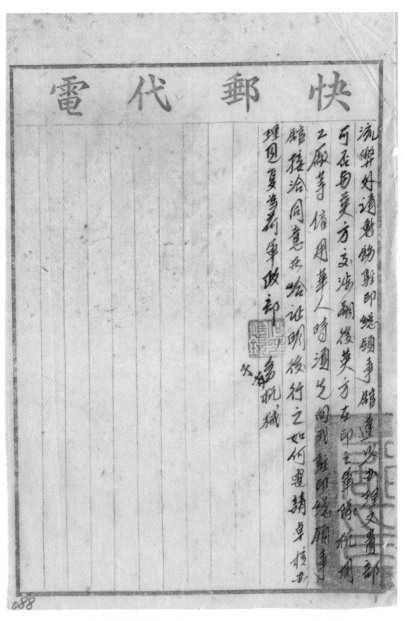

資料來源：〈駐印度國軍法權管轄問題〉，《外交部》，國史館藏，數位典藏號：020-011903-0017。

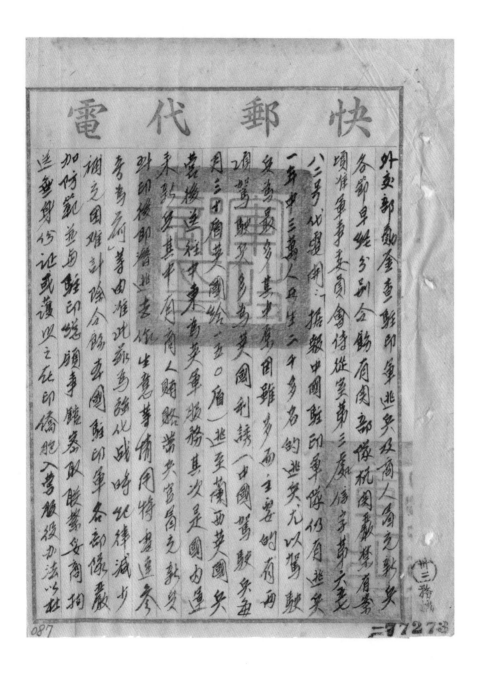

快郵代電

外交部勛鑒查駐印軍逃兵及商人會充勤兵
各節疊皋迭分別令飭商有關部隊統問嚴禁有案
頃據軍事委員會侍從室第三處傳字第六號
八三號代電開⋯據報中國駐印軍隊仍有逃英
一年中三萬人以生二千多名約逃英尤以駕駛
兵為最多其次為團雖多而主要的有再
項駕駛敺買多為英國利誘（中國駕駛兵為
見三十個英國給三五〇盾）逃至蘭西英國兵尤
嵩接丘種平東為英軍服務其次是國內運
來勤兵其中有商人賄賂英官員充軍受
對印後卽轉逃走⋯生意等備團特書運參
事為嗣苧由惟此⋯為強化戰時紀律減少
補充困難計除令駐印軍各部隊嚴
加防範並鈐印筋頒事⋯客取聯絡妥商拘
送無身份证或護收之在印僑胞入告械役办法以杜

087

二七二七三

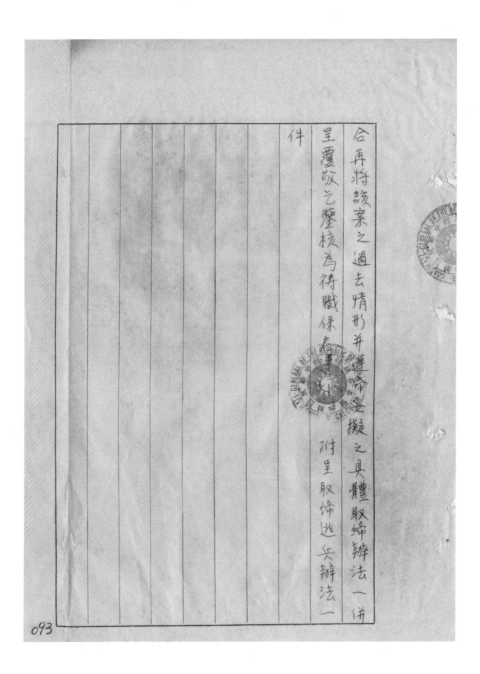

合再將該案之過去情形并遵命擬之具體取締辦法一併

呈覆敬乞鑒核為禱職保　　附呈取締逃兵辦法一

件

093

駐加爾各答總領事館代電

遞達機關　外交部
由事
附件　抄件一
中華民國三十三年　六月九日發
加字33第二三六號

部次長鈞鑒奉歐33字第二二號鈞電以我國駐印軍隊時有

潛逃并有商人冒充新兵到印後即逃出隊另作生意飭妄

擬取締辦法具報等因奉此查我國駐印軍隊自前年到印駐

紮以來確時有逃兵發現其逃往印度東部各區者均經本館

依法續捕而當地政府亦頗予協助每拘捕輒送來館均經彙

解藍伽軍部訊辦本館無不隨時相機嚴密協助取締現在似

已較前減少至於僑胞方面亦曾有不法之徒勾引逃兵者本

館亦已嚴予撤底清理使逃兵逛勇無法混迹僑社所有各情

均經於各次報告中呈報在案查杜除逃風治本之策仍應由

指揮部方面從嚴管束蓋於止較拘處為直心兹奉電前因理

第　頁

092

（四）請軍政部令知指揮部切實與總領館合作（平時并非不合作）

并隨時互通消息凡有僑民雖非軍人而有與逃兵事有關經

總領館通知者亦應受理。

（乙）治標辦法。

（一）由本館知照當地政府不得僱用無身份証及護照之中國僑民并

注意其身份証有無塗改及掉換照片情事。

（二）請當地政府切實注意無居留証身份或護照之中國僑民并

隨時與總領館合作。

095

取締逃兵辦法

（甲）治本辦法：

（一）嚴查交運特別注意昆明及丁江兩站以免有冒充軍人或商人混跡於士兵之間。

（二）請軍政部飭令我國駐印軍部對部隊嚴加約束切實管理以遏逃風。

（三）請軍政部飭令我國駐印軍各級長官不得隨意准部下長假其必須准給長假者應設法送返祖國否則亦應妥擬適當之安插辦法以免其流落更免逃兵以請准長假為藉口而在外

逍遙。

軍乃委員會蔣公厘公鑒：關於英印刑乃法庭对家
國軍乃人員之裁判权问题一案，貴厘本年五月十九
日蘇四二外字第1866號代电暨附件均敬悉，本部經將
该印警昌通知原文抄凡一係封達英國大使館查
蘇，至關於英國大使館轉達印度政府所提議嗣收
以遇任何一案件之發生，其裁判权问题之断定均拟以
被控者立于犯法律时之身份地位为取决之根拟一
節，愛應对本部本年四月廿四日出文所引述之中英協
定（軍運）第二條规定，课为其東真，性事期別情形及當地乙
級軍官同真权，僅指武嚴法第七條第八條之場合而

154

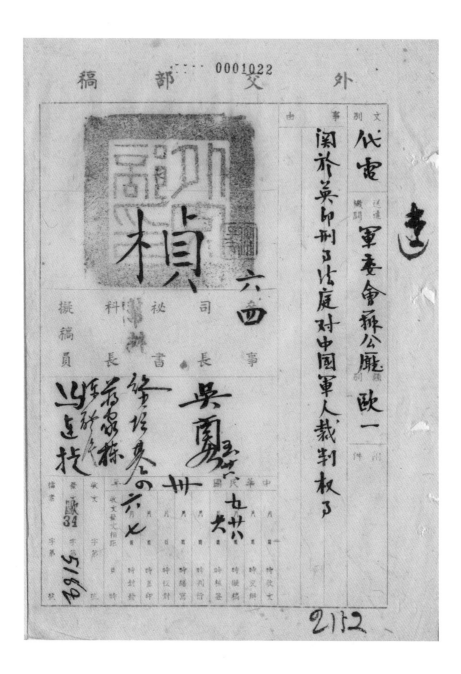

一九四三年美英國於軍隊國外法权之後[?]對日亦有同樣之規定似不全先例，

知[?]即應另先例文一[?]目，所如指疾國賊略第[?]兩條

如場合即重，其而指特別原因自不止一端，而以逃逸善

通习法審判為目的而入伍之欧之歐著業件，而以業件又為

嚴重之刑罰性者[?]目為特珠原由因之一本部諡愛所

称「以逞失該部将的而指陳之已实发生，其情節嚴重

者当可援用此规定以期獲以逞害之救應」本章即措用

以應之，阅於裁判权問題之断定英印而提議之辦法

古一般通似不合，豪国自难同真，貴属素文而引述之家

國陸海空軍審判法第十六、條规定至为恰当，本部抄

挑此點並復英國大使館唯為祛除英方之顧慮便易

言頭諉當地任何高級軍官有權同意將本團軍人歸外

國法院管轄似覺言此先例．查戒嚴法第七、八兩條由明文

規定戒嚴時設習法，務設歸司令官掌管司法官應

受習令官指揮並未提及司令官可同真地方法院行

使管轄權以與中英協定草案第二條所指之情形

似毫何聯繫．按一九四三年五月廿一日中美換文內亦有

與中英協定第二條之同樣規定且諮調更當明晰．英文

載稱其間有以特別原因美國政府軍了當局或認為此項

頭中英協定第二條之同樣規定且諮調更當明晰．英文

裁判以不受理為宜．則建議各項均應以書面經由外交

金徑通知中國政府俾可由中國當局從事裁判。

丁4（192×272公厘）

達於接近之程度起見，查本部對英國大使館復照由

茲扣述現正商訂中之中英合軍人員互享待遇有關

品外治权協定，以便獲得部之嚴重。獲得遣專之澈查

准憲前由，相應復請查照為荷。外交部啟

丁4（192×272公厘）

156

檔案 23：國際公法摘要

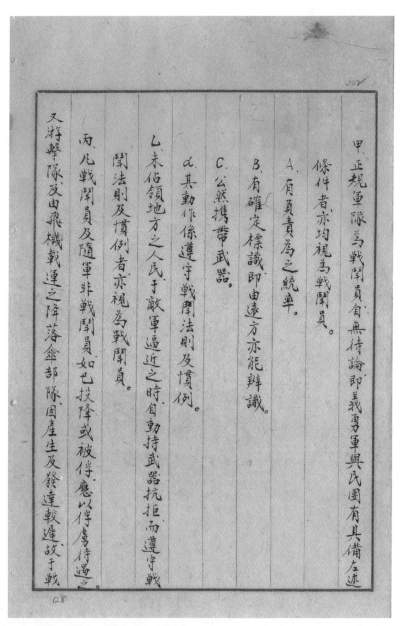

甲、正規軍隊為戰鬥員自無待論，即義勇軍與民團有具備左述
條件者亦均視為戰鬥員。

A. 有員責為之統率。

B. 有確定標識即由遠方亦能辨識。

C. 公然攜帶武器。

d. 其動作係遵守戰鬥法則及慣例。

乙、未佔領地方之人民于敵軍逼近之時自動持武器抗拒而遵守戰
鬥法則及慣例者亦視為戰鬥員。

丙、凡戰鬥員及隨軍非戰鬥員如已投降或被俘應以俘虜待遇之。

又游擊隊及由飛機載運之降落傘部隊，因產生及發達較遲故于戰

資料來源：「遠征手冊」，〈遠征軍司令長官任內資料（一）〉，《陳誠副總統文物》，國史館藏，
數位典藏號：008-010701-00068-002。

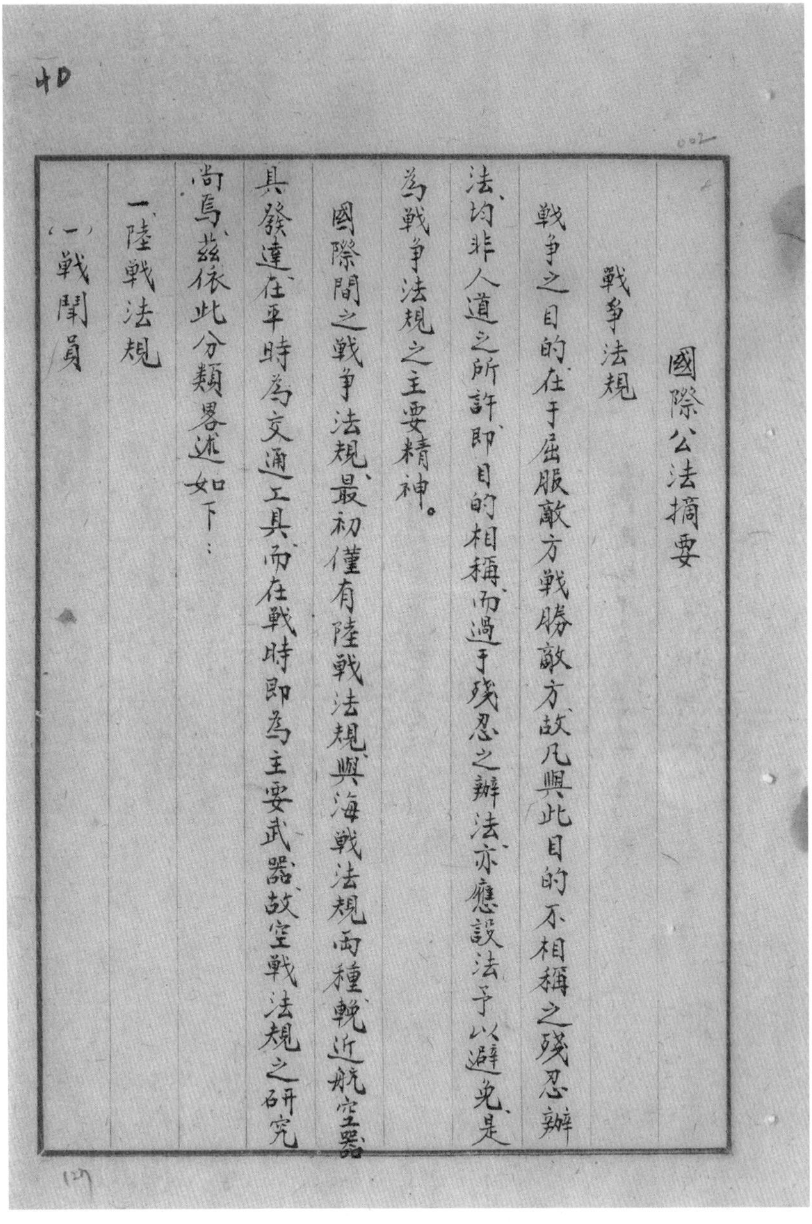

40

002

國際公法摘要

戰爭法規

戰爭之目的在于屈服敵方戰勝敵方、故凡與此目的不相稱之殘忍辦法、均非人道之所許、即目的相稱、而過于殘忍之辦法、亦應設法予以避免、是為戰爭法規之主要精神。

國際間之戰爭法規、最初僅有陸戰法規、與海戰法規兩種、輓近航空器具發達、在平時為交通工具、而在戰時即為主要武器、故空戰法規之研究尚焉、茲依此分類畧述如下：

一、陸戰法規

(一)戰鬥員

127

據軍事官長之命令將其數目點明後方得取去并須製給收據

取去之銀錢應列入各有關俘虜之賬內俘虜之身份証書官階証

章勳章及貴重物品不得取去之。

丁所有戰時俘虜均應于俘獲後最短時間內移送于距戰線較遠

之收容所以避危險。

戊俘虜所居住之處所均應担保其適于衛生與健康俘虜之食物須

與本國軍隊食物質量相同俘虜之服裝鞋襪應按期更新鋄修補之。

己俘虜中之軍官及軍官得由收容國鋄給與該國軍隊內同級軍官

相等之餉薪但此餉薪不得超過彼等在其本國軍隊內應領之

數目。

41

爭法規中尚無明白規定然依上述甲乙兩項規定衡之自仍應視為戰鬥

員而于被捕獲時予以俘虜待遇．

(二)俘虜之待遇

甲、俘虜始終應受人道之待遇，並應保護，不受虐待及民眾之侮

辱，除因職別健康情形，職務能力，男女性別外，不得有不同之待遇。

乙、詢問俘虜時，不得施用強迫手段，以為取得關于其本軍或本國

情形消息之用，俘虜之拒絕答覆者，不得施以任何恫嚇侮辱或予

以任何不快不利之待遇．

丙、凡俘虜自用之服裝及物件，除軍器馬匹軍裝軍用文件外，應仍

歸俘虜保持，又鋼盔及防毒面具亦然，俘虜所帶之銀錢必須根

129

護之。用尾一交戰國軍隊之傷者病者落于他交戰國之手時應以俘虜待遇之。

丙、每次戰後佔戰場者、應設法搜覓傷者病者、并防止搶掠及虐待。

丁、所收容或發現傷者病者及死者之姓名應即報告最高長官以便彙集通知敵方。

戊、醫生護士及教士應受保護、其人民組織之救護團体、而曾被承認者、亦應受同樣待遇。

己、任何隔于敵方活動救護隊得保存其用品與輸運工具及車伕。但主管機關有權收為救護傷者病者之用。

庚、單行或群行用為救療搬移之醫務車輛、應與活動救療隊同庚、對于重病重傷之俘虜不論階級及數目應于其能受運送時送歸其本國或交由中立國招待所有送歸及移送之費用自收容國之界。

一、其本國或交由中立國招待所有送歸及移送之費用自收容國之界。

起概由俘虜曾服役之國担任。

辛、俘虜之遺囑應照收容國軍人同樣辦法為之接收并予備案關于証明死亡之文件亦同樣辦理之。

(三)戰地傷者病者之待遇

甲、凡軍隊內之軍人及其他正式隨軍服務之人員受傷或生病時，應不分國籍概予遵重并給人道之待遇及救護。

乙、急迫退却時、不得已而抛棄傷者病者應在在軍務情形可能範圍內將救護人員及醫藥材料之一部份留為該傷者病者救軍使及其隨從之號兵旗手及譜譯員等，均享有不可侵犯權。

乚、敵方軍使之來他方并無必乎接受之義務，可揚不接受之信號命

其退回住其退回之途程中，不得襲擊或停虜之。

丙軍使雖有不可侵犯之特權但司令官得採取一切必要手段以防止其窺

探軍情（如規定路線或遮掩其耳目等辦法是）軍使濫用特權或欺詐

行為時，得不以軍使待遇，而暫時扣留之。

（六）投降

甲、投降條件，于雙方軍事當局議訂時切勿傷及軍隊之榮譽。

乚、投降條件一經議訂應誠實遵守之。

（七）休戰

樣待遇。

辛，用白地加紅十字于中心作為軍隊內救療機關之特別符號紅十字

旗只可掛于應受保護之建築物或機關之上不得冒用濫用且應

同時懸掛本國國旗。

（四）間諜

甲、凡以詭秘行動或喬裝或作虛偽之陳述投入交戰他方刺探或法

刺探軍情者，始得認為間諜。

乙、被捕之間諜，非經審訊不得處罰。

（五）軍使旗

甲、奉交戰一方之命令，欲與交戰地他方交涉并高揚白旗者為軍使、

A. 得徵收賦稅捐稅等惟應依原有稅率辦理一切行政費用亦應照舊負担又如此外另有徵收則應以軍事上及地方行政上之必要為限。

B. 得為實物及力役之徵用為應以軍事之必要為限且于被徵用團体或個人之員担能力亦應與予顧及又徵用命令必須以司令官之名義行之對于所徵用之物品應設法給以現金以資補償否則必須給與收據以為憑証。

C. 得佔用一切屬于敵國國家所有之款項証券軍火庫交通工具及足供軍用之動產。

d. 得佔用一切交通工具軍用品貨倉等此類物品縱使屬于私

甲、休戰條件一經議定雙方即應暫停敵對行為至其停戰期間應

于停戰條件內明白規定之。

乙、休戰條件或為一般的或為局部的均無不可。

丙、休戰條件經一方之破壞他方即可將其廢棄惟如此項破壞行為係

出于個人則僅能要求對方查明處罰。

(八)軍事佔領

甲、凡一地方在交戰中事實上入于對方軍隊之管領即為軍事佔領。

乙、佔領方之軍事當局應採取一切手段以恢復并維持當地之安寧秩

秩序并應于可能範圍內對于當地法律予以遵重。

丙、佔領方之軍事當局得為如左之措置：

二、空戰法規

(一)軍隊軍事工程軍需工廠及存儲所、兵工廠、軍械局、軍事交通、及其連運路線、雖得作為轟炸目標但如目必須殃及居民時、應避免轟炸之。

(二)戰場附近之城市鄉村住宅及建築物必因其為軍力集中之重要地點、始得予以轟炸但居民因而蒙受之危險亦應予以顧及。

(三)此外復經定有如下之限制、

　果不得轟炸距戰場較遠之城市鄉村住宅及建築物。

e、凡宗教機關慈善機關教育機關所有財產不論是否國家所有應一律視為私有財產不得予以扣押或毀壞。

人亦仍得佔用之，惟于埃復和平後應予返還并給付償金。

e.得佔用屬于敵國國家所有之一切建築物、地產、森林農其等物，惟應以使用收益人之態度時妥為保護。

丁、佔領方之軍事當局所為各項措置應受如左之限制。

A、不得強迫居留人民提供其本國之軍情，亦不得強迫宣誓效忠于己。

B、家庭榮譽、個人生命與權利、私有財產、宗教信仰、及其他習慣應予遵重。

C、不得放縱掠奪，不得沒收私有財產。

d、不得因個人行動而對整個社會為財產上或其他科罰。

乙、不得以轟炸恐嚇平民毀壞私人財產住宅及建築物。

丙、不得以轟炸為強制徵用軍餉及軍需之手段。

丁、不得轟炸宗教藝術科學慈善各機關之建築物歷史紀念品、衛生船隻醫院及傷者病者之集合處所。

中英軍事合作與「中緬印戰區」（1940-1945）：英國檔案中的觀察 *

鄺智文
香港浸會大學歷史系副教授

一、前言：英國在亞洲與太平洋戰場的角色

「中緬印戰區」（China Burma India Theater, CBI）一語，最早來自美國陸軍於 1942 年 3 月在此地區的指揮機構「中緬印美國陸軍司令部」（Headquarters, American Army Forces, China, Burma and India, AAF CBI），這個名稱顯示太平洋戰爭初期美國陸軍的領導和計劃當局對此戰區的理解。[1] 可是，這並非唯一的理解方式，因為此戰區亦與中、英兩國有莫大之關係，三國對此戰區的性質、重要性、作戰目標，以及戰鬥手段均有不同甚至互相衝突的理解。1942 年 7 月英印陸軍總司令部關於國軍遠征軍實力的一份報告，提到中英兩軍「對戰鬥時的時間和空間概念不盡相同」（Their conception of time and space factors in battle is different from ours），因此難以合作。[2] 雖然報告作者當時正討論戰術問題，實則此問題在中、英、美三國的戰略合作中亦時有出現。

不少論者研究中緬印戰區時，大多集中於中緬印戰區的「中、緬」部分，特別是地面戰鬥，少有注意印緬邊境、印度洋，甚至空中戰場，以及相關後勤體系與中緬戰局的關係。本文希望指出，討論中緬印戰區時，實有必

---

* General Research Fund provided by the Research Grants Council of Hong Kong (project title "The Japanese 'Total-State' Experiment in Hong Kong, 1942-1945," project no. 12600219).

1 CBI Order of Battle: Lineages and History, http://www.cbi-history.com (accessed 10 June 2020).

2 "The Chinese Army in Burma," 6 July 1942, WO 208/384, TNA.

要留意它與世界其他戰區的關聯，特別是與地中海—中東—印度洋戰局的
關係。對英方而言，中緬印戰區包含數個互相關連的區域：中國、東南亞、
印度、印度洋、中東，以及太平洋和大洋洲等。由於印度是中國戰區和中緬
前線的大後方，印度洋則是印度與世界其他地區的連接處，因此英國在此戰
區的重要性絕不應被忽略。[3] 至 1944 年 6 月，緬甸前線的英軍第 11 集團軍
（11th Army Group）屬下的第 14 軍團（Fourteenth Army），共有 3 個軍，計
有 14 個師、1 個獨立旅，與「欽迪特突擊隊」（Chindits）[4] 等龐大兵力，其時
在緬北的美軍有 65,784 人，國軍有 147,396 人，可見英國對緬甸戰區之投入
和重視程度。[5]

　　齊錫生在《劍拔弩張的盟友》[6] 中，曾全面討論中美在中緬印戰區一面共
同作戰，一面磨擦不斷的複雜關係。本文則嘗試拋磚引玉，以英國國家檔案
局（The National Archives, TNA）所藏之檔案史料，討論中、美、英三國對
日作戰時遇到的各種問題和困難、三國的合作和衝突，以及英國軍政領導
階層對此戰區的不同理解。除了三國之間的張力外，本文亦希望指出英國政
府內部，包括首相邱吉爾（Winston Churchill, 1874-1965）、外交部、海陸空
三軍，與身在亞洲的指揮官們，對戰況和相應策略的理解亦時有出入，因此
不應概括地將英國不同部門和部隊，簡化為方向和意志相同的整體。本文先
簡介英國國家檔案局所藏的中緬印戰區相關檔案，然後以 26 件檔案資料為

3　其實，即使美軍自身亦於 1944 年 10 月史迪威離開後，將此司令部分拆為美軍中國戰區
　　（United States Army Forces, China Theater, USF CT），以及美軍印緬戰區（United States
　　Forces, India, Burma Theater, USF IBT）。

4　港譯「殲敵部隊」。

5　"Appendix D: Skeleton Order of Battle, 11 Army Group, South-East Asia Command, 22nd
　　June 1944," in John Grehan and Martin Mace, *The Battle for Burma 1943-1945: From Kohima
　　& Imphal Through to Victory* (Barnsley: Pen and Sword Books, 2015).

6　齊錫生，《劍拔弩張的盟友：太平洋戰爭期間的中美軍事合作關係（1941-1945）》（臺
　　北：中央研究院近代史研究所、聯經出版事業公司，2011 年）。英文的相類研究可
　　參看 Hans van de Ven, *China at War: Triumph and Tragedy in the Emergence of the New
　　China* (Cambridge, MA: Harvard University Press, 2018); Christopher Bayly and Tim Harper,
　　Forgotten Armies: The Fall of British Asia, 1941-1945 (London: Allen Lane, 2004).

例，討論英國與中緬印戰區的幾個問題：太平洋戰爭爆發前英國對國民政府在交通和軍事方面的支援、太平洋戰爭初期的中英軍事合作，以及英國在戰爭末期對國民政府抗戰能力的判斷等。

二、英國國家檔案局藏中緬印戰區相關檔案簡介

英國國家檔案局所藏的中緬印戰區相關檔案，除常用的外交部檔案（Records of the Foreign Office），主要來自內閣檔案（Records of the Cabinet Office）、陸軍部檔案（Records of the War Office），以及特殊作戰執行部檔案（Records of Special Operations Executive）這3個系列，其中相關的檔案細目如下述：

（一）內閣檔案

內閣檔案收錄了1863至2018年間英國內閣和屬下委員會的檔案，包括會議紀錄和參考資料，計有384個檔案系列。與中緬印作戰相關的是CAB 79參謀首長委員會會議紀錄（War Cabinet and Cabinet: Chiefs of Staff Committee: Minutes. Minutes of Meetings，共92卷，涵蓋1939至1946年）和CAB 80參謀首長委員會備忘錄系列（War Cabinet and Cabinet: Chiefs of Staff Committee: Memoranda，共107卷，涵蓋1939至1946年）。參謀首長委員會由海、陸、空三軍參謀長組成，包括第一海務大臣（First Sea Lord）、帝國總參謀長（Chief of Imperial General Staff），以及空軍總參謀長（Chief of the Air Staff）組成。參謀長委員會於1923年成立，為首相和內閣分析軍事問題，並提供建議，亦為三軍提供合作溝通的機會。其屬下有聯合計劃小組（Joint Planning Sub-Committee），由三軍計劃人員做成，為參謀首長委員會提供詳細分析和計劃。

（二）陸軍部檔案

陸軍部（War Office）檔案收錄了所有英國陸軍相關的檔案，涵蓋時段為 1568 至 2007 年，其中與第二次世界大戰中緬印戰區相關者為 WO 106、WO 172、WO 193、WO 203 及 WO 208 檔案系列，其詳細內容如下：

1. WO 106 陸軍部作戰與軍事情報處檔案（War Office: Directorate of Military Operations and Military Intelligence）系列屬於陸軍部作戰處檔案，涵蓋時間為 1837 至 1962 年。與第二次世界大戰相關的機構，包括陸軍部作戰與情報處（Directorate of Military Operations and Intelligence, 1922-1939）、陸軍部作戰與計劃處（Directorate of Military Operations and Plans, 1939-1943）、陸軍部作戰處（Directorate of Military Operations, 1943-1964），以及陸軍部計劃處（War Office, Directorate of Plans, 1943-1964）。此系列共有 6,402 個卷宗，但與中緬印戰區相關的部分有限。與中國有關的檔案收錄在數個「中國」（China）資料夾，和中國抗戰和中緬印戰區相關的檔案主要是 WO 106/3533 至 WO 106/3591、WO 106/118 至 WO 106/128，以及 WO 106/5249 至 WO 106/5254。

2. WO 172 第二次世界大戰英國陸軍東南亞部隊作戰日誌（War Office: British and Allied Land Forces, South East Asia: War Diaries, Second World War）系列收入 1939 至 1946 年間，英國陸軍被派到亞太地區的所有部隊的作戰日誌（War Diaries）和相關資料，共有 11,401 個卷宗。每次作戰後，英軍各兵種和部隊均會撰寫作戰日誌，有時不同兵種的作戰日誌，會以戰略單位（軍團、軍、師、旅）被整合起來，成為一個完整的作戰日誌，但不同兵種和部隊亦會保留自己的日誌。例如，1941 年香港作戰後，駐港英軍的指揮官們撰寫了「要塞日誌」（Fortress War Diary），屬下的步兵旅亦撰寫了作戰日誌，各步兵營、砲兵團、工兵，以及後勤部隊等，亦有保留各自的作戰日誌。由於守軍戰敗，不少檔案在投降時被毀，因此以上日誌的內容只靠記憶重組。這個情況在馬來亞和香港作戰中被消滅的部隊較為常見，但其後的作戰日誌則較為完整。要尋找關於與國軍共同作戰的英國陸軍部隊，以及 204 使團（Mission 204）等部隊的作戰日誌，可參看「緬甸1942」（Burma 1942）自 WO 172/369 至 WO 172/1457（25 個卷宗，約 1,000 份檔案）、「緬甸 1944」（Burma 1944）自 WO 172/4145 至 WO 172/11339（55 個卷宗，約 7,000 份檔案）。要尋找相關檔案，最好能先確定部隊的名稱和番號。

3. WO 193 陸軍部作戰與計劃處檔案（War Office: Directorate of Military Operations and Plans）系列收入 1934 至 1958 年，關於陸軍報作戰及計劃處，以及其前身組織的參照檔案（Collation Files），共有 1,008 個卷宗。與中緬印相關的檔案在「遠東」（Far East）部分，包括 WO 193/863 至 WO 193/869、WO 193/892 至 WO 193/898、WO 193/915 至 WO 193/922 等，大多關於中、英兩國在戰前和開戰初期的軍事聯絡。

4. WO 203 東南亞戰區司令部檔案（War Office: South East Asia Command: Military Headquarters Papers, Second World War）系列收入 1932 至 1949 年間，關於盟軍東南亞戰區司令部及其前身組織的檔案，共有 6,472 個卷宗。包含了 1940 年成立的遠東總司令部（Commander-in-Chief Far East）、第 1943 年成立的盟軍東南亞戰區司令部，以及盟國東南亞地面部隊的通訊。此系列共有 6,742 個卷宗，內容有關亞太地區英國陸軍各部關於情報、行政、組織、裝備、訓練、戰俘，以及戰爭罪行的資料。

5. WO 208 陸軍部作戰與軍事情報處檔案（War Office: Directorate of Military Operations and Intelligence, and Directorate of Military Intelligence; Ministry of Defence, Defence Intelligence Staff）系列收入 1907 至 1990 年間，關於陸軍部情報處的檔案，共有 5,661 個卷宗。陸軍部情報處於兩次大戰期間曾進行多次改組：1922 至 1939 年，是陸軍部作戰與軍事情報處（War Office, Directorate of Military

Operations and Intelligence），大戰爆發至 1964 年，則是陸軍部軍事
情報處（War Office, Directorate of Military Intelligence）。在第二次世
界大戰期間，軍事情報處屬下最多設有 14 個分支，是為 MI1-15（軍
情 1 處至軍情 15 處，沒有 13 處），分別負責行政（MI1）、中東、遠
東、斯堪的那維亞、美國、蘇聯、中南美洲（MI2）、東歐、波羅的
海（MI3）、地圖（MI4）、反滲透（MI5）、國外情報（MI6）、宣傳
（MI7）、截聽與通訊安全（MI8）、戰俘與脫出者救援（MI9）、技術
情報（MI10）等。與中緬印戰區相關的軍事情報檔案，例如英印陸
軍情報處（Directorate of Military Intelligence, Indian Army）與英軍
服務團（British Army Aid Group）的檔案複件均收入於此。

（三）特殊作戰執行部檔案

特殊作戰執行部（Special Operations Executive, SOE）於 1940 年成
立，最初是為了在歐洲淪陷區進行特殊作戰和情報戰，其後在亞洲亦開始活
動。SOE 在亞洲的人員包括大量戰前已活躍於亞洲的商人、行政人員，甚
至傳教士等。在中國最主要的工作為進行貨幣交易和商品走私（行動代號為
「悔恨行動」，Operation Remorse）、協助訓練國軍游擊隊（參與 204 使團任
務），亦有部分人員在英軍服務團工作。HS 1 特殊作戰執行部遠東檔案系列
（HS 1: Special Operations Executive: Far East）收入關於特殊作戰執行部，
在中國、印度，以及東南亞的組織、行政，以及行動的檔案，其涵蓋年分為
1940 至 1947 年，共有 350 個卷宗。

三、從英國國家檔案局資料看英國與中緬印戰區

（一）太平洋戰爭爆發前英國對華支援（交通線方面）

英國擁有緬甸、馬來亞、新加坡、香港等殖民地，中緬印戰區對英國

而言極為重要。自 1930 年代起，英國的計劃者已開始考慮英國在歐洲作戰時，如何應對日本入侵其亞洲殖民地。其中，馬來亞和新加坡被視為英國在東南亞防務的核心，陸空軍打算以馬來半島（時稱「馬來屏障」，Malay Barrier）為據點，保護正在興建的新加坡海軍基地（於 1941 年初完成）。香港則被視為「前哨」（Outpost），其守軍將盡力拖延日軍進攻，直至彈盡援絕或皇家海軍的增援艦隊抵達。緬甸則由於有泰國為緩衝區，因此少有軍事方面的準備。可是，戰前的計劃者已明確指出，如歐洲開戰，則英國將沒有足夠力量抵禦日軍在亞太地區的攻勢。

　　1937 年 7 月中日兩國開戰後，英國容許國民政府經香港輸入戰略物資到中國境內，是為對國府的間接支援。另一方面，英國亦調整其亞太地區的防衛政策，例如在 1938 年 7 月縮減了加強香港防務的計劃，並於 1939 年 2 月向國民政府提供貸款。此外，英國亦嘗試拉攏美國，使其向日本施壓以制止日本南侵。可是，日本不斷向英國施壓，前者更於 1938 年 10 月占領廣州，使國民政府只能依賴走私從香港輸入物資到內陸，運輸能力大打折扣。其後，雖然日本仍不斷向英國施壓要其關閉滇緬公路，但國民政府仍能由此路從各地輸入戰略物資。1940 年 1 月 22 日，英國駐騰越領事經英國駐上海公使向倫敦報告：1939 年 2 月 19 日至 1939 年 12 月 31 日期間，國民政府利用滇緬公路從外國（包括香港），輸入了 31,047 箱武器，包括槍炮和飛機零件，以及 358,667 箱各式彈藥和彈藥車等相關裝備。[7]

7　"Enclosure in Tengyueh Despatch to Embassy, Shanghai No. 8 of 22nd January, 1940," 22 January 1940, *Allied military assistance: tonnages supplied via the Burma Road*, WO 208/278, TNA. WO 208/278「盟國軍事援助：經緬甸援助量」（Allied military assistance: tonnages supplied via the Burma Road）資料夾收入太平洋戰爭爆發前，經滇緬公路輸入中國的戰略物資之統計和相關文件，時間為 1939 年 3 月至 1942 年 2 月。

檔案 1：英國駐騰越領事致上海總領事報告（1940 年 1 月 22 日）

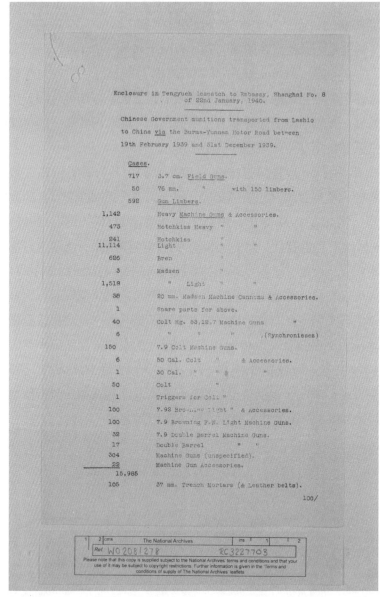

Enclosure in Tengyueh despatch to Embassy, Shanghai No. 8
of 22nd January, 1940.

Chinese Government munitions transported from Lashio
to China via the Burma-Yunnan Motor Road between
19th February 1939 and 31st December 1939.

Cases.

717	3.7 cm. Field Guns.
50	76 mm. " with 150 limbers.
592	Gun Limbers.
1,142	Heavy Machine Guns & Accessories.
473	Hotchkiss Heavy " "
241	Hotchkiss " "
11,114	Light " "
626	Bren " "
3	Madsen " "
1,518	" Light " "
38	20 mm. Madsen Machine Cannons & Accessories.
1	Spare parts for above.
40	Colt Mg. 53,18.7 Machine Guns "
6	" " " (Synchronises)
150	7.9 Colt Machine Guns.
6	50 Cal. Colt " & Accessories.
1	30 Cal. " " "
50	Colt "
1	Triggers for Colt "
100	7.92 Browning Light " & Accessories.
100	7.9 Browning F.N. Light Machine Guns.
32	7.9 Double Barrel Machine Guns.
17	Double Barrel " "
304	Machine Guns (unspecified).
22	Machine Gun Accessories.
15,985	
105	37 mm. Trench Mortars (& Leather belts).

100/

資料來源："Enclosure in Tengyueh Despatch to Embassy, Shanghai No. 8 of 22nd January, 1940,"
22 January 1940, *Allied military assistance: tonnages supplied via the Burma Road*, WO 208/278,
TNA.

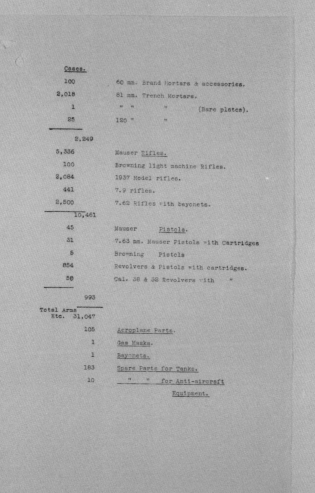

<u>Cases.</u>

100	60 mm. Brand Mortars & accessories.
2,018	81 mm. Trench Mortars.
1	" " " (Bare plates).
25	120 " "
2,249	
5,336	Mauser <u>Rifles.</u>
100	Browning light machine Rifles.
2,084	1937 Model rifles.
441	7.9 rifles.
2,500	7.62 Rifles with bayonets.
10,461	
45	Mauser <u>Pistols.</u>
31	7.63 mm. Mauser Pistols with Cartridges
8	Browning Pistols
854	Revolvers & Pistols with cartridges.
58	Cal. 38 & 32 Revolvers with "
993	

Total Arms
Etc. 31,047

105	<u>Aeroplane Parts.</u>
1	<u>Gas Masks.</u>
1	<u>Bayonets.</u>
183	<u>Spare Parts for Tanks.</u>
10	" " for Anti-aircraft Equipment.

Cases.	Ammunition Etc.
4,571	Bombs.
34,913	T. N. T.
2,835	Fuses.
95	Detonators.
860	Tetryl.
22	Tracers.
15,714	11.5 cm. shells.
1,536	Charges for shells.
23,621	7.62 cm. shells.
15,700	3.7 cm. shells.
1,200	" " gunpowder.
0	7.5 " shells.
200	" " gunpowder.
400	7.7 " "
7,862	7.5 " Anti-aircraft shells
1,007	3.7 " Mortar shells.
13	37 mm. Practice shells.
2,160	60 " Brandt "
1,200	60 " shells.
5,479	81 " Mortar "
11,867	" Brandt "
101	120 mm. " "
800	Gunpowder for Mortar shells.
1,745	4.7 cm. Anti Tank "
4	Brandt Cartridges & fuses.
1,292	13.2 mm. Cartridges.
65,408	7.92 " "
600	" " Cartridge Links.
4,644	" smk Cartridges.
969	7.9 " "

38,592/

Cases.	Ammunition Etc.
38,592	7.9 s.s. Cartridges.
31,997	" mm. "
63,312	7.62 mm. "
3,922	Safety "
10	23 mm. "
240	Madsen Cartridges.
5,822	2 cm. Madsen Cartridges.
200	Gunpowder for 2 cm. Cartridges.
1,000	Mauser Cartridges.
141	Mauser Pistol Cartridges.
55	9.m.(Browning Pistol) Cartridges.
13	Revolver & Pistol Cartridges.
62	Winchester Shot Gun Cartridges.
1	32 cal. Cartridges.
610	Cartridges (unspecified).
5,750	Smokeless Gun Powder.
58	Ammunition Wagons.
26	Metallic wooden cases for projectiles.

Total Ammunition Etc: 358,667

Grand Total   390,014 Cases.

　　可是，歐洲方面於 1939 年 9 月開戰，使英國自顧不暇。其後，歐洲戰局在 1940 年中急轉直下：法國於 6 月被迫投降、義大利宣布參戰，使地中海成為戰區、英國本土遭到直接威脅，更使英國在亞太地區的地位危如累卵。日本即加強向英法兩國施壓，迫使英國宣布關閉滇緬公路。英國則繼續嘗試鼓勵美國對日本採取更強硬的態度。可是，由於當時正值雨季，關閉公路的象徵意義大於實際，但的確使國民政府難以大量輸入物資。當時英國在亞洲防務極為薄弱，如日本當時開戰，則英國在亞洲的殖民地將更快淪陷。至年底，歐洲戰況好轉，英國取得不列顛作戰（Battle of Britain）勝利並穩住地中海局勢，英國政府即重開滇緬公路。

　　至 1941 年中，由於歐洲和地中海戰區的局勢對英國有利，加上美國對日本逐漸採取強硬態度，並願意與英國在軍事上展開協調，因此英國即使面對日本空襲滇緬公路的威脅，仍繼續開放公路予國民政府輸入戰略物資。8 月，參謀首長委員會撰寫關於滇緬公路的報告予內閣，提到公路對中國的重要性、日方可能採取的行動，以及英國可以選擇的反應等。參謀首長委員會認為由於德軍進攻蘇聯，因此滇緬公路成為中國唯一的對外交通線，其他路線均需要至少兩年才可完成，因此公路變得更為重要。可是，針對日軍對滇緬公路的行動，參謀首長委員會認為由於仍然需要避免與日本開戰，因此英國可以回應的手段不多，只能提供游擊隊訓練、防空武器，以及國際航空隊（正在成立的美國志願航空隊及由英國人員組成的轟炸機隊）。委員會又認為向國民政府提供游擊隊訓練將可能導致日本宣戰，因此不宜立即進行，但英國可以容許國際航空隊在緬甸進行訓練。[8]

8　"The Burma Road Report," 20 August 1941, C.O.S.(41)481, *War Cabinet and Cabinet: Chiefs of Staff Committee: Memoranda*, CAB 80/29/81, TNA, pp. 2-3.

檔案 2：英國參謀首長委員會紀錄，「滇緬公路報告」(1941 年 8 月 20 日)

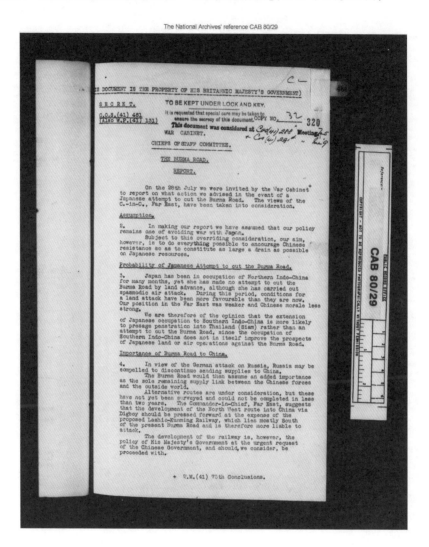

The National Archives' reference CAB 80/29

資料來源："The Burma Road Report," 20 August 1941, C.O.S.(41)481, *War Cabinet and Cabinet: Chiefs of Staff Committee: Memoranda*, CAB 80/29/81, TNA.

The National Archives' reference CAB 80/29

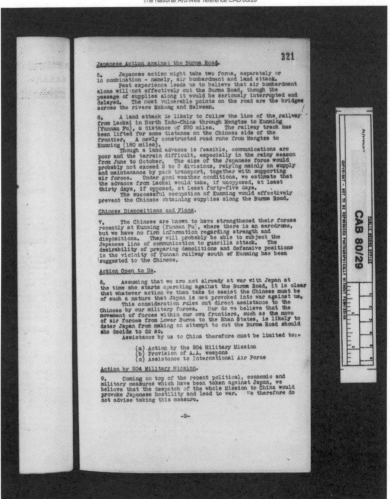

321

Japanese Action against the Burma Road.

5.   Japanese action might take two forms, separately or in combination - namely, air bombardment and land attack.
Past experience leads us to believe that air bombardment alone will not effectively cut the Burma Road, though the passage of supplies along it would be seriously interrupted and delayed. The most vulnerable points on the road are the bridges across the rivers Mekong and Salween.

6.   A land attack is likely to follow the line of the railway from Laokai in North Indo-China through Mengtze to Kunming (Yunnan Fu), a distance of 290 miles. The railway track has been lifted for some distance on the Chinese side of the frontier. A newly constructed road runs from Mengtze to Kunming (180 miles).
Though a land advance is feasible, communications are poor and the terrain difficult, especially in the rainy season from June to October. The size of the Japanese force would probably not exceed 2 to 3 divisions, relying mainly on supply and maintenance by pack transport, together with supporting air forces. Under good weather conditions, we estimate that the advance from Laokai would take, if unopposed, at least thirty days, if opposed, at least forty-five days.
The successful occupation of Kunming would effectively prevent the Chinese obtaining supplies along the Burma Road.

Chinese Dispositions and Plans.

7.   The Chinese are known to have strengthened their forces recently at Kunming (Yunnan Fu), where there is an aerodrome, but we have no firm information regarding strength and dispositions. They will probably be able to subject the Japanese line of communication to guerilla attack. The desirability of preparing demolitions and defensive positions in the vicinity of Yunnan railway south of Kunming has been suggested to the Chinese.

Action Open to Us.

8.   Assuming that we are not already at war with Japan at the time she starts operating against the Burma Road, it is clear that whatever action we then take to assist the Chinese must be of such a nature that Japan is not provoked into war against us.
This consideration rules out direct assistance to the Chinese by our military forces. Nor do we believe that the movement of forces within our own frontiers, such as the move of air forces from Lower Burma to the Shan States, is likely to deter Japan from making an attempt to cut the Burma Road should she decide to do so.
Assistance by us to China therefore must be limited to:-

          (a) Action by the 204 Military Mission
          (b) Provision of A.A. weapons
          (c) Assistance to International Air Force

Action by 204 Military Mission.

9.   Coming on top of the recent political, economic and military measures which have been taken against Japan, we believe that the despatch of the whole Mission to China would provoke Japanese hostility and lead to war. We therefore do not advise taking this measure.

-2-

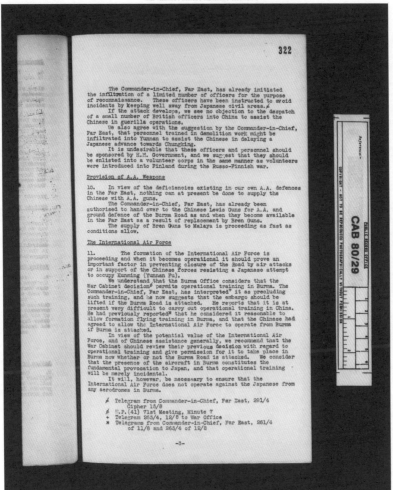

322

The Commander-in-Chief, Far East, has already initiated the infiltration of a limited number of officers for the purpose of reconnaissance. These officers have been instructed to avoid incidents by keeping well away from Japanese civil areas./

If the attack develops, we see no objection to the despatch of a small number of British officers into China to assist the Chinese in guerilla operations.

We also agree with the suggestion by the Commander-in-Chief, Far East, that personnel trained in demolition work might be infiltrated into Yunnan to assist the Chinese in delaying a Japanese advance towards Chungking.

It is undesirable that these officers and personnel should be sponsored by H.M. Government, and we suggest that they should be enlisted into a volunteer corps in the same manner as volunteers were introduced into Finland during the Russo-Finnish war.

Provision of A.A. Weapons

10.　In view of the deficiencies existing in our own A.A. defences in the Far East, nothing can at present be done to supply the Chinese with A.A. guns.

The Commander-in-Chief, Far East, has already been authorised to hand over to the Chinese Lewis Guns for A.A. and ground defence of the Burma Road as and when they become available in the Far East as a result of replacement by Bren Guns.

The supply of Bren Guns to Malaya is proceeding as fast as conditions allow.

The International Air Force

11.　The formation of the International Air Force is proceeding and when it becomes operational it should prove an important factor in preventing closure of the Road by air attacks or in support of the Chinese forces resisting a Japanese attempt to occupy Kunming (Yunnan Fu).

We understand that the Burma Office considers that the War Cabinet decision/ permits operational training in Burma. The Commander-in-Chief, Far East, has interpreted+ it as precluding such training, and he now suggests that the embargo should be lifted if the Burma Road is attacked. He reports that it is at present very difficult to carry out operational training in China. He had previously reportedx that he considered it reasonable to allow formation flying training in Burma, and that the Chinese had agreed to allow the International Air Force to operate from Burma if Burma is attacked.

In view of the potential value of the International Air Force, and of Chinese assistance generally, we recommend that the War Cabinet should review their previous decision with regard to operational training and give permission for it to take place in Burma now whether or not the Burma Road is attacked. We consider that the presence of the aircraft in Burma constitutes the fundamental provocation to Japan, and that operational training will be merely incidental.

It will, however, be necessary to ensure that the International Air Force does not operate against the Japanese from any aerodromes in Burma.

　/　Telegram from Commander-in-Chief, Far East, 291/4
　　　Cipher 13/8
　/　W.P.(41) 71st Meeting, Minute 7
　+　Telegram 263/4, 12/8 to War Office
　x　Telegram from Commander-in-Chief, Far East, 261/4
　　　of 11/8 and 263/4 of 12/8

-3-

323

<u>Action recommended in the event of a Japanese attack being successful or partially successful.</u>

12.　　The Commander-in-Chief, Far East suggests certain measures which might be taken as palliatives in the event of a Japanese attack on the Burma Road being successful or partially successful.　He suggests –

　　(a) The lifting of the embargo on export of petrol and the development of methods of smuggling from Hong Kong to China.
　　　　We do not recommend this, as it seems unlikely materially to improve Chinese ability to operate and is almost certain to lead to incidents which might result in war.

　　(b) The development of the North West Route into China via Digboi.
　　　　This we have dealt with in paragraph 4 above.

　　(c) Assistance in operating an air transport service from Burma to Chinese aerodromes.
　　　　Our resources in transport aircraft are insufficient at present for us to inaugurate an air transport service.

　　(d) Investigations into the possibility of supplying material to China via Vladivostock Railway and via Persia and Central Asia.
　　　　In view of the requirements of the Russians we do not consider that any important quantity of material could be supplied by these routes.
　　　　Such small supplies as could be passed through Vladivostock could best be arranged by the United States Government. Supply via Persia would appear to be impracticable as a serious project.

<u>Conclusions.</u>

13.　　It is apparent that in the present situation, where the basic principle of our policy in the Far East lies in avoiding war with Japan, there is little direct action we can take to prevent a determined attempt to close the Burma Road.　The measures we can take to assist the Chinese if the attack develops appear to be limited to infiltrating a limited number of British personnel into China to assist the Chinese in guerilla operations and demolition work;　these should not be sponsored by H.M.G., but should be "volunteers".

14.　　We recommend that the War Cabinet should extend their present policy of assisting the International Air Force by giving permission for operational training in Burma now.

　　　　　　　　　　　(Signed) DUDLEY POUND
　　　　　　　　　　　　　　　　J.G. DILL
West George Street, S.W.1.,　　　　　C. PORTAL
20th August, 1941.

　　　　　　　　-4-

　　1941 年下半年，英國對支援國民政府的抗戰變得更為積極。9 月，英國開始於密支那（Myitkyina）興建機場，以空運物資到中國。印度與緬甸事務大臣（Secretary of State for India and Burma）雅馬厘（Leo Amery, 1873-1955）於 1941 年 9 月向內閣報告，國民政府將從美國獲得 20 架 DC 式飛機，可以在雲南和密支那之間進行空運任務。英屬緬甸當局正為國民政府興建機場，平整跑道的工程已經進行。工程由英方出資，但國民政府則負責飛機庫的資金。[9] 從這些文件可以看出，雖然英國忙於應付歐洲和地中海的戰爭，但亦能嘗試在交通方面支援國民政府對日作戰。

9　"Burma-China Communications," 3 September 1941, C.O.S.(41)548, *War Cabinet and Cabinet: Chiefs of Staff Committee: Memoranda*, CAB 80/30/48, TNA, p. 1.

檔案 3：英國參謀首長委員會紀錄，「緬中聯絡」（1941 年 9 月 3 日）

The National Archives' reference CAB 80/30

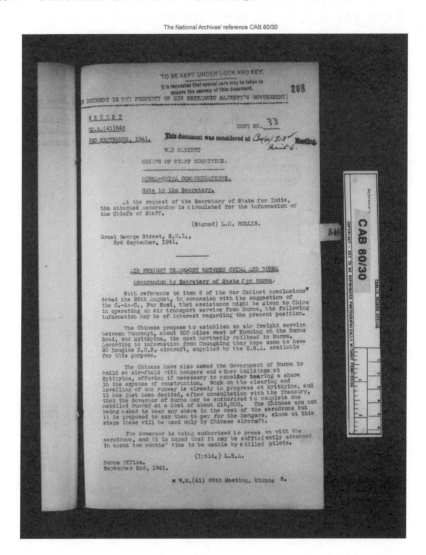

© Crown Copyright

資料來源："Burma-China Communications," 3 September 1941, C.O.S.(41)548, *War Cabinet and Cabinet: Chiefs of Staff Committee: Memoranda*, CAB 80/30/48, TNA.

（二）太平洋戰爭爆發前英國對華支援（陸空軍方面）

　　1940 年底英國本土情況大致穩定後，英國政府隨即嘗試加強英國在亞洲的軍力並建立聯盟，以威懾日本使其放棄開戰。可是，英軍仍受制於歐洲、地中海，以及大西洋等戰區的需要，因此在亞洲缺乏飛機和裝甲部隊。有鑑於此，遠東總司令樸芳（Robert Brooke-Popham, 1878-1953）力主加強和中、美、荷加強軍事合作。1941 年 2 月，帝國副總參謀長海寧（Robert H. Haining, 1882-1959）中將向內閣呈交備忘錄，內容關於派員到國民政府訓練游擊隊和為國民政府提供空軍支援，並在緬甸集中相關的人員和物資。海寧提到訓練部隊規模為 36 名英國軍官和 260 名士兵。派員到中國協助訓練游擊隊的計畫之結果，即為後來不太成功的「204 使團」。[10]

---

[10] "Assistance to China: Note by the Vice Chief of the Imperial General Staff," 24 February 1941, C.O.S.(41)120, *War Cabinet and Cabinet: Chiefs of Staff Committee: Memoranda*, CAB 80/26/20, TNA. 此外，此文件亦收錄了 1941 年 2 月遠東總司令和駐華大使卡爾（Archibald C. Kerr, 1882-1951）致英國政府的電文，內容均關於利用緬甸支援國民政府。

檔案 4：「帝國副總參謀長呈對華支援之備忘」（1941 年 2 月 24 日）

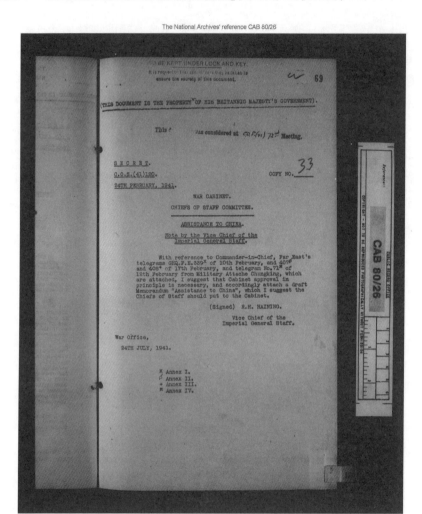

The National Archives' reference CAB 80/26

© Crown Copyright

資料來源："Assistance to China: Note by the Vice Chief of the Imperial General Staff," 24 February 1941, C.O.S.(41)120, *War Cabinet and Cabinet: Chiefs of Staff Committee: Memoranda*, CAB 80/26/20, TNA.

70

ASSISTANCE TO CHINA.

Draft Memorandum by the Chiefs of Staff.

The War Cabinet (W.M.(40) 288th Meeting, Conclusion 4)
approved in principle closer co-operation with China.
A more Senior Military Attaché, Major General Dennys, has
since been appointed with an expanded staff and has now
submitted his proposals which have the support of the
Commander-in-Chief, Far East.

There are two main features -

    (a) a fighting mission initially of 36 British
        Officers and 260 other ranks, whom he suggests
        should be mostly Ghurkas to assist in and
        organise Chinese guerilla activities.

    (b) a preliminary base and maintenance organisation
        primarily for the development of air assistance
        to China.

The Commander-in-Chief, Far East proposes to assemble
the necessary personnel equipment and stores in Burma.

The approval of the Cabinet, in principle, is now
sought to the collection of the Mission in Burma and to the
assembly there of the base and maintenance organisation in
anticipation of war with Japan.

ANNEX I.

Copy of a telegram dated 10th February, 1941, from the
Commander-in-Chief, Far East to the War Office (repeated
to Commander-in-Chief, India and General Officer Commanding,
Burma.

15686 cipher 10/2.

    G.H.Q.F.E./83/1/2. Following for Chiefs of Staff.
Reference your 94384 (M.O.2.) of 26/12. Since preparation
of mission will take several months consider its preparation
should be initiated immediately Dennys reports it to be
desirable and without waiting to settle detailed composition.
Propose that General Officer Commanding Burma under me
should be responsible for all preparations and that
personnel and stores should be assembled in Burma. Governor
and General Officer Commanding agree. Understand that
cost of project will be borne by His Majesty's Government
whatever final size of mission may be it should include
R.A.F. Officers able to organise aerodromes. Officers
able to get results from Chinese Guerillas, O.R. to
provide small personal escorts for these officers, some
administrative staff and interpreters. Many of above would

-1-

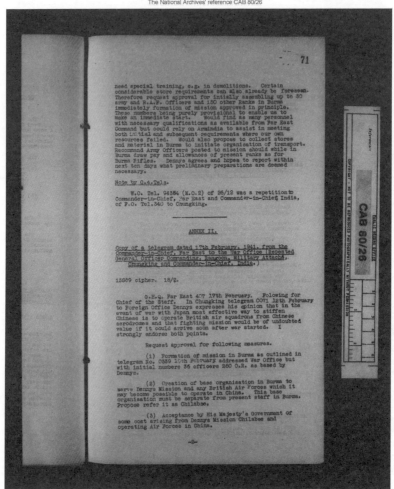

71

need special training, e.g. in demolitions.   Certain
considerable store requirements can also already be foreseen.
Therefore request approval for initially assembling up to 30
Army and R.A.F. Officers and 150 other Ranks in Burma
immediately formation of mission approved in principle.
These numbers being purely provisional to enable us to
make an immediate start.   Would find as many personnel
with necessary qualifications as available from Far East
Command but could rely on Armindia to assist in meeting
both initial and subsequent requirements where our own
resources failed.   Would also propose to collect stores
and material in Burma to initiate organisation of transport.
Recommend Army Officers posted to mission should while in
Burma draw pay and allowances of present ranks as for
Burma Rifles.   Dennys agrees and hopes to report within
next ten days what preliminary preparations are deemed
necessary.

Note by G.4.Tels.

W.O. Tel. 94384 (M.O.2) of 26/12 was a repetition to
Commander-in-Chief, Far East and Commander-in-Chief, India,
of F.O. Tel.340 to Chungking.

ANNEX II.

Copy of a telegram dated 17th February, 1941, from the
Commander-in-Chief, Far East to the War Office (Repeated
General Officer Commanding, Rangoon, Military Attaché,
Chungking and Commander-in-Chief, India.)

15889 cipher. 18/2.

G.H.Q. Far East 407 17th February.   Folowing for
Chief of the Staff.   In Chungking telegram OO71 12th February
to Foreign Office Dennys expresses his opinion that in the
event of war with Japan most effective way to stiffen
Chinese is to operate British air squadrons from Chinese
aerodromes and that fighting mission would be of undoubted
value if it could arrive soon after war started.   I
strongly endorse both points.

Request approval for following measures.

(1) Formation of mission in Burma as outlined in
telegram No. 0389 10th February addressed War Office but
with initial numbers 36 officers 260 O.R. as based by
Dennys.

(2) Creation of base organisation in Burma to
serve Dennys Mission and any British Air Forces which it
may become possible to operate in China.   This base
organisation must be separate from present staff in Burma.
Propose refer it as Chilabse.

(3) Acceptance by His Majesty's Government of
some cost arising from Dennys Mission Chilabse and
operating Air Forces in China.

-2-

72

(4) Provision of ample supplies of money to be
sent to Dennys immediately war with Japan breaks out.

(5) Building up dumps of material in Burma and
obtaining and organising lorry transport ready to carry
material forward.

ANNEX III.

Copy of a telegram dated 17th February, 1941, from the
Commander-in-Chief, Far East to the War Office (Repeated
General Officer Commanding, Burma, Military Attaché,
Chungking, and Commander-in-Chief, India.)

15868 cipher. 17/2.

G.H.Q., Far East telegram No. 406 17th February
addressed War Office repeated Rangoon Chungking Delhi.

Reference paragraph 2 G.H.Q. Far East telegram
No. (?407) 17th February CHI(?LABSE) must be capable of
expansion as necessary. Framework as follows.
Rangoon H.Q. Chi(?labse) with general staff for
Intelligence and Training Q. staff for supply and
transportation forward of rail or river head in Burma
a staff for personnel and (? expert) (? engineers) for
construction of accommodation and dumps and for
maintenance of road. Lashio base depot with commander
and adjutant stores section and transport section.
Maymyo training centre with commander adjutant and
instructors to train in guerilla warfare demolitions, etc.

Reference paragraphs 3 and 4 G.H.Q. Far East 407
17th February as C.M.A. Burma is already overwhelmed by
war expansion strongly urge accounts staff for Chi(?labse)
should be provided from United Kingdom and kept separate
from military accounts organisation in Burma. If you
agree military accounts officer to take charge should be
flown out early.

ANNEX IV.

Copy of a telegram dated 18th February, 1941, from
Sir A. Clark Kerr (Chungking).

No. 71.

Following for the War Office and the Air Ministry from
Dennys.

Part 1. Following appreciation is based on the assumption
of war between Britain and Japan. In addition to bad
economic situation and probable food shortage in some
areas the Chinese military situation is worse than I

-3-

The National Archives' reference CAB 80/26

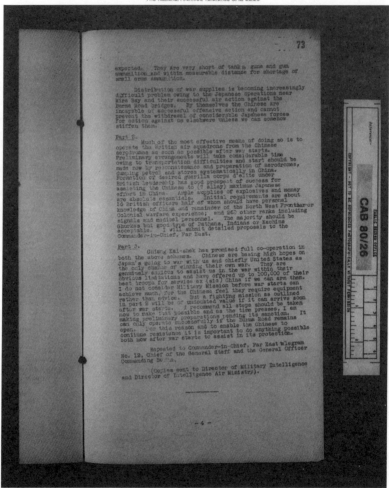

　　可是，雖然樸芳對中英軍事合作頗有希望，但英國軍方對此卻抱持較謹慎的態度。1941 年 6 月，帝國總參謀長迪爾（John G. Dill, 1881-1944）上將向參謀首長委員會提交報告，討論英國援華問題。迪爾認為英方要小心不能被國民政府捲入亞洲的戰爭，亦要盡力拉攏美國以威懾日本。他又認為應該鼓勵國民政府以游擊戰拖住日本，因為亞洲戰局的最終結果，只能取決於英國在歐洲擊敗德國。迪爾認為：「我們的目標一直是而且應該繼續是避免和日本開戰」，而且「蘇德開戰使日本南進的危機增加而非減少」。他又指出：「美國的態度是阻止日本開戰的最大阻力，而且我們現時比美國在計劃和實質幫助〔中國〕方面走得更前」。可是，他強調「給予中國的支援必需能同時加強我們的防衛……因此，與中國的討論需要以我們的遠東作戰計劃為依據，而非中國即時的戰術需要。中國的未來仰賴我們贏得戰爭。」迪爾的態度象徵著英國軍方對整體形勢和中國在戰爭中的角色之判斷。在他眼中，中國在當時的角色是拖住日軍，使之不能對英美開戰。[11] 由於英國軍政高層大多抱此態度，因此英國未有對蔣中正（1887-1975）在戰前向英方提出派兵支援香港和緬甸等提案有實質回應。

11　"Assistance to China: Memorandum by the Chief of the Imperial General Staff," 28 June 1941, C.O.S.(41)401, *War Cabinet and Cabinet: Chiefs of Staff Committee: Memoranda*, CAB 80/29/1, TNA.

檔案 5：「帝國總參謀長對華支援備忘錄」（1941 年 6 月）

The National Archives' reference CAB 80/29

© Crown Copyright

資料來源："Assistance to China: Memorandum by the Chief of the Imperial General Staff," 28 June 1941, C.O.S.(41)401, *War Cabinet and Cabinet: Chiefs of Staff Committee: Memoranda*, CAB 80/29/1, TNA.

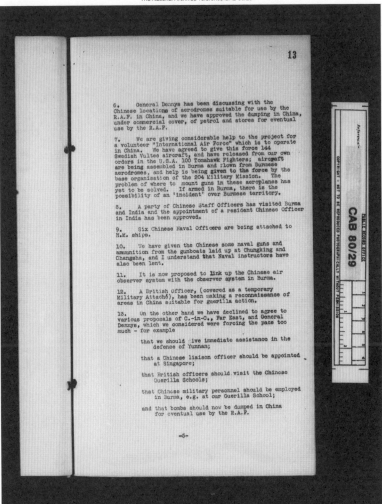

13

6.　General Dennys has been discussing with the Chinese locations of aerodromes suitable for use by the R.A.F. in China, and we have approved the dumping in China, under commercial cover, of petrol and stores for eventual use by the R.A.F.

7.　We are giving considerable help to the project for a volunteer "International Air Force" which is to operate in China.　We have agreed to give this force 144 Swedish Vultee aircraft, and have released from our own orders in the U.S.A. 100 Tomahawk Fighters; aircraft are being assembled in Burma and flown from Burmese aerodromes, and help is being given to the force by the base organisation of the 204 Military Mission.　The problem of where to mount guns in these aeroplanes has yet to be solved.　If armed in Burma, there is the possibility of an 'incident' over Burmese territory.

8.　A party of Chinese Staff Officers has visited Burma and India and the appointment of a resident Chinese Officer in India has been approved.

9.　Six Chinese Naval Officers are being attached to H.M. ships.

10.　We have given the Chinese some naval guns and ammunition from the gunboats laid up at Chungking and Changsha, and I understand that Naval instructors have also been lent.

11.　It is now proposed to link up the Chinese air observer system with the observer system in Burma.

12.　A British Officer, (covered as a temporary Military Attaché), has been making a reconnaissance of areas in China suitable for guerilla action.

13.　On the other hand we have declined to agree to various proposals of C.-in-C., Far East, and General Dennys, which we considered were forcing the pace too much - for example

that we should give immediate assistance in the defence of Yunnan;

that a Chinese liaison officer should be appointed at Singapore;

that British officers should visit the Chinese Guerilla Schools;

that Chinese military personnel should be employed in Burma, e.g. at our Guerilla School;

and that bombs should now be dumped in China for eventual use by the R.A.F.

-5-

The National Archives' reference CAB 80/29

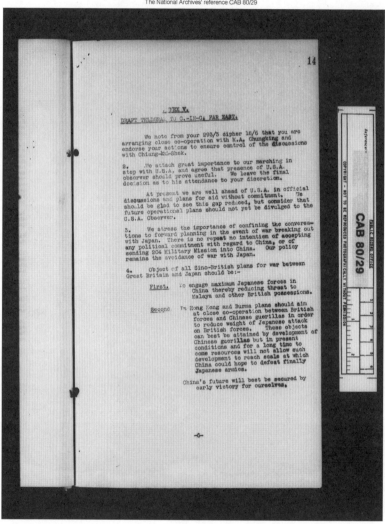

14

ANNEX V.

DRAFT TELEGRAM TO C.-IN-C. FAR EAST.

We note from your 293/3 cipher 18/6 that you are arranging close co-operation with M.A. Chungking and endorse your actions to ensure control of the discussions with Chiang-Kai-Shek.

2. We attach great importance to our marching in step with U.S.A. and agree that presence of U.S.A. observer should prove useful. We leave the final decision as to his attendance to your discretion.

At present we are well ahead of U.S.A. in official discussions and plans for aid without commitment. We should be glad to see this gap reduced, but consider that future operational plans should not yet be divulged to the U.S.A. Observer.

3. We stress the importance of confining the conversations to forward planning in the event of war breaking out with Japan. There is no repeat no intention of accepting any political commitment with regard to China, or of sending 204 Military Mission into China. Our policy remains the avoidance of war with Japan.

4. Object of all Sino-British plans for war between Great Britain and Japan should be:-

First. To engage maximum Japanese forces in China thereby reducing threat to Malaya and other British possessions.

Second In Hong Kong and Burma plans should aim at close co-operation between British forces and Chinese guerillas in order to reduce weight of Japanese attack on British forces. These objects can best be attained by development of Chinese guerillas but in present conditions and for a long time to come resources will not allow such development to reach scale at which China could hope to defeat finally Japanese armies.

China's future will best be secured by early victory for ourselves.

-6-

　　隨著美國在 1941 年陸續加強菲律賓防務，並把美國太平洋艦隊調到珍珠港（Pearl Harbor），英國亦嘗試協助國民政府作戰，從側面支援香港、馬來亞，以及緬甸的守軍。1941 年 9 月 9 日，陸軍部通知遠東總司令樸芳，指示他可以就派員到中國指導游擊戰進行相應計劃，但必須保密，而且英國此時只能以此回應日本攻擊滇緬公路。陸軍部特別提到這些人員僅可被視為「志願者」，類似英國派往芬蘭的人員。當時，英國正陸續調兵增援亞洲，不能有其他動作予日本開戰之口實，使英國尚未準備好即要被迫作戰。[12]

---

12 "War Office to C-in-C Far East," 9 September 1941, *Assistance to China in the event of a Japanese attempt to cut the Burma road*, WO 106/3536, TNA, p. 1. WO 106/3536「如日本嘗試切斷滇緬公路英國對中國之援助」(Assistance to China in the event of a Japanese attempt to cut the Burma road）資料夾收入太平洋戰爭爆發前，英國對日本若切斷滇緬公路時，英方可能對國民政府提供援助的討論，時間為 1941 年 10 至 11 月。

檔案 6：英國陸軍部致遠東總司令電（1941 年 9 月 9 日）

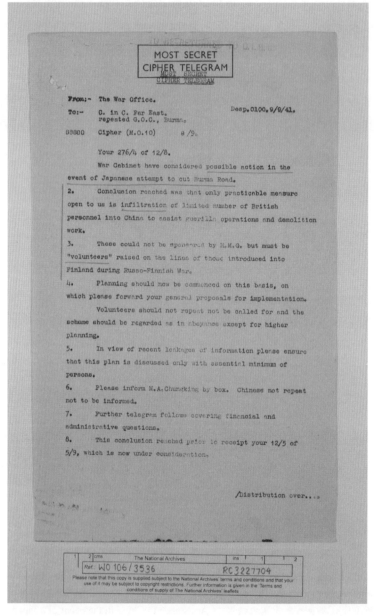

資料來源："War Office to C-in-C Far East," 9 September 1941, *Assistance to China in the event of a Japanese attempt to cut the Burma road*, WO 106/3536, TNA.

　　至 1941 年秋，英、美、荷已儼然形成對日軍事同盟的態勢，在英、美協調下，由美軍飛行員組成，陳納德（Claire L. Chennault, 1893-1958）上校指揮的「美國志願航空隊」（American Volunteer Group, AVG）成軍，即飛虎隊（Flying Tigers），在樸芳安排下已在緬甸受訓，準備到中國戰區助戰。[13] 可是，亞洲的英美軍尚未準備好之時，日美交涉已瀕臨決裂。其時，皇家海軍雖然已制定計劃，但尚未集合足夠兵力增援亞洲。同時，馬來亞已有逾十萬英、印、澳地面部隊，但其重裝備不足，而且缺乏空中兵力。緬甸方面的防務更無從談起。在英方決策當局眼中，當務之急是加強空中力量。1941 年 11 月，參謀首長委員會就英國協助建立志願空軍以支援中國一事，指示遠東總司令樸芳。參謀首長委員會提到即將建立一個中隊的布倫亨中型轟炸機（Bristol Blenheim）和一個中隊的水牛式戰鬥機（Brewster F2A Buffalo）。邱吉爾看到參謀首長委員會草擬給樸芳的草稿後，認為應向後者直言「除非你強烈反對，否則我們將即時派出水牛機和布倫亨機中隊」。[14] 邱吉爾在東南亞英軍亦需要大量飛機時，決意派機到中國，顯示他對援華一事之重視。

13　這批戰鬥機由英方提供。參見 Eugenie Buchan, *A Few Planes for China: The Birth of the Flying Tigers* (Lebanon, NH: ForeEdge, 2017).

14　"Far East-Air Assistance to China," 11 November 1941, C.O.S.(41)670, *Far East. Assistance to China. Minute by Prime Minister on draft telegram to C.-in-C., Far East*, CAB 80/31/70, TNA.

檔案 7：英國參謀首長委員會紀錄，「遠東：對華空中支援」（1941 年 11 月 11 日）

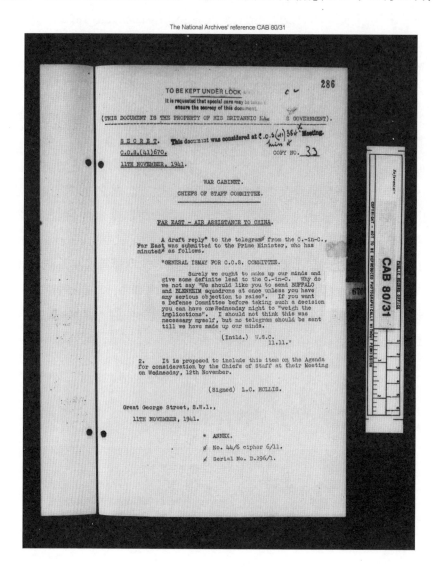

The National Archives' reference CAB 80/31

© Crown Copyright

資料來源："Far East-Air Assistance to China," 11 November 1941, C.O.S.(41)670, *Far East. Assistance to China. Minute by Prime Minister on draft telegram to C.-in-C., Far East*, CAB 80/31/70, TNA.

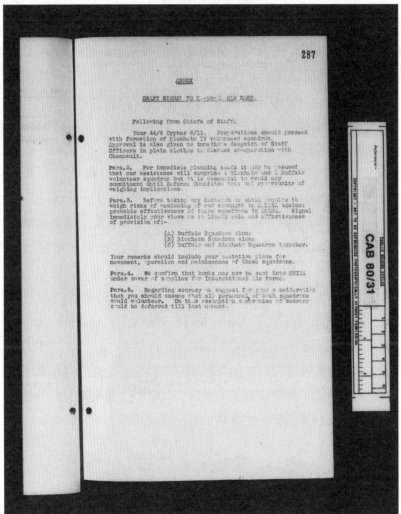

287

ANNEX

DRAFT SIGNAL TO C.-in-C. FAR EAST.

Following from Chiefs of Staff.

Your 44/6 Cypher 6/11. Preparations should proceed
with formation of Blenheim IV volunteer squadron.
Approval is also given to immediate despatch of Staff
Officers in plain clothes to discuss co-operation with
Chennault.

Para.2. For immediate planning needs it may be assumed
that our assistance will comprise 1 Blenheim and 1 Buffalo
volunteer squadron but it is essential to avoid any
commitment until Defence Committee have had opportunity of
weighing implications.

Para.3. Before taking any decision we shall require to
weigh risks of weakening of our strength in MALAYA against
probable effectiveness of these squadrons in CHINA. Signal
immediately your views as to likely role and effectiveness
of provision of:-

(A) Buffalo Squadron alone.
(B) Blenheim Squadron alone.
(C) Buffalo and Blenheim Squadron together.

Your remarks should include your tentative plans for
movement, operation and maintenance of these squadrons.

Para.4. We confirm that bombs may now be sent into CHINA
under cover of supplies for International Air Force.

Para.5. Regarding secrecy we suggest for your consideration
that you should assume that all personnel of both squadrons
would volunteer. On this assumption compromise of secrecy
could be deferred till last moment.

（三）太平洋戰爭初期中英軍事合作

　　1941 年 11 至 12 月，英、美、中三國對日協調初見成效，但距離建立堅實的軍事同盟仍尚有距離。與此同時，英軍繼續增援亞洲，特別是加強馬來屏障的防務。11 月中，加拿大援軍兩營抵達香港；12 月初，英國增援亞洲的艦隊陸續抵達，其前鋒 Z 艦隊（Z Force）已在新加坡，東洋艦隊（Eastern Fleet）司令湯菲力（Tom Phillips, 1888-1941）上將亦已和美國亞洲艦隊司令討論共同行動。可是，日本在 12 月 8 日發動進攻，使英國在亞太地區的防務部署在數月內崩潰。戰爭開始不久，英軍即加強和國民政府方面的協調。12 月 9 日，駐港英軍派出香港義勇防衛軍（Hong Kong Volunteer Defence Corps, HKVDC）副司令曉士（Harry Owen-Hughes, 1901-1984）上校到重慶與國軍聯絡，後者正組織援軍救援香港。可是，英國在亞洲的戰況隨即急轉直下：12 月 10 日，Z 艦隊覆滅，湯菲力上將陣亡；日軍於 12 月 18 日登陸香港島，守軍已然絕望。此外，日軍在馬來亞亦長驅直入，使新加坡和緬甸面對直接威脅。英軍在此時痛感空中力量的不足，因此美英荷澳聯軍司令（American-British-Dutch-Australian Command, ABDACOM）魏菲爾（Archibald P. Wavell, 1883-1950）[15] 上將於 12 月 16 日，向邱吉爾詢問能否使用尚在緬甸的國際志願空軍的轟炸機和戰鬥機，又希望可以控制已經成軍的美國志願航空隊，以集中這個地區的航空兵力。他強調「空防對緬甸和東印度至為重要，而且需求甚急。」[16]

15　港譯「韋維爾」。

16　"Defence of Burma," 16 December 1941, C.O.S.(41)279(O), *Defence of Burma. Note by Secretary*, CAB 80/60/49, TNA, p. 1.

檔案 8：英國參謀首長委員會紀錄，「緬甸防務」（1941 年 12 月 16 日）

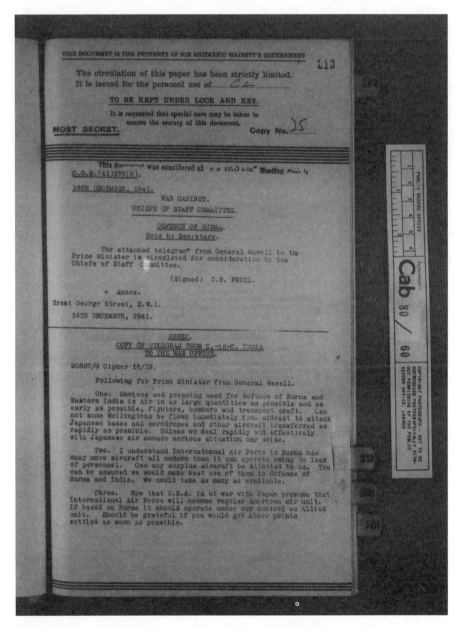

資料來源："Defence of Burma," 16 December 1941, C.O.S.(41)279(O), *Defence of Burma. Note by Secretary*, CAB 80/60/49, TNA.

　　在此背景下，中英雙方開展高層協調和合作。17 日，英國參謀首長委員會指示魏菲爾上將到重慶和蔣中正會談，並要駐華大使館武官格林斯岱（Gordon E. Grimsdale, 1893-1950）向蔣指出歡迎蔣參與有關盟國戰略的討論並派出代表。[17] 約一週後，魏菲爾上將和副司令美國陸軍勃蘭德（George H. Brett, 1886-1963）少將與蔣中正於重慶商討軍事合作的內容。會面於 23 日開始，先由魏菲爾和勃蘭德與蔣中正手下將領會面，蔣中正於下午加入討論，兩人再於 24 日和蔣共進早餐。24 日，格林斯岱發電報至陸軍部，提到魏菲爾、勃蘭德，以及蔣中正之間的會面。由於事關機密，蘇聯和荷印的代表均未有列席。會議決定中英美軍的首要任務為保護仰光（Rangoon）和緬甸，並應該開始向日本發動空中攻勢。英美代表承諾繼續為國民政府提供軍火，使之可以建立攻擊能力，後者的部隊則繼續嘗試拖住日軍，並攻擊其交通線。格林斯岱暗示與會者同意將繼續舉辦英、美、中代表會議，並把內容呈上盟國軍事會議供參考。[18]

---

17 "Minutes of Meeting held on Wednesday, 17th December, 1941 at 5.0 pm," 17 December 1941, C.O.S.(41)426th, *War Cabinet and Cabinet: Chiefs of Staff Committee: Minutes. Minutes of Meetings*, CAB 79/16/26, TNA.

18 "Military Attaché, Chungking to the War Office," 24 December 1941, *China: co-ordination between Chinese and British authorities*, WO 193/922, TNA. WO 193/922「中國：中英合作」（China: co-ordination between Chinese and British authorities）資料夾收入太平洋戰爭爆發後至緬甸淪陷後不久，關於中英合作的檔案，時間為 1941 年 12 月至 1942 年 7 月。

檔案 9：英國駐華大使館武官致陸軍部電文（1941 年 12 月 24 日）

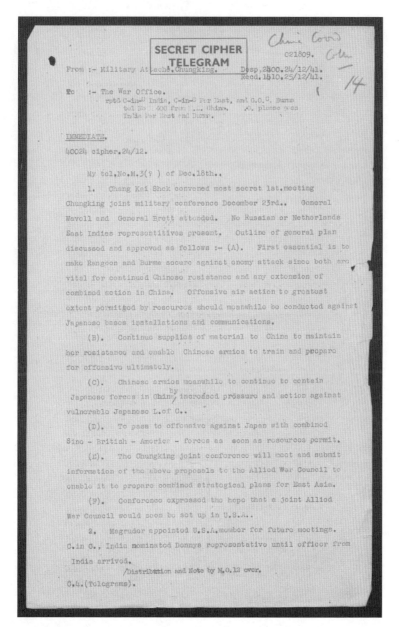

資料來源："Military Attaché, Chungking to the War Office," 24 December 1941, *China: co-ordination between Chinese and British authorities*, WO 193/922, TNA.

- 2 -

```
        To:-    M.O. 12 (for action)

    Copies to:-    S. of S.
                   C.I.G.S.
                   V.C.I.G.S.
                   D.H.O.S.P.
                   D.D.M.O.(O)
                   D.P. (2 copies)
                   M.O.1.2.10.12.
                   D.M.I.D.D.M.I.(I) (O)
                   M.I.2   2a.  2c.
                   D.S.D.
                   C.N.S. (Admlty.)
                   D. of Plans Admlty.
                   Head of War Reg. (Admlty.)
                   C.A.S.(Air Min.)
                   D. of Plans Air Min.
                   Col. Jacob (Cab. Offices)
                   Sec. J.P.S.(Cab. Offices)
                   India Office (Col. McCay)
                   Burma Office (Maj. Upson) (3 copies)
                   For. Office (Mr.Sterndale Bennett)
                   N.A.B .
```

Note by M.O.12.

    1. It is presumed that the telegram referred to in the first sentence is M.A. Chungking's No.M.348 of 15 Dec.

    2. Telegram has been repeated to C. in C. India, C. in C. Far East and G.O.C.Burma.

　　可是，魏菲爾實際上對中英合作之信心不大。26 日，魏菲爾向倫敦和緬甸方面報告他與國軍參謀人員和蔣中正夫婦見面的感受。他在給與迪爾上將的私信中，開首即提到 23 日的會面「漫長而令人不滿」。他指出：「會面極不專業，人太多，沒有地圖，翻譯差勁」。會上，英美代表希望國軍方面明白仰光的重要性，又提出容許英軍使用部分尚在仰光的租借物資，並把美國志願航空隊留在仰光作戰。在信中，魏菲爾聲稱自己曾嘗試與國軍領導曾討論實際作戰的問題，提出國軍第 5 軍能否暫緩進入緬甸，因英方不能確保它能擁有獨立的交通線。可是，中方只將其建議轉交蔣中正。魏菲爾認為，蔣中正只對一個問題真正感到興趣：在重慶建立盟國軍事會議，以協調英、美、中三國的行動。他提到相關討論「冗長而不特別有意義」，而且認為在重慶建立這種會議，對情報保密方面將是個大問題。他又提到蔣希望得到美援（特別是飛機）後於 1942 年發動反攻，擊敗日本，並對魏菲爾和勃蘭德不能提供確實時間表感到失望。他對國民政府的軍事效率沒有太大信心，認為蔣中正和宋美齡雖然「極為聰明」，但在軍事方面卻「雙腳不沾地面」。他又觀察到國軍內部士氣似乎不高，而且一方面希望得到裝備，另一方面卻無相關使用的組織和計劃。他特別提到雖然他和勃蘭德強調緬甸的重要性，但國軍和蔣中正方面似乎「對我的問題沒有太大興趣」。[19] 另一方面，《事略稿本》提到蔣中正於 24 日的早餐會上，向魏菲爾和勃蘭德聲言：「遠東對倭作戰，端在中國之陸軍，以配合英美之海空軍而協同作戰」。蔣中正甚至對「英人之貪詐與自私，毫無協同作戰之誠意，不禁痛憤無已」。[20] 這些發言某程度上反映了魏菲爾對蔣中正的觀察。[21]

---

19 "Governor of Burma to Secretary of State for Burma," 25 December 1941, *China: co-ordination between Chinese and British authorities*, WO 193/922, TNA.

20 「蔣中正與英大使卡爾談經濟問題」(1941 年 12 月 24 日)，〈事略稿本—民國三十年十二月〉，《蔣中正總統文物》，國史館藏，數位典藏號：002-060100-00159-024。

21 「蔣中正在嘉陵賓館歡宴九中全會出席委員並以本黨抗戰之成就與幹部同志革命建國之要道為題致訓詞又召集英美軍事代表團團長及魏菲爾勃蘭德等開第一次會議並通過遠東聯合軍事行動初步計畫六條等要案」(1941 年 12 月 23 日)，〈事略稿本—民國三十年十二月〉，《蔣中正總統文物》，國史館藏，數位典藏號：002-060100-00159-023。

檔案 10：緬甸總督致緬甸部長轉交魏菲爾信（1941 年 12 月 25 日）

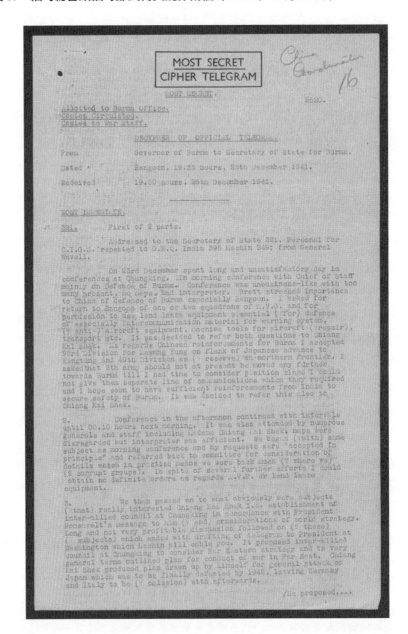

資料來源："Governor of Burma to Secretary of State for Burma," 25 December 1941, *China: co-ordination between Chinese and British authorities*, WO 193/922, TNA.

He proposed to cable this plan to Washington separately.

4.　　　　We breakfasted and had final interview with Chiang Kai Shek this morning (26th December). He slightly held forth on necessity to finish Japanese war in 1942 and said that if (? sufficient) air support from United States of America was forthcoming (? Chinese) forces could carry out (? General) offensive by June next year at the earliest or by October at the latest.

5.　　　　Comments follows in part 2 of this telegram. Our departure from Chungking was typical apparently of Chinese methods. At least four Generals came to see us off but no one seems to have given orders for last night's plane to be ready, so we waited nearly four hours and left at 1400 instead of 1030. By 1210 we were back at Chungking pilot having returned on report of Japanese planes about and being unable to obtain reliable information. By 2000 hours succeeded in getting fresh start in plane and eventually reached Rangoon midday 28th December.

Second and last part. Following is part 2 of my cable and contains comments on visit to Chungking (.)

　　　　From the little I saw of Chinese military machine and from discussion with our own and American Missions feel we can place little reliance on Chinese (corrupt group) against Japan. Chiang Kai Shek and his wife are highly intelligent, idealistic and determined but have not feet firmly on ground and inclined to be unpractical and visionary in military plans. Chinese morale probably not very high and opinion of foreign (? observers) seem to be that they are capable of one more big effort and one only and that not unless supported (? by) North America status (sic) forces. They look to Americans to supply Air Force and equipment for this effort but have little conception of organisation needed to maintain Air Forces. They are at present buoyed up with hopes of large scale American assistance and speedy end of their war which has lasted so long. If these hopes are disappointed it might have serious effect on their morale. Chiang Kai Shek kept insisting on necessity for definite dates when he might expect assistance and was obviously disappointed that none could be given.

　　　　Main assistance that Chinese can afford in near future is by action against Japanese lines of communication in China which are obviously vulnerable. Therefore Mission 204 should be completed and start work as early as possible. It would have been invaluable at this time if ready. Will send separate cable about deficiencies.

3.　　　　In spite of able and continuous support from Brett doubt if I really impressed Chinese with importance to them and urgency of defence of Burma. I had difficult and play as I had nothing to give and was asking for some of their precious supplies of Air and (omission) equipment while they looked to Americans as universal providers. They were polite but not really interested in my problems.

4.　　　　As regards A.V.G., Chennault who accompanied us to Chungking is unwilling to send more squadrons to Rangoon and is asking for despatch to China of squadron already there since he regards warning system and facilities as inadequate. It will be difficult to resist this demand if pressed since he is not under my orders. But will examine question on arrival Rangoon.

5.　　　　As regards Lend-Lease equipment MacGruder has instructions from Washington only to release to us with Chinese agreement. I think this can be obtained but slowly and reluctantly and time presses. If I consider (? it) necessary on return to Rangoon shall take most essential requirements in

/anticipation of....

MOST SECRET
CIPHER TELEGRAM

anticipation of permission.

6.   As regards 5th army am doubtful of their value, their
supply will be embarrassment and very much prefer to send
reinforcements from India if possible. Will cable further
after discussions at Rangoon.

7.   Do not think inter-allied war council at Chungking
will accomplish much but it may be useful clearing house for
information. Security of plans will be difficult problem and
Council may prove embarrassment rather than aid. It seems
however inevitable.

Distribution by M.O.12:-

S. of S.
C.I.G.S.
V.C.I.G.S.
D.M.O. & P.
D.P. (2).
D.D.M.O.(O).
M.O.1.10.12.
D.D.I.F.
D.M.I.
D.D.M.I.(I).
M.I.2. (3).

　　魏菲爾於 1941 年 12 月 25 日回到仰光當日，香港淪陷，英國失去在華南的據點。同時，馬來半島於 1942 年 1 月亦幾乎澈底失陷，新加坡危在旦夕。邱吉爾意識到中英兩軍似乎難以合作，因此於 1 月 20 日致函參謀首長委員會，聲言滇緬公路與緬甸甚至比已經失去戰略作用的新加坡更為重要，又對魏菲爾上將拒絕國軍的增援表示疑問。[22] 這個文件顯示邱吉爾始終以海空作戰與後勤角度理解戰爭，在太平洋戰爭初期，甚至有借助國軍陸軍作地面作戰主力的傾向，此與蔣中正的想法不謀而合。可是，他的意見與當時身在亞洲的英軍指導層對國軍實力的理解有所出入，而他似乎亦沒有注意到後勤方面的困難。他竟然認為：「如果新加坡守不住，我們可以快速把部隊轉移到緬甸」。實際上英軍在該區已無預備兵力，最重要的援軍第 18 步兵師（18th Infantry Division）於 1 月底抵達新加坡，並於數星期內成為俘虜。與此同時，英國軍方則加緊研究緬甸和中國陸路交通，並於 1942 年 2 月提交報告，詳列緬甸和中國連接的道路和鐵路。[23]

---

22 "Defence of Burma," 20 January 1942, C.O.S.(42)37, *War Cabinet and Cabinet: Chiefs of Staff Committee: Memoranda*, CAB 80/33/37, TNA

23 "Preliminary Report on Routes Between India-Burma-China (Reference C.O.S.(42) 51st Meeting 15 February 1942)," 27 February 1942, *China: co-ordination between Chinese and British authorities*, WO 193/922, TNA. (Map)

檔案 11：英國參謀首長委員會紀錄，「緬甸防務」（1942 年 1 月 20 日）

The National Archives' reference CAB 80/33

TO BE KEPT UNDER LOCK AND KEY

It is requested that special care may be taken to ensure the secrecy of this document.

Cv 163

(THIS DOCUMENT IS THE PROPERTY OF HIS BRITANNIC MAJESTY'S GOVERNMENT).

This document was considered at C.O.S.(42) 23rd Meeting, Item 6.

S E C R E T.

C.O.S. (42) 37.

20th JANUARY, 1942.

COPY NO. 33

WAR CABINET.

CHIEFS OF STAFF COMMITTEE.

DEFENCE OF BURMA.

Note by Secretary.

The following minute by the Prime Minister is circulated in connection with C.O.S.(42) 33, for consideration by the Chiefs of Staff at their meeting to-morrow Wednesday, 21st January, 1942.

Prime Minister's Personal Minute
Serial No.D.5/2.

"General Ismay for C.O.S. Committee.

This is surely a matter for the Supreme Commander, but an opinion should be expressed by the C.O.S. Committee. Obviously nothing should distract us from the battle of Singapore, but should Singapore fall, quick transference of forces to Burma might be possible. As a strategic object, I regard keeping the Burma Road open as more important than the retention of Singapore. What is the truth of the story about Wavell having refused Chiang-Kai-Shek's large offers of Chinese troops.

(Intld). W.S.C.
20.1.42."

(Signed) L.C. HOLLIS.

Great George Street, S.W.1.,

20th January, 1942.

⌀ Annex IV to C.O.S.(42) 33
(Telegram No.63 of 19/1/42 from Governor of Burma).

CAB 80/33

© Crown Copyright

資料來源："Defence of Burma," 20 January 1942, C.O.S.(42)37, *War Cabinet and Cabinet: Chiefs of Staff Committee: Memoranda*, CAB 80/33/37, TNA.

檔案 12：印、緬、中聯絡道之初期報告（1942 年 2 月 27 日）

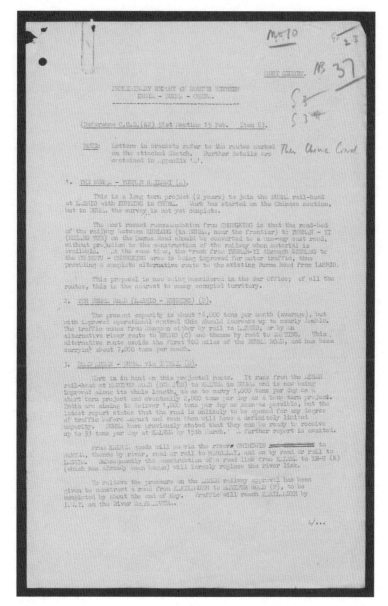

資料來源："Preliminary Report on Routes Between India-Burma-China (Reference C.O.S.(42) 51st Meeting 15 February 1942)," 27 February 1942, *China: co-ordination between Chinese and British authorities*, WO 193/922, TNA.

-2-

4. ROAD ASSAM - CHINA. via (FORT HERTZ) N.MULO, MYITKYINA, TENGYUEH, LUNGLING (G).

This route has been agreed by INDIA and CHINA. as an alternative to Route (D) for the carriage of Lease-Lend supplies to CHINA. Financial approval has been obtained and work will begin as soon as possible, CHINA having agreed to find most of the labour for the BURMA section. Traffic will come via rail-head and river-head at LEDO and MYITKYINA. It is estimated here that the road could be completed in about a year.

5. ROAD ASSAM - CHINA via LIGKING (J).

This route is common to route (G) as far as FORT HERTZ, but then continues eastward across most difficult country. This is a long term project and for the time being has been abandoned.

6. AIR FREIGHT TRANSPORT ROUTE LEDO - MYITKYINA - YUNNAN-YI (K).

This proposal is now under consideration. The suggestion is that the aeroplanes (provided by America) should carry stores into CHINA from INDIA and return with loads of tungsten.

Although a Washington telegram states that 100 aeroplanes will have a carrying capacity of 10,000 tons a week, it is considered here the figure should read 1,000 tons a week.

Representatives from INDIA and CHUNGKING are now in MYITKYINA discussing this project.

7. ROUTES SIBERIA - CHINA via LANCHOW (L).

There are various routes connecting the TURK - SIB railway with CHINA, and these converge on LANCHOW. Though they cannot carry a large capacity they form a secure route from U.S.S.R. to CHINA. Diplomatic action would be necessary before these routes could be used. The question of the capacity of this route is under investigation.

8. SUMMARY.

(a) Projects already approved:-

	Short Term.	Long Term.
Road MANIPUR - BURMA ROAD }	30,000	60,000
Road IMPHAL - KALEWA }		
Road ASSAM - TCHU		6,000 *
Road LEDO - LUNGLING		
(b) Projects under consideration:-		
Road LEDO - ZIGLING		6,000 *
Route TURK - SIB Railway - LANCHOW		3,000 *
Air Ferry DINJAY - MYITKYINA - YUNNANYI		?

* War Office estimate.

M.O.12(b)
27.2.42.

APPENDIX "A"　　　　　　　　　　　　　　　　　MOST SECRET

1.　BURMA - YUNNAN RAILWAY (LASHIO - KUNMING) (A).

　　　　Under construction in part but is not likely to be
completed before May 1944 (Governor Burma's telegram 144 of
9/2). Work cannot be continued during the summer months owing
to rain and floods.

　　　　War Office have ruled that the present work of survey
and railway construction on the BURMA section shall not cease
(War Office telegram 60664 (M.O.10) of 5/2).

2.　ROAD ASSAM - BURMA via IMPHAL (D).

　　　　An existing metalled road joins ASSAM rail-head at
MANIPUR ROAD (DIMAPUR) with IMPHAL. War Office telegram 68664
(M.O.10) of 5/2 approved road construction IMPHAL - KALEWA
(the Burmese river-head on the River CHINDWIN).

　　　　INDIA are working with all speed on the section IMPHAL -
TAMU and have asked BURMA to be prepared to receive deliveries
at KALEWA by the end of March. Initial deliveries will be small
but it is hoped to deliver 1,000 tons per day as soon as possible.
BURMA have been asked to aim at clearing 2,000 tons per day at
KALEWA, (India's telegram 2075/4 of 31/1).

　　　　BURMA started work on the alignment TAMU - KALEWA in
December and are hastening the work to the utmost within the
limits imposed by lack of labour, equipment and P.W.D. personnel.
Enemy occupation of a large part of the Tenasserim Division has
released a considerable number of P.W.D. personnel for this
work. BURMA estimates that the alignment can be cleared and
made ready for surfacing by the end of May and a river shingle
coat might be laid by the end of August, but INDIA has asked for
the date to be advanced (telegram from Governor of India, E.A.
Dept., KLL/649 of 14/2).

　　　　The greatest difficulties to be faced are bridging,
about which reliable data is not yet available, and the problem
of keeping labour on the job during the rains. The region is
virulently malarious (Governor Burma's telegram 156 of 12/2).

　　　　Onward transport from KALEWA can at present be undertaken
by the Rivers CHINDWIN and IRRAWADY to MANDALAY, thence by
river or rail to BHAMO or LASHIO. Approval has, however, been
given for road construction to the Burmese rail-head at YE-U
(Burma's telegram G(M) 94 of 17/2). INDIA has requested BURMA
not to delay work on the sector TAMU-KALEWA in order to press
on with KALEWA - YE-U.

3.　ROAD KAKILAMUKH - DIMAPUR (MANIPUR ROAD) (F).

　　　　War Office telegram 70607 .(Ops) of 13/2 approved
this road which will enable material transported by I.W.T. from
CALCUTTA to KAKILAMUKH to reach the MANIPUR ROAD terminal of
the IMPHAL - KALEWA road.

　　　　This will avoid one transhipment, as CALCUTTA is not on
the Indian metre gauge railway to MANIPUR ROAD. It will also
supplement the limited capacity of the latter.

　　　　The distance is approximately 85 miles, and INDIA hope
to be able to complete the work before the Monsoon comes
(early in June) (India's telegram VVY/2784/4 of 11/2).

　　　　　　　　　　　　　　　　　　　　　　　　/ 4 ....

4. ROAD ASSAM - CHINA via FORT HERTZ - LANGTAO - KYITKYINA
    TENGYUEH AND LUNGLING.

        INDIA have agreed with the Generalissimo that the
    immediate construction of a road from the ASSAM rail and river-
    heads at SADIYA and LEDO, thence FORT HERTZ, LANGTAO, SAMPROBUM,
    MYITKYINA, TENGYUEH to LUNGLING is necessary both for operational
    purposes in the event of the loss of RANGOON and for the supply
    of Lease/Lend stores to CHINA.   Work to start from both ends
    and CHINA to supply labour for the section LUNGLING - FORT HERTZ
    (India's telegram 3163/Q of 16/2).

        As a result of General Chiang Kai Shek's visit to DELHI,
    INDIA have agreed that effort should now be concentrated on this
    road, subject to the concurrence of His Majesty's Government
    (which has been obtained), and of the BURMA Government.

        The distance is approximately 360 miles and the estimated
    capacity and date of completion are not known.   There is,
    however, a road of sorts between SAMPROBUM and MYITKYINA, and the
    rest of the route, though difficult, is passable.   It is,
    therefore, possible that the work might be completed within a
    year.   The average initial monthly capacity will probably be not
    more than 6,000 tons.

5. ROAD ASSAM - CHINA via SICHANG (J).

        All routes so far mentioned have the disadvantage of
    feeding the BURMA road West of the vulnerable bottleneck in the
    area of the SALWEEN and MEKONG river crossings.

        A road has been proposed which would join ASSAM with
    SICHANG, which is on a new motor road now under construction
    between KUNMING and CHENTU, thus avoiding the Burma Road.   The
    proposed route is from SADIYA or LEDO to FORT HERTZ, i.e. the
    same for the first 150 miles as Route (Q); thence KUTIEN -
    CHUNGTIEN - SICHANG. Even so the road traverses most formidable
    country, including three major rivers, and could hardly be
    completed within two years.   The average monthly capacity would
    be not more than 6,000 tons.   The total distance is about 530
    miles.

        The Government of India have now agreed with General
    Chiang Kai Shek that this road should be abandoned for the time
    being in favour of Route (Q) (telegram from Government of
    India, E.A. Dept 1184 of 17/2).

6. ROUTES SINKIANG - CHINA via LANCHOW (R).

        Early in 1941 it was estimated that about 2,500 tons
    per month were delivered to LANCHOW by four roads running East
    from the TURK - SIB railway; it is possible that with improved
    facilities and additional lorries and/or pack transport the
    capacity of these roads might be increased to about 3,000 tons
    per month.

        These routes have all been used regularly by M.T., as
    well as camels and donkeys.   They were organised by the Russians
    to supply war materials to CHINA, but this traffic stopped in
    June 1941.   Traffic was small in the winter, but the roads were
    not closed.

　　中英美三國在緬甸的軍事合作尚未有機會磨合，前線的情況已急速惡化。1942 年 2 月 15 日，新加坡淪陷，英國在亞洲的勢力遭到重大打擊。在緬甸，雖然國民政府於 2 月派出遠征軍到緬甸東部協防，其時英印軍將大量部隊送往仰光前線，但部隊逐旅抵達戰場頗為紊亂，後勤上更難以兼容國軍加入。雙方尚未能建立合作，前線即已潰敗。3 月 7 日，英軍自仰光撤出，國民政府不但失去對外交通樞紐，更失去在緬甸的大量物資。[24] 時至 5 月，中英兩軍已退至緬印邊境。可是，英國在 4 月的印度洋海戰（Indian Ocean raid）中雖然承受一定損失，但東洋艦隊卻仍然完整，保住了盟軍對印度洋的控制。由於英軍繼續控制印度和印度洋，中國戰區的後方得以維持，並保有反攻基地。雖然從印度到中國的運輸，在 1945 年 1 月雷多公路（Ledo Road）完成前，只能依賴駝峰空運，但英軍繼續控制印度洋，亦使盟國得以繼續從波斯和伊朗，把大量戰略物資和租借裝備送到蘇聯，對蘇聯在 1942 至 1943 年得以維持起著一定作用。[25]

　　緬甸淪陷後，本已缺乏信任的中英雙方幾乎決裂，互相指責。5 月 28 日，即中英兩軍被趕出緬甸後不久，英國駐華大使薛穆（Horace J. Seymour, 1885-1978）發電報至外交部，提到緬甸淪陷使國民政府對英美頗感失望。薛穆提到「中國人現時並不完全相信美國和英帝國，在擊敗德國後有決心和日本作戰到底」。他建議儘快為國民政府提供其最重視的航空援助，雖然他和澳洲駐華總領事艾格登（Frederic W. Eggleston, 1875-1954）均認為中方趁機要求他們用不著的飛機。可是，薛穆以為由於緬甸戰敗對中國士氣影響不少，因此亦應該滿足中方要求。[26] 其後，英美兩國達成共識，決定由美國

24　Hans van de Ven, *China at War Triumph and Tragedy in the Emergence of the New China, 1937-1952* (London: Profile Books, 2017), p. 163.

25　Andrew Boyd, *The Royal Navy in Eastern Waters: Linchpin of Victory 1935-1942* (Barnsley: Pen & Sword Books, 2017); Ashley Jackson, *Persian Gulf Command: A History of the Second World War in Iran and Iraq* (New Haven, CT: Yale University Press, 2018).

26　"Chungking to Foreign Office," 28 May 1942, *China: co-ordination between Chinese and British authorities*, WO 193/922, TNA.

負責中國戰區的空戰，因此皇家空軍在戰爭期間並無派機到中國作戰，此舉
對後來英國在華情報和軍事活動影響不少。

檔案 13：英國駐華大使館致外交部電（1942 年 5 月 28 日）

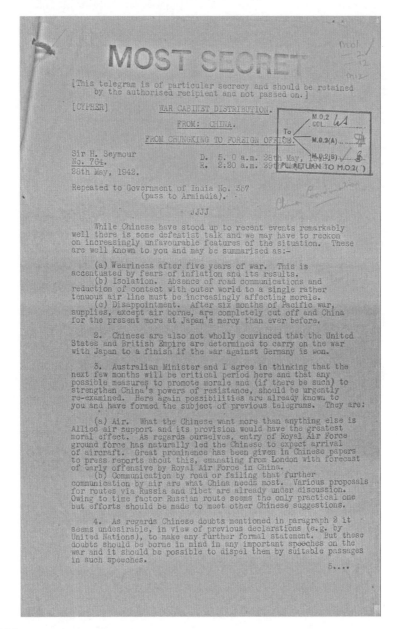

資料來源："Chungking to Foreign Office," 28 May 1942, *China: co-ordination between Chinese and British authorities*, WO 193/922, TNA.

5. Even at some cost to ourselves we should avoid friction over financial matters.

6. <u>Confidential</u>.

Australian Minister and I have discussed all this with United States Ambassador. His views appear to be

(a) that it is very doubtful whether Allied Air Forces could operate here more than such additional aircraft as are being supplied to A.V.G.

(b) He also, I think, feels that Chinese are trying to cash in on their present situation by extracting promises from the Allies of help in the form of aircraft etc. which they may not make full use of. As regards (a) bases, supplies and maintenance arrangements exist now for operation of British fighter aircraft over and above A.V.G. requirements. As regards (b) I do not say this opinion is altogether unfounded but the present situation must in time produce its effects on Chinese morale and if there is any stimulant we can give we should certainly do so.

　　另一方面，英軍則認為國軍的實力強差人意，似乎印證了戰前英國情報部門以及戰爭初期英軍高層對國軍戰力的估計。1942 年 7 月 6 日，英印陸軍總司令部的軍事情報處長（Director of Military Intelligence, General Headquarters India）哥富倫（Walter J. Cawthorn, 1896-1970），將一份由一名曾於緬甸前線作戰的英軍軍官撰寫的報告，轉交陸軍部軍事情報處。報告對國軍士氣、軍紀、戰術和訓練均多所批評。報告指出：「中國軍隊剛抵達緬甸時看來軍容鼎盛」，但報告作者聲言中國軍隊紀律不佳，其士兵時有搶掠，又干預鐵路運作，甚至擎槍指嚇鐵路人員。報告又指緬甸的國軍部隊士氣參差，但亦提到孫立人（1900-1990）的新編第 38 師士氣不俗，而且認為有戰意的國軍部隊在作戰時頗為勇敢，特別在擁有裝甲部隊支援的時候。另一方面，報告特別提到第 6 軍甘麗初（1901-1950）部士氣低落，部隊快速瓦解。在戰術方面，報告亦提供不少細緻的觀察，包括經常被指出的參謀作業問題，但亦提到國軍官兵行軍能力頗強，而且對空隱蔽工作極佳。可是，報告點出中英兩軍不能在戰鬥中合作，因為雙方「對戰鬥時的時間和空間概念不盡相同」。[27] 最主要之原因，應是雙方對後勤安排和行軍路線要求的不同，加上緬甸大部分地區缺乏基礎設施，使兩軍在作戰層面對難以合作。

27　"The Chinese Army in Burma," 6 July 1942, *Chinese Army Units in India and Burma*, WO 208/384, TNA. WO 208/384「印度與緬甸的中國陸軍部隊」（Chinese Army Units in India and Burma）資料夾收入關於在緬印地區的中國軍隊的情報，有助從英軍的角度和標準理解國軍個別部隊的狀態和英方人員的評價，時間為 1942 至 1943 年。

檔案 14：「中國陸軍在緬甸」報告（1942 年 7 月 6 日）

資料來源："The Chinese Army in Burma," 6 July 1942, *Chinese Army Units in India and Burma*, WO 208/384, TNA.

THE CHINESE ARMY IN BURMA.

Generally speaking the behaviour and value of Chinese troops bore
the forecasts of those who had seen them or followed their actions in
China.

DISCIPLINE.

On first arrival the Chinese forces were impressive. They were smart,
answered readily to command and their military discipline was as good off
parade as on. This was doubtless due to the effect of the very strict
injunctions laid down by the Generalissimo from CHUNGKING. Later their
more normal characteristics re-asserted themselves, many accidents, and discipline off
parade deteriorated badly. Looting became very common and interference
with the working of the railways, including the holding up at the point of
the pistol of some of the highest railway authorities in Burma, resulted
in large desertions of subordinate staffs, many accidents, and a final
breakdown of the whole system. But their discipline "on parade" remained
good and such matters as military security of H.Qs were at all times
excellent.

MORALE.

Morale varied with commanders and divisions. The 38 Div was as
uniformly good as 55 Div was bad. When morale was good the Chinese showed
high personal courage, self-confidence, tenacity in defence, and, when
co-operating with tanks, daring in attack. When morale collapsed, as it
did with almost the whole of the 6th Army, it did so with surprising
rapidity and completeness and with very little justification.

TACTICS & TRAINING

Details of the tactics used by the Chinese have been difficult to
obtain. Minor tactics were generally reputed to be poor and reliance
placed more on mass effort than individual initiative. The Chinese proved
as susceptible to road-blocks as ourselves and it was road-blocks that
cut off 55 Div and so led to the complete collapse of Chinese resistance
in the SHAN States front.

Commanders varied as was to be expected with the political appointments
which had necessarily to be made. Staffs were nearly always poor, and,
through bad administrative arrangements, heavily overworked. Officers and
men lacked education which hampered their ability to improve their military
training. All troops were exceptionally hardy and were capable of long
marches. M.T. discipline was bad but concealment from the air always
excellent.

Close co-operation in battle with the Chinese cannot be relied upon.
Their conception of time and space factors in battle is different from
ours.

INTELLIGENCE.

Chinese communiques and statements are issued with the one overruling
idea of selling Chinese resistance to the world. The ones in Burma were
no exception to this rule, though tempered slightly by the fact that
British and American observers were in some position to check the accuracy
of the statements made. After the Chinese collapse in the Shan States
the Chinese military spokesmen at Chungking, to cover this disaster,
referred glibly to British forces surrounded in Burma, echoed equally
glibly by All India Radio and the BBC.

Provision of intelligence by the Chinese was very poor. No documents
were ever handed over after scrutiny for perusal by us, and very few items
of information were ever passed. This was partly inability to realise
the value of information and partly the determination to receive all
possible credit at CHUNGKING by dispatching all captured material there.

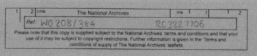

（四）英國在戰爭末期對國民政府抗戰能力的判斷

1942 年下半年，由於日軍在中途島大敗，加上與美澳軍在南太平洋進行消耗戰，因此對印度洋與印緬方面未有多大動作。該年底，英印軍曾向緬甸北部反攻，但被日軍逐回印緬邊境。其時，英軍曾組織「長距離滲透部隊」（Long Range Penetration Unit），又稱「欽迪特突擊隊」（Chindits），以支援英軍作戰。[28] 與此同時，英美物資繼續沿東非—印度洋抵達印度，退到印度的國軍（編成為駐印軍）亦接受美軍裝備和訓練。在華南和香港，英軍服務團則成為當地最成功的情報機構之一，不但為美國第 14 航空隊提供情報，亦維持了英國在該地的聲望和影響力。[29] 國民政府則繼續利用駝峰空運，從英屬印度獲得物資和補給。至 1943 年下半年，盟國逐步整理東南亞和中國戰區的指揮體系，準備將來反攻。

1943 年 7 月三軍情報委員會（Combined Intelligence Committee）撰寫「中國對盟國戰略貢獻及日本意圖」（Contribution of China to Allied Strategy and Japanese Intentions）報告呈交參謀首長委員會。報告列出了包括糧食、金融、士氣等問題對國府持續抵抗的影響。報告認為雖然國民政府與日本單獨求和的可能性非常低，但如果盟軍不能繼續援助國府，或在其周邊地區贏得軍事勝利以鼓舞其士氣，則國民政府可能與日本出現「不宣而和」（undeclared peace）的狀態，使盟軍難以利用中國大陸為反攻日本的基地之一。另一方面，報告指出中國當時拖住日本大量兵力，又為盟軍提供空軍基地打擊日本，而且在道義和政治上均是重要盟友，因此不可或缺。國軍雖然戰鬥力有限，但在中央控制下仍是重要的人力資源。報告總結，對國民政府持續抗戰的最大支援，是盟軍在其國境附近（即緬甸）贏得軍事勝利，特別是重奪滇緬公路。報告點出如果盟國不能提供足夠誘因，即使中日兩國「很

---

28 Brett Van Ess, "Wartime Tactical Adaptation and Operational Success: British and Japanese Armies in Burma and India, 1941-45" (Ph. D. dissertation, King's College London, 2019).

29 Edwin Ride, *BAAG: Hong Kong Resistance, 1942-1945* (Hong Kong: Oxford University Press, 1981).

不可能」會停戰，但危機仍然存在。[30] 這個報告反映了當時盟軍（特別是英國的參謀與計畫人員）頗為擔心國民政府因為缺乏支援而和日本單方面溝和，但缺乏裝備和海軍兵力，卻使東南亞的盟軍不能快速利用海路進行反攻，因此只能繼續從陸路反攻緬北。

---

[30] "Contribution of China to Allied Strategy and Japanese Intentions," 16 July 1943, C.O.S.(43)382(O), *War Cabinet and Cabinet: Chiefs of Staff Committee: Memoranda*, CAB 80/71/52, TNA.

檔案 15：英國參謀首長委員會紀錄，「中國對盟國戰略貢獻及日本的意圖」報告（1943 年 7 月 16 日）

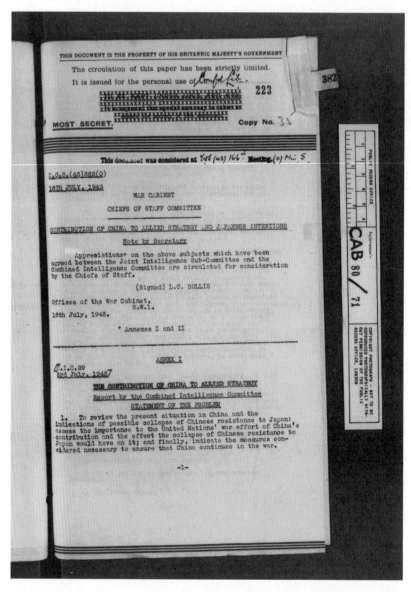

資料來源："Contribution of China to Allied Strategy and Japanese Intentions," 16 July 1943, C.O.S.(43)382(O), *War Cabinet and Cabinet: Chiefs of Staff Committee: Memoranda*, CAB 80/71/52, TNA.

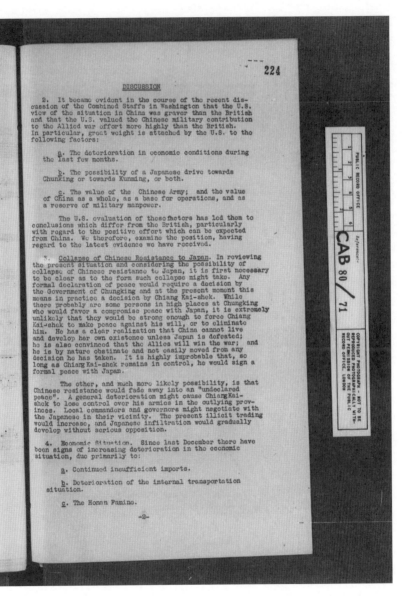

224

DISCUSSION

2.　It became evident in the course of the recent discussion of the Combined Staffs in Washington that the U.S.
view of the situation in China was graver than the British
and that the U.S. valued the Chinese military contribution
to the Allied war effort more highly than the British.
In particular, great weight is attached by the U.S. to the
following factors:

a.　The deterioration in economic conditions during
the last few months.

b.　The possibility of a Japanese drive towards
Chunking or towards Kunming, or both.

c.　The value of the Chinese Army; and the value
of China as a whole, as a base for operations, and as
a reserve of military manpower.

The U.S. evaluation of these factors has led them to
conclusions which differ from the British, particularly
with regard to the positive effort which can be expected
from China. We therefore, examine the position, having
regard to the latest evidence we have received.

3.　Collapse of Chinese Resistance to Japan.　In reviewing
the present situation and considering the possibility of
collapse of Chinese resistance to Japan, it is first necessary
to be clear as to the form such collapse might take.　Any
formal declaration of peace would require a decision by
the Government of Chungking and at the present moment this
means in practice a decision by Chiang Kai-shek.　While
there probably are some persons in high places at Chungking
who would favor a compromise peace with Japan, it is extremely
unlikely that they would be strong enough to force Chiang
Kai-shek to make peace against his will, or to eliminate
him.　He has a clear realization that China cannot live
and develop her own existence unless Japan is defeated;
he is also convinced that the Allies will win the war; and
he is by nature obstinate and not easily moved from any
decision he has taken.　It is highly improbable that, so
long as Chiang Kai-shek remains in control, he would sign a
formal peace with Japan.

The other, and much more likely possibility, is that
Chinese resistance would fade away into an "undeclared
peace".　A general deterioration might cause Chiang Kai-
shek to lose control over his armies in the outlying prov-
inces.　Local commanders and governors might negotiate with
the Japanese in their vicinity.　The present illicit trading
would increase, and Japanese infiltration would gradually
develop without serious opposition.

4.　Economic Situation.　Since last December there have
been signs of increasing deterioration in the economic
situation, due primarily to:

a.　Continued insufficient imports.

b.　Deterioration of the internal transportation
situation.

c.　The Honan Famine.

-2-

225

d. Japanese raids on food-producing areas in Chekiang and Kiangsi, and in the Ichang and Tungting Lake areas.

e. Continued inflation which affects soldiers and wage earners and is especially severe in its effect upon the official and educated classes.

Crops in Szechwan, however, seem to be good, although it is still too early to forecast the size of the final harvest.

Neither the food situation nor the inflation are serious enough at present to cause Chiang Kai-shek to give up the struggle, or to break his power.

5. Possibility of Japanese Attacks. The prospects of a Japanese attack on Kunming from Indo-China are now being examined in detail. It is a possible operation but hazardous. The Japanese show no signs of attempting it at present and we consider that they will not spare troops to undertake it unless they feel that a serious threat to their position in China is being created by the increasing use of the air ferry service which terminates at Kunming. The natural difficulties of the route which the Japanese would have to follow are so great that if the Chinese forces stationed in Yunnan put up a determined opposition there would be little likelihood of the Japanese succeeding.

The chances of a Japanese advance to capture Chungking are also being carefully examined. This operation also is possible but difficult. The Yangtze River has many rapids between Ichang and Chungking and there is a considerable hill barrier both north and south of the river. Even if Chungking were captured Chiang Kai-shek could move his capital further into the interior of China, though his position would then be greatly weakened and his ability to make any contribution to Allied strategy correspondingly reduced.

In general the capture of Chungking and Kunming would mean major military operations and represent a major increase in Japanese commitments in China, both for garrison and L. of C. troops and for air forces. Japan would be particularly unwilling to engage in further air commitments. Her troops are substantially occupied either in garrisoning the more important cities or in holding the long and vulnerable lines of communication.

6. Morale.

a. Fighting Forces. There are a number of factors which cause a low state of morale in the Chinese Army and so reduce its fighting value. These are the lack of equipment and ammunition, the lack of good N.C.O.'s and officers, particularly senior officers, the lack of military tradition in the Chinese nation and the Chinese inability ever to withstand a determined Japanese attack. Recently this situation has been aggravated by shortage of food.

b. Home Front.

(1) Official and Educated Classes. The shortage of food, inflation, and general war weariness are all lowering the morale of the official and educated classes. It is probable that economic conditions are better

-3-

226

for these classes in the Japanese occupied territory, and this combined with the effect of the present Japanese policy of seeking their ends by cajolery and propaganda rather than by offensive military operations tend to reduce the will to resist. On the other hand, it can be assumed that these factors will be to some extent counterbalanced by national pride and aversion to subjugation under a foreign soldiery.

(2) The Masses. The morale of the uneducated classes will depend almost entirely on whether or not they have food to eat; and at present there is a food shortage. They are, however, in any case accustomed to endure famines from time to time and are not in a position to influence the political situation. It is at present unlikely that the peasants who form a large majority of the population will stop producing food for the market.

In general, doubt as to whether adequate Allied assistance will arrive in time, and the lack of striking Allied success in any area of immediate interest to China are further important factors affecting mainly the educated classes and fighting forces.

The decline in morale is probably the most serious factor of the Chinese situation today. Morale, however, may have recently improved as a result of the successful Chinese operation in the middle Yangtze valley and recent developments in the Pacific.

7. Importance to the War Effort of the United Nations of China's Contribution. There are three main Chinese contributions to the war effort of the United Nations:

a. China forms a serious occupational and maintenance commitment for Japan, amounting at present to 22 divisions and 14 mixed brigades. This commitment is due partly to the Chinese armed forces but primarily to the size and topography of China.

b. China provides possible air bases for future air attacks against Japan and Japanese communications. The area most suited for attack against Japan proper by long range bombers is the province of Chekiang, where suitable airfields already exist. The two most suitable airfields (Chuhsien and Lishui) are temporarily unserviceable but could readily be restored whenever adequate protection could be provided.

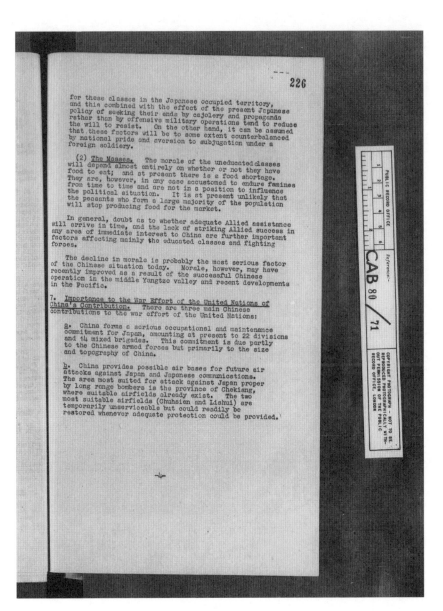

227

They are not at present in the area occupied by the
Japanese.   The province is partly mountainous, and
airfield development on a large scale in the parts not
occupied by the Japanese would present considerable
difficulty.   A chain of airfields extending into
W. China is in existence and a number of these places
have runways of from 1,400 to 2,000 yards.

c. A very important current contribution of China as
a member of the United Nations lies in the moral and
political fields.

8. Chinese Army.   The Chinese Army numbers more than 2¼
million men, but is almost entirely deficient in modern
equipment (except rifles), in aircraft and administrative
services.   Still more important there is a serious
shortage of trained commanders and staffs, and scarcely
any military tradition.   It is not at present capable of
offensive operations, other than guerrilla warfare, except
in conjunction with Allied forces.   The latest evidence
suggests that the fighting value of the Chinese armies as
a whole is probably less than it was six months ago.

Chinese military units, specially trained and equipped
by the American and/or British would be of greater fighting
value.   Such troops would be more valuable as light
infantry for reconnaissance and wide outflanking movements,
always provided that for some time to come at least, they
are not expected to operate as the main or independent
striking forces.   However, this light infantry role,
while limited, should be of particular importance in any
operations in the mountains and jungle of Burma, Thailand,
Malaya and Indo-China.

While comparatively small forces can be trained to carry
out the light infantry role suggested above, to bring the
present Chinese Army as a whole up to any reasonable standard
of military efficiency would be an undertaking so vast that
it could only be accomplished in a period of years.   We do
not think it would be possible for Chinese formations and
units to be commanded by American or British officers.
Considerations of nationalistic sentiment, quite apart from
difficulties of language, would preclude this.

Provided the Chinese Army remains under centralized
control, it should be of very great value to Allied operations in China, if only as a source of manpower and labor
for the L. of C. and for work on airfields and as a guerrilla
screen restricting Japanese activities in subsidiary theaters.

-5-

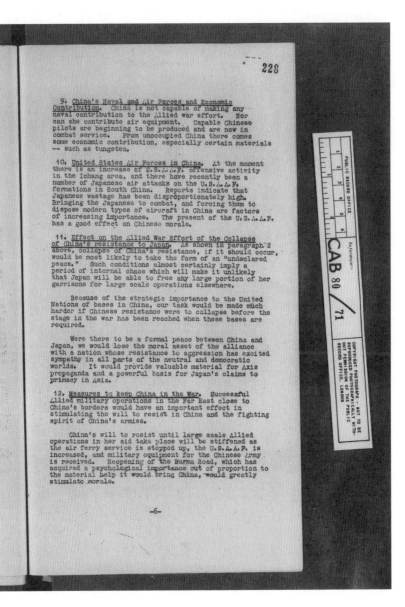

228

9. China's Naval and Air Forces and Economic Contribution. China is not capable of making any naval contribution to the Allied war effort. Nor can she contribute air equipment. Capable Chinese pilots are beginning to be produced and are now in combat service. From unoccupied China there comes some economic contribution, especially certain materials -- such as tungsten.

10. United States Air Forces in China. At the moment there is an increase of U.S.A.A.F. offensive activity in the Ichang area, and there have recently been a number of Japanese air attacks on the U.S.A.A.F. formations in South China. Reports indicate that Japanese wastage has been disproportionately high. Bringing the Japanese to combat, and forcing them to dispose modern types of aircraft in China are factors of increasing importance. The present of the U.S.A.A.F. has a good effect on Chinese morale.

11. Effect on the Allied War Effort of the Collapse of China's resistance to Japan. As shown in paragraph 2 above, collapse of China's resistance, if it should occur, would be most likely to take the form of an "undeclared peace." Such conditions almost certainly imply a period of internal chaos which will make it unlikely that Japan will be able to free any large portion of her garrisons for large scale operations elsewhere.

Because of the strategic importance to the United Nations of bases in China, our task would be made much harder if Chinese resistance were to collapse before the stage in the war has been reached when these bases are required.

Were there to be a formal peace between China and Japan, we would lose the moral asset of the alliance with a nation whose resistance to aggression has excited sympathy in all parts of the neutral and democratic worlds. It would provide valuable material for Axis propaganda and a powerful basis for Japan's claims to primacy in Asia.

12. Measures to keep China in the War. Successful Allied military operations in the Far East close to China's borders would have an important effect in stimulating the will to resist in China and the fighting spirit of China's armies.

China's will to resist until large scale Allied operations in her aid take place will be stiffened as the air ferry service is stepped up, the U.S.A.A.F. is increased, and military equipment for the Chinese Army is received. Reopening of the Burma Road, which has acquired a psychological importance out of proportion to the material help it would bring China, would greatly stimulate morale.

-6-

CONCLUSION   229

13.   In view of the fact that very little direct
military pressure is being exerted against China on
land or in the air, we do not consider that the
factors already mentioned - lack of food, inflation
and decline in morale - are sufficient at present to
cause the collapse of China's resistance.   But a
continuation of the present rate of deterioration might
do so.   Nevertheless, we consider that, for the next
12 months at least, formal peace between China and
Japan is extremely unlikely.   In the absence, however,
of some Allied action to stimulate Chinese morale there
is a danger that we might be faced with a situation
amounting to an "undeclared peace" between China and
Japan.

A formal peace would adversely affect the
United Nations' prestige and public opinion.   Even an
undeclared peace would make much more difficult the
use of bases in China and would deprive the United
Nations of the present and potential contribution to the
war effort of the Chinese army.

A new and large scale Japanese offensive in
China is unlikely.   Japan may, however, appreciate that
the increasing use of the air ferry service to Kunming
is indicative of the build-up of a serious threat to her
whole position in China.   The danger period for a
possible new Japanese offensive in China is therefore
likely to lie between the moment when this service is
substantially stepped up and the moment when Japan
becomes seriously apprehensive of a major Allied offensive
threatening from some other direction her position in
occupied territories.   When the second of these points
is reached, the likelihood of a new Japanese offensive
in China will probably quickly diminish.

The measures most likely to ensure continuance
of Chinese resistance are successful Allied military
operations close to China;   the increased delivery of
supplies, particularly military equipment;   the build-up
of the American Air Force in China;   and, on psychological
rather than on practical grounds, the reopening of the
Burma Road.

_____

ANNEX II

U.S. SECRET
BRITISH MOST SECRET

C.I.C. 28

3rd July, 1943.

JAPANESE INTENTIONS

Report by the Combined Intelligence Committee

STATEMENT OF THE PROBLEM

1.   To review previous appreciations and to report on
present Japanese strategy and Japan's probable intentions.

-7-

1943 年 8 月，「盟軍東南亞戰區司令部」(South East Asia Command, SEAC) 成立，由蒙巴頓 (Louis Mountbatten, 1900-1979) 出任盟軍東南亞戰區總司令 (Supreme Allied Commander South East Asia, SACSEA)，史迪威 (Joseph W. Stilwell, 1883-1946) 中將出任副司令。「中國戰區」則以蔣中正為總司令，史迪威為參謀長。本來同時控制中東、錫蘭，以及印緬前線的印度總司令部則只控制印度。東南亞戰區總司令部的主要地面部隊為第 11 集團軍屬下在印緬前線的第 14 軍團。1944 年春，中、英、美軍開始對緬北反攻，同時日軍緬甸方面軍亦對英帕爾地區進攻。英軍的欽迪特突擊隊則於日軍後方擾亂其交通線，拖住包括日軍第 53 師團等兵力，使其不能援助正和中、英、美軍作戰的前線日軍。至年中，中、美聯軍逐步進入緬北，於 6 月下旬與英軍共同占領交通樞紐孟拱 (Mogaung)，並於 8 月占領密支那。英帕爾 (Imphal) 的英軍亦逐走當面的日軍，向仰光方向推進。

　　雖然前線戰局尚算理想，但英、美、中三國在此戰區的領導層卻摩擦不斷。部分原因是史迪威個人性格和他與蔣中正的衝突使然，但主要原因是中緬印戰區確實過大，而且其地形極為複雜。1944 年 6 月，盟軍東南亞總司令參謀長鮑樂 (Henry R. Pownall, 1887-1961) 中將，撰寫「與將來於緬甸可能之作戰相關的指揮架構」(Future Organization of Command in Relation to Probable Future Operations in Burma) 備忘錄，呈交盟軍東南亞總司令和參謀首長委員會，直言：「現時的困難情況主要是源自於史迪威將軍的多重角色」。鮑樂認為，史迪威是蒙巴頓的副手，又是蔣中正的參謀長，使他應該同時身處錫蘭和重慶。他指出當時中緬印戰區的指揮架構，經 1943 年 8 月的改動後仍然過分臃腫，建議應予以廢除，以中國與東南亞兩個戰區取代。史迪威應該專注輔助蔣中正，把緬北前線的指揮工作交由另一位美國將領負責。[31]

31　"Future Organization of Command in Relation to Probable Future Operations in Burma," 3 June 1944, C.O.S.(44)488(O), *War Cabinet and Cabinet: Chiefs of Staff Committee: Memoranda*, CAB 80/84/17, TNA.

檔案 16：英國參謀首長委員會紀錄,「與將來於緬甸可能之作戰相關的指揮架構」備忘錄(1944 年 6 月 3 日)

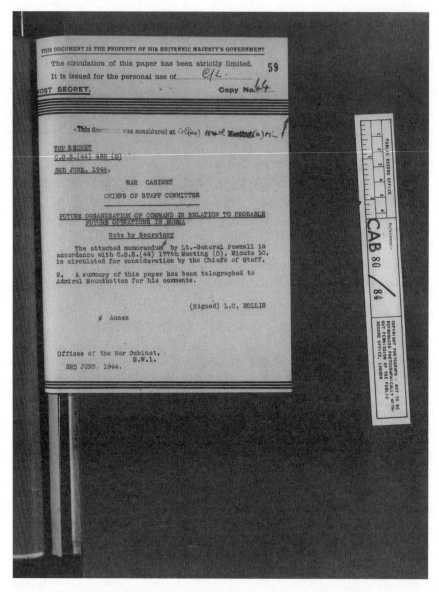

資料來源:"Future Organization of Command in Relation to Probable Future Operations in Burma," 3 June 1944, C.O.S.(44)488(O), *War Cabinet and Cabinet: Chiefs of Staff Committee: Memoranda*, CAB 80/84/17, TNA.

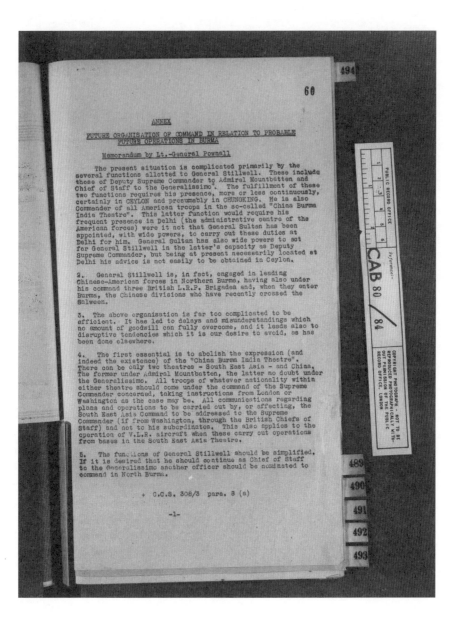

60

ANNEX

FUTURE ORGANISATION OF COMMAND IN RELATION TO PROBABLE FUTURE OPERATIONS IN BURMA

Memorandum by Lt.-General Pownall

The present situation is complicated primarily by the several functions allotted to General Stillwell. These include those of Deputy Supreme Commander to Admiral Mountbatten and Chief of Staff to the Generalissimo. The fulfillment of these two functions requires his presence, more or less continuously, certainly in CEYLON and presumably in CHUNGKING. He is also Commander of all American troops in the so-called "China Burma India Theatre". This latter function would require his frequent presence in Delhi (the administrative centre of the American forces) were it not that General Sultan has been appointed, with wide powers, to carry out these duties at Delhi for him. General Sultan has also wide powers to act for General Stillwell in the latter's capacity as Deputy Supreme Commander, but being at present necessarily located at Delhi his advice is not easily to be obtained in Ceylon.

2. General Stillwell is, in fact, engaged in leading Chinese-American forces in Northern Burma, having also under his command three British L.R.P. Brigades and, when they enter Burma, the Chinese divisions who have recently crossed the Salween.

3. The above organisation is far too complicated to be efficient. It has led to delays and misunderstandings which no amount of goodwill can fully overcome, and it leads also to disruptive tendencies which it is our desire to avoid, as has been done elsewhere.

4. The first essential is to abolish the expression (and indeed the existence) of the "China Burma India Theatre". There can be only two theatres - South East Asia - and China. The former under Admiral Mountbatten, the latter no doubt under the Generalissimo. All troops of whatever nationality within either theatre should come under the command of the Supreme Commander concerned, taking instructions from London or Washington as the case may be. All communications regarding plans and operations to be carried out by, or affecting, the South East Asia Command to be addressed to the Supreme Commander (if from Washington, through the British Chiefs of Staff) and not to his subordinates. This also applies to the operation of V.L.R. aircraft when these carry out operations from bases in the South East Asia Theatre.

5. The functions of General Stillwell should be simplified. If it is desired that he should continue as Chief of Staff to the Generalissimo another officer should be nominated to command in North Burma.

+ C.C.S. 308/3 para. 8 (a)

-1-

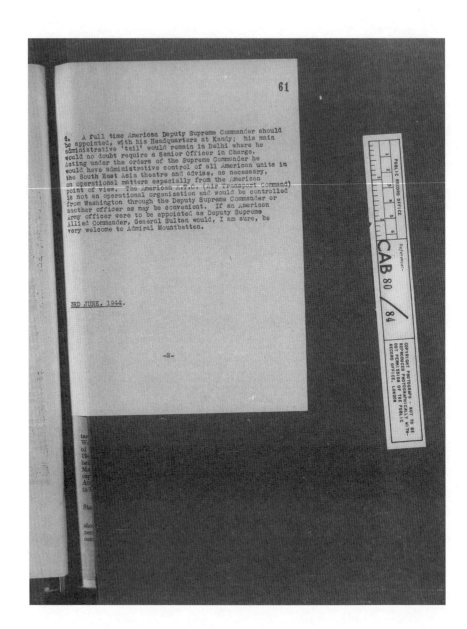

61

6.   A full time American Deputy Supreme Commander should be appointed, with his Headquarters at Kandy; his main administrative 'tail' would remain in Delhi where he would no doubt require a Senior Officer in Charge. Acting under the orders of the Supreme Commander he would have administrative control of all American units in the South East Asia theatre and advise, as necessary, on operational matters especially from the American point of view. The American A.T.C. (Air Transport Command) is not an operational organization and would be controlled from Washington through the Deputy Supreme Commander or another officer as may be convenient. If an American Army officer were to be appointed as Deputy Supreme Allied Commander, General Sultan would, I am sure, be very welcome to Admiral Mountbatten.

3RD JUNE, 1944.

-2-

　　同時，英國亦在研究下一步行動。1944 年 8 月 8 日，參謀長委員會討論緬甸戰況以及將來的策略，參與會議者包括首相邱吉爾、外相艾登（Anthony Eden, 1897-1977）、三軍參謀長，以及身在倫敦的蒙巴頓和他的參謀長，美國陸軍少將魏德邁（Albert C. Wedemeyer, 1897-1989）。當時，魏德邁尚未替史迪威。會議前半部分，蒙巴頓和魏德邁未有參與，邱吉爾等討論蒙巴頓提出的兩個方案，其中「冠軍計劃」（Champion）預計盟軍由密支那和英帕爾地區同時南進，從陸路規復緬甸；「先鋒計劃」（Vanguard）則由海路直取仰光。邱吉爾頗為憂慮緬甸戰役（Burma campaign）[32] 的英軍傷病問題，因此傾向由海路進攻仰光。他指出英國在此戰區的目的，應該是「奪回我們在此地區的重要據點」（應指仰光、新加坡、香港等地）。可是，當時盟軍在諾曼第（Normandy）和中太平洋馬里亞納群島（Marianas Islands），均在進行大規模的兩棲作戰，因此盟軍已無登陸船隻在緬甸進行兩棲作戰，而且與會者均同意仍要分兵保護印度到中國的航空交通線。結果，會議雖然沒有實質決定，但與會者均傾向繼續向以仰光為目標的地面進攻，並加派皇家海軍到太平洋作戰。[33] 1944 年 10 月，史迪威離職，「中緬印美國陸軍司令部」即被「美軍中國戰區」和「美軍印緬戰區」兩個司令部取代。11 月，盟國東南亞地面部隊（Allied Land Forces South East Asia, ALFSEA）成立，取代了第 11 集團軍的建制，簡化了英軍的指揮體系。

32　緬甸戰役（Burma campaign）在國軍戰史上，分為 1942 年的第一次緬甸作戰，以及 1943 至 1945 年的第二次緬甸作戰，但之於英軍的立場，是 1941 至 1945 年期間，在殖民地緬甸發生的一系列作戰。英國檔案與英方論述，亦沒有第一次與第二次之分，因此本文依使用的檔案進行解讀時，均以緬甸戰役稱之，謹此敘明。

33　"Minutes of the 264th Meeting of the Chiefs of Staff Committee," 8 August 1944, C.O.S.(44)(O)264th, *War Cabinet and Cabinet: Chiefs of Staff Committee: Minutes. Minutes of Meetings*, CAB 79/79/4, TNA.

檔案 17：英國參謀首長委員會第 264 次會議紀錄（1944 年 8 月 8 日）

The National Archives' reference CAB-79-79-4_1.jpg

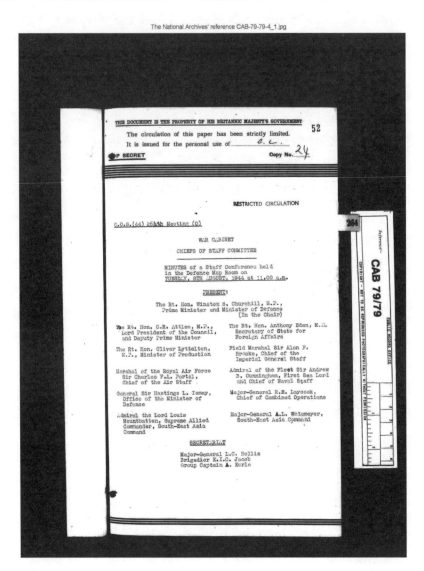

© Crown Copyright

資料來源："Minutes of the 264th Meeting of the Chiefs of Staff Committee," 8 August 1944, C.O.S.(44)(O)264th, *War Cabinet and Cabinet: Chiefs of Staff Committee: Minutes. Minutes of Meetings*, CAB 79/79/4, TNA.

53

CAB 79/79

OPERATIONS IN BURMA

SIR ALAN BROOKE said that the Chiefs of Staff had discussed with Admiral Mountbatten two alternative plans for operations in Burma after the present monsoon. If we were to maintain our present position in Burma, we must undertake offensive operations when the monsoon ended. If we did not do so, the Japanese might well seize the initiative and prejudice our whole position as they had done during the last campaigning season. Admiral Mountbatten's first plan, "CHAMPION", envisaged an advance southwards from the Mogaung-Myitkyina area supported by a parallel advance from the Imphal area. Even if these operations were successfully completed, it was likely that we should find that we were compelled to advance still further south.

Admiral Mountbatten's second plan, "VANGUARD", was for an operation to recapture Rangoon. He (C.I.G.S.) preferred this plan, which offered the best prospects of recapturing Burma. Smaller forces would be required to hold Burma on the Thailand frontier than were now required to hold the Assam border to maintain our position covering the air route over the "Hump". He therefore felt that we should undertake plan "VANGUARD" at the earliest possible moment with a view to recapturing Burma and thus releasing forces for operations elsewhere.

Admiral Mountbatten had insufficient resources in South-East Asia Command to carry out the operation and would require additional land forces, air transport and landing craft. The necessary forces could not be made available in time for the operation to be launched before March 1945, and only then if the situation in Europe at the beginning of October was such that we could afford to transfer resources from that theatre to the Far East.

In addition to a decision as to future operations in Burma, a decision was required regarding our general strategy for the war against Japan. The operations envisaged by Admiral Mountbatten would not absorb all the forces available. Considerable naval forces could be spared now and air forces would become available after the defeat of Germany. His own view was that we should undertake as much of plan "CHAMPION" as was necessary to maintain our position covering the air route over the "Hump" during the period between the end of the monsoon and March, 1945, and should launch "VANGUARD" at the earliest possible moment, which under present conditions would probably be not before March, 1945. At the same time we should send what naval forces we could spare to the Pacific to work in conjunction with Australian land forces as a British task force operating under General MacArthur. We should press on with preparations for increasing the size of this task force as additional land forces and air forces could be provided from Europe, and should arrange with the Americans for General MacArthur's operations to come under the direction of the Combined Chiefs of Staff. An early decision was required both as regards operations in Burma and our general strategy in the Far East.

-1-

The National Archives' reference CAB-79-79-4_3.jpg

54

THE PRIME MINISTER said that an operation for the capture
of Rangoon would result in the diversion of Japanese forces
from Northern Burma, whereas an operation such as "CULVERIN"
would not. He preferred "VANGUARD" to "CHAMPION" since the
latter appeared likely to commit us to a laborious reconquest
of Burma from the north. He did not think that the Japanese
fleet was likely to return to Singapore and agreed that we
should therefore be able to spare naval forces from the Indian
Ocean. He had no objection to such forces working with the
United States forces in the Pacific, providing that the Americans
could make the necessary maintenance facilities available and
desired our help in this theatre. He was horrified to learn
that "VANGUARD" could not be launched before the spring of
1945 and felt that the possibility of speeding up the
operation should be examined. Rangoon was in itself an
important objective and its capture would open up possibilities
of further operations such, for example, as an advance on
Moulmein or Bangkok or to the Kra Isthmus or Malay Peninsula.
The possibility of using Australian divisions in the operation
should not be overlooked.

As regards our general strategy in the Far East, he
suggested that this might be to recapture the many valuable
possessions we had lost in that area.

/At this point the Deputy Prime Minister, the Foreign
Secretary, the Minister of Production, Admiral
Mountbatten and General Wedemeyer entered the
meeting/.

ADMIRAL MOUNTBATTEN described with the aid of maps the
outline plans for operations "CHAMPION" and "VANGUARD".

He said that under his present directive he was responsible
for safeguarding and developing the air route over the "Hump"
and for exploiting any success against the Japanese, with a
view to opening the overland route to China. The first part
of his directive was already practically accomplished, and
"CHAMPION", if successful, would result in opening the overland
route to China for the intermittent supply of such items as
heavy guns and tanks, which could not be transported by air,
by February, 1945. It was proposed to construct two 4-inch
and one 6-inch pipelines alongside the road, the first 4-inch
line, which would deliver some 13,600 long tons of P.O.L.
per month, should be completed by July, 1945. The road would
not be completed as a two-way all-weather route for the
regular delivery of supplies to China until July, 1946, when
it should carry some 20,000 tons per month. The present air
lift over the "Hump" was 13,500 tons per month and it was
hoped to increase this to 20,000 tons per month.

General Stilwell had estimated that five divisions would
be required to defend the road and pipelines. As long as it
required such defence the road could not be a remunerative
route of supply to China, since the bulk of its capacity would
be required to support the forces guarding it.

-2-

CAB 79/79

The National Archives' reference CAB-79-79-4_4.jpg

55

The primary object of developing the supply routes to China was to build up a stockpile of P.O.L. for the United States 14th Air Force, which was required to support American operations for the capture of Formosa and subsequent operations against Japan. The value of the road would depend upon the progress of American operations in the Pacific. If it were not completed until after a port had been opened through which supplies could be carried to China, it would be too late, since one "Liberty" ship could carry nearly as much as could be transported by the road in a month.

"VANGUARD" was not so certain a way of opening the overland route as "CHAMPION", since it was dependent for its success on the Japanese reaction. On the other hand, it offered the prospect of the earliest possible recapture of the whole of Burma. If adequate forces were employed, he believed that the Japanese must react violently and rapidly. Our occupation of the Rangoon-Pegu area would sever all the lines of communication on which his forces in Burma depended, with the exception of one difficult and indifferent route. If the Japanese reacted as he believed, they would, our forces in the north would be able to advance rapidly southwards; we should be relieved of the necessity to guard the road and pipelines; we should be able to re-open the old Burma road, thus greatly increasing supplies to China, and the way would be open for the recapture of Burma.

THE PRIME MINISTER said that while he agreed that we were under an obligation to protect the air route to China, he deprecated a policy which would result in the whole effort of the British/Indian forces being bogged down in Burma. He thought the effort required to guard the air route was disproportionately costly, though he agreed that this must be maintained as, if supplies were cut off, the Generalissimo's forces would wither. He pointed out that the present lift over the "Hump" was 12,500 tons per month, whereas that over the old Burma road had been only 2,500 tons per month. It was hoped that the new road would have a capacity of 20,000 tons per month but this would not be available until 1946. He suggested that we should inform the Americans that we refused to concern ourselves with the development of the road or the pipelines, though we would faithfully adhere to our obligation to guard the air route.

SIR ALAN BROOKE said that at present, we had to protect the Assam frontier and maintain our position covering the air route. At some time or other we must recapture Burma. "CHAMPION" held out the gloomy prospect of "eating the porcupine quill by quill". He considered it would be to our advantage to capture Rangoon and to clear Burma at the earliest possible date, since this would secure the air route, open overland routes to China, give us an easier frontier to defend and thus release forces for operations elsewhere.

He was therefore in favour of "VANGUARD". As sufficient forces for this operation could not be made available before March, some operations would have to be undertaken in the Mogaung-Myitkyina area between the end of the monsoon and that date. Such operations would, however, contribute to the ultimate clearance of Burma. Once Rangoon had been captured, it would be necessary to go ahead and clear Burma of the Japanese remnants.

-3-

The National Archives' reference CAB-79-79-4_5.jpg

56

THE PRIME MINISTER said he had understood that once Rangoon had been captured, it would be possible to leave the Japanese remaining in Burma to rot away and to release forces for other operations. He had not realised that it was the intention that after capturing Rangoon, we should then proceed with operations to recapture the whole of Burma. His object was to reduce to the smallest possible limits British forces operating in the swamps of Burma, and once Rangoon was captured, he would prefer to bye-pass the remaining Japanese forces and launch operations in other directions.

SIR ALAN BROOKE said that so long as Japanese forces remained in Burma, we should have to provide forces to defend the air route. The quickest way therefore of releasing forces for operations in other theatres was, after the capture of Rangoon, to press ahead and clear up the Japanese remaining in Burma.

In reply to a question, ADMIRAL MOUNTBATTEN said he estimated that it would take some six months after the capture of Rangoon to recapture the remainder of Burma. He suggested that this was satisfactory, since forces would be released about November, which was the beginning of the campaigning season in South-East Asia. Difficulties had been experienced in preparing India as a base for operations, owing to the fact that it was the policy to restrict supplies to "approved operations". India had done everything that was possible, and "VANGUARD" could be launched from India provided that certain items of equipment were now supplied on high priority. Still more equipment would be required if India was to be the base for a later large scale amphibious operation.

THE PRIME MINISTER said that no decision had as yet been taken as to the base from which future large scale amphibious operations would be launched. As a result of conversations at "SEXTANT", the possibility of using Australia as a base had been examined. There had, however, been great changes in the situation since that date, in particular, the American programme for operations in the Pacific had been greatly speeded up. Whilst the employment of British forces in the Pacific might not affect "VANGUARD", it would certainly prevent the exploitation of the capture of Rangoon by further thrusts against Moulmein, Bangkok, the Kra Isthmus or Malaya. It now appeared that no large scale amphibious operation would be possible until November, 1945. If this was so, then the decision not to divert resources to develop India as a base, at a time when our shipping position was very strained and all available resources were required for "OVERLORD", was surely a wise one.

MR. ATTLEE asked what modification of our strategy in Burma, with a view to releasing forces for operations elsewhere, would be possible on the assumption that we continued to fulfill our obligation to secure the air route to China.

ADMIRAL MOUNTBATTEN pointed out that in order to secure the air route, we had to hold a very long front, and gave it as his view that so long as we had this obligation to fulfil, no forces could be released. The quickest way to release forces was to recapture the whole of Burma and the capture of Rangoon as a first step offered the quickest means to this end.

-6-

57

THE PRIME MINISTER said that of the two plans, he preferred "VANGUARD", but it now appeared that whichever course we adopted, we were committed to the laborious reconquest of Burma, swamp by swamp. He drew attention to the very large proportion of our casualties in that theatre which were due to disease and not to enemy action, and reminded the meeting that after our last campaign in Burma, we had decided emphatically against any operation for the reconquest of that country from the north. We had also previously turned down a suggested operation for the recapture of Rangoon.

SIR ALAN BROOKE said that conditions had changed greatly since we had decided against a seaborne assault on Rangoon. We now had air superiority in Burma. We had learned much about the capabilities of airborne forces and such forces could be made available. The plan now under consideration involved the large scale use of these forces and not a seaborne assault.

THE PRIME MINISTER said it appeared clear that the British/ Indian army could do nothing but reduce Burma, and that there was no chance of their playing a part in amphibious operations in other areas until the end of 1945. It might be, however, that when Rangoon had been captured, the situation would be such that it would be considered better to march to the east than to stop and mop up Burma, and that the forces which would become available from Europe should be employed in recovering territory such as Singapore, which we had lost to the Japanese.

THE CONFERENCE:-

    Agreed to meet later in the day to consider
    the part to be played by British forces
    in the war against Japan.

Offices of the War Cabinet,
        S.W.1.

  8TH AUGUST, 1944

-5-

　　與此同時，英軍內部亦提到英國特殊作戰機構和美軍在印度和中國戰區的關係。1944 年 12 月，英國特殊作戰執行部提交一份報告予處長吉賓士（Colin McVean Gubbins, 1896-1976）少將，提及特殊作戰執行部在中國少有直接行動，因此與戰略情報局（Office of Strategic Services, OSS）在中國沒有合作。可是，戰略情報局在印度的分支則接受英方的援助，並在英國東南亞戰區的範圍內活動。報告認為史迪威是雙方合作困難的障礙，直言：「有史迪威擔任中緬印戰區〔美軍〕司令一日，他將想盡辦法阻止英美軍在任何層面有任何合作」，因此雙方合作始終有限。不過，報告亦提到史迪威離職後，合作情況即有改善。特殊作戰執行部甚至認為史迪威的繼任人魏德邁將會改變態度，使合作成為可能。可是，實際情況將令英方大失所望。[34]

---

[34] "OSS and SOE Relations in the Far East," 8 December 1944, *OSS Burma and Siam*, HS 1/307, TNA.

檔案 18：「OSS 與 SOE 在遠東之關係」備忘錄（1944 年 12 月 8 日）

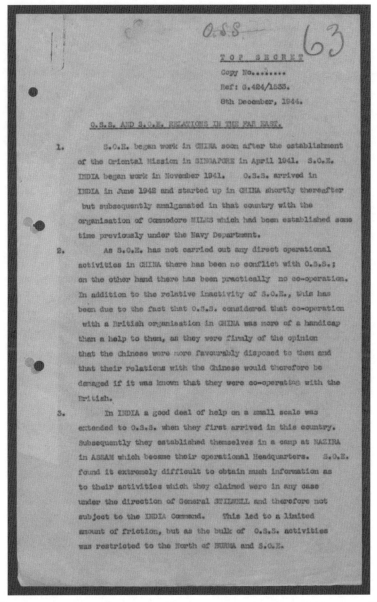

資料來源："OSS and SOE Relations in the Far East," 8 December 1944, *OSS Burma and Siam*, HS 1/307, TNA.

- 2 -

deliberately therefore reduced the scale of their activities there, there was relatively little trouble.

4.　　　With the founding of S.E.A.C. O.S.S. INDIA was set up with a Headquarters at KANDY, but the active operational section, which was Detachment 101 based on NAZIRA was made part of O.S.S. CHINA and continued to consider itself only under the orders of General STILWELL in his capacity as Commanding General of the C.B.I. theatre.　General DONOVAN subsequently agreed that any operational activities of O.S.S. CHINA into S.E.A.C. territory should be cleared beforehand through P. Division S.E.A.C., being put up to P. Division by O.S.S. INDIA on behalf of O.S.S. CHINA.　This in fact never took place as O.S.S. CHINA never kept O.S.S. INDIA sufficiently advised for this procedure to be carried out.

5.　　　O.S.S. INDIA, starting relatively so late in the theatre, found themselves up against the difficulty that various areas were already being worked by S.O.E., and as they very definitely did not wish to be considered a junior partner it made co-operation in these areas somewhat difficult.

6.　　　There is no doubt that from the point of view of S.O.E. the main difficulties have been:

　　(a)　　that as long as General STILWELL was Commanding General of the C.B.I. theatre he did everything possible to prevent co-operation between British and American officers in any organisation and at any level.　This inevitably affected O.S.S. as it affected every other American organisation in the theatre.

　　(b)　　O.S.S. personnel in this theatre have on the whole been lacking not only in local knowledge but also in knowledge of S.O.E. technique. There has therefore been a justifiable feeling

- 3 -

of distrust among S.O.E. operational staff
officers as to the competence and reliability
of O.S.S. plans and performance.

(c)　　the Co-ordinator of P. Division has, in
accordance with instructions from S.A.C.,
done everything possible to win the confidence
of O.S.S. and to give them the feeling that
they were being given a square deal and more
than a square deal. In so doing he has
hesitated to make decisions which would be
unpopular with the Americans, even when it was
clear that such decisions would have to be
made. This has sometimes had the opposite
result to that intended, e.g. the OATMEAL-JUKEBOX
incident where there is little doubt that if
the Co-ordinator had made an earlier decision
the effect on O.S.S./S.O.E. relations would
have been better, regardless of what the
decision had been. As it was, the Co-ordinator,
having decided in his own mind to award the
priority to S.O.E., went on trying to obtain
a compromise until the very last minute
which inevitably resulted in creating an undue
competitive spirit between the operational
staff officers of the two organisations and made
the final decision still less acceptable to
O.S.S. than it would otherwise have been.

7.　　With regard to 6 (a). There has been a rapid improvement since General STILWELL's removal. It must be remembered,
however, that this influence was allowed to permeate
American Military circles for over 2 years and it will take
time for the recovery to be complete.

8.　　The division of the CHINA and BURMA/INDIA American
theatres should also assist. There is every reason to believe

- 4 -

that with General WHEELER as Deputy S.A.C. at KANDY and
General WEDEMEYER, as American Commander - and we expect
at a later stage S.A.C. - in CHINA a different spirit will
gradually spread and this will make easier the co-operation
between O.S.S. and S.O.E.

9.   With regard to 6 (b).   O.S.S. is of course learning
by experience and presumably more experienced personnel will
join them from the European and Mediterranean theatres.

10.   With regard to paragraph 6 (c).   It is difficult to know
in which direction our advantage lies.   If a stronger and
more efficient Co-ordinator were to be appointed, it would
probably assist co-ordination in certain directions.   On the
other hand there would be a grave danger that the officer
so appointed would be tempted to exercise control over the
organisations and more particularly the British organisations
concerned.   We have always felt that from the S.O.E.
point of view this would be disastrous.   The Co-ordinator
is at present hopelessly understaffed and if closer long
range co-ordination is to be achieved his staff must be
strengthened.   We understand that this is being done.

11.   With regard to what would suit us best in the way of
co-ordination, it is clear that we are in the stronger
position in S.E.A.C. and O.S.S. are in the stronger position
in CHINA.   At this time of writing the position in CHINA
is fluid and the outcome obscure.   If the present regime,
or some modification of it, continues, the Americans will
undoubtedly be the controlling influence and, particularly
in connection with the provision and employment of aircraft,
we shall have to obtain American assistance.   If, on the
other hand, CHINA collapses all present American organisation
in CHINA is likely to disappear unless of course they swing
right over and instal themselves with the Communists in YENAN.
This step seems hardly likely, particularly as geographically
it will be very difficult for the Americans to obtain

- 5 -

adequate contacts. In the event of such a collapse S.O.E.
activities would become decidedly more important although
extremely difficult. Activities would divide into two main
classes:

    (a)   Continuation of our present proposals for the
            influencing of Puppets and other guerillas
            in coastal areas in order to assist eventually
            American landings, and

    (b)   Long term activities directed towards improving
            the position of GREAT BRITAIN in CHINA when
            some form of order is finally re-extablished.
            This would mean maintaining contact with
            various groups and factions in CHINA and
            giving assistance where possible to those
            who seem most indicated.

12.   (a) in paragraph 11 above will require a C.C.O.S.
directive. (b) in paragraph 11 above would require a
Foreign Office directive.

13.   For the purpose of this paper we will assume that
American influence in CHINA will continue and therefore we
wish to have for course (a) in paragraph 11 above as much
American support as we can obtain. In this event it would
probably pay us to aim at an agreement whereby we were
considered the senior partner in S.E.A.C. territories and
O.S.S. became senior partners in CHINA. This would still
leave the position of F.I.C. open to argument.

14.   We are convinced that the best way of handling the
F.I.C. problem in relation the the Americans is to
concentrate on obtaining a pronouncement from them with
regard to the BLAIZOT Mission. If they accept the BLAIZOT
Mission they accept by implication the fact that clandestine
activities in F.I.C. are primarily controlled from S.E.A.C.
It is true that this would only be so as far as the French
are concerned, but the chances of the Americans being able

- 6 -

to do anything effective in F.I.C. without the French is in
our opinion small. If on the other hand they do not accept
the BLAIZOT Mission, they will by such a refusal put
themselves out of court as far as the French are concerned
and will therefore eliminate themselves to a large extent
from effective activity in F.I.C.

15.   If co-ordination, as recently envisaged, takes place
in CHINA we shall undoubtedly be faced with the problem that
the American co-ordinator in CHINA will wish to co-ordinate
F.I.C. activities on the argument that as far as American
troops are concerned F.I.C. is in the CHINA theatre. This
we must refuse, even though it will result in O.S.S. CHINA
refusing then to be co-ordinated at all for F.I.C. We do
not believe that this would cause us any embarrassment.

16.   It would, of course, be necessary to define somewhat
more clearly what the rights of a junior partner are. We
imagine that it would mean that co-ordinated plans would
be worked out to the extent of seeing that there was no
undue duplication and that in any areas in which the senior
partner had a specific interest the senior partner would

(a)   have to agree to the junior partner operating
       in that area, and

(b)   the junior partner would have to follow
       general policy indications laid down by the
       senior partner.

The principal safeguard for the junior partner would
presumably be the Theatre Commander who would see to it that
his interests were served in the best way and would not allow
the senior partner to act unduly in a dog-in-the-manger
fashion.

17.   We believe that an arrangement on these lines would be
definitely to our advantage. In CHINA we expect to require
American assistance and the coastal area to be dealt with
is so large and our resources relatively so small that we

- 7 -

do not think there should be any difficulty.　We should try
to reserve primarily to ourselves the HONGKONG and adjacent
area.

18.　　　It may well be of course that O.S.S. will not accept
the proposal that they should be a junior partner in this
theatre.　If that is so, our general interest would be to have
that minimum of co-ordination in this theatre which would
prevent their activities upsetting ours and which would at the
same time support our case for obtaining American co-operation
in CHINA.　This means that everything should be done to
assist the Americans in this theatre with transport, training,
special supplies, etc. so that a quid pro quo can be demanded
in CHINA.

19.　　　O.S.S. INDIA decided some time ago to concentrate
primarily on Intelligence and Morale Operations in non-British
territories.　This did not mean that they in any way renounced
their right to operate equally with S.O.E. throughout the
theatre.　We consider that whether the principle of senior
and junior partner is accepted or not, it would be to our
advantage to encourage them to concentrate on the lines
they themselves have proposed.　They are also going to have
Maritime Units.　These are not competitive with S.O.E.,
although they may be with S.O.G.S. and their activities on
this side should also be encouraged.

20.　　　Whether the general principle of senior and junior
partners is accepted or not, it is we believe essential that
S.O.E. should be accepted as the senior partner in relation
to resistance movements in British territories.　This
proposal has in fact been accepted by O.S.S., but we think
should be accepted more formally.

DISTRIBUTION:　　　　Copy No:

C.D. (LONDON)　　　　1
D/B (LONDON)　　　　2
A.D.　　　　　　　　3
File (2)　　　　　　4 & 5

　　1944 年下半年，英國發現國民政府在日軍「一號作戰」（一号作战，Operation Ichigo）攻勢下形勢頗為危急。10 月，駐華大使館武官格林斯岱向陸軍部報告，指雲南實力派龍雲（1884-1962）曾向英美求助，甚至要求給與火砲，「以抵擋日本裝甲部隊」。[35] 對此，英國政府的態度則頗為明確。早於 1944 年夏，格林斯岱已因為英軍服務團司令賴廉士（Lindsay T. Ride, 1898-1977）和廣西的李濟深（1885-1959）過從甚密，對其作出訓誡。[36] 對於影響力比李濟深更弱的龍雲，英方自然興趣不大。10 月 20 日，陸軍部回覆格林斯岱，對龍雲的實力頗有疑問，認為：「我們的情報不能確認雲南軍比中國遠征軍是更好的部隊」，直言如果雲南軍質素甚佳，則何以未被派往緬甸助戰。陸軍部又指龍雲要求火砲支援，可能只是為了日後不戰而退預先製造理由，即使他願意作戰，最終亦可能浪費了裝備。因此陸軍部拒絕為他提供武器，暗示英國將不會理會他和國民政府之間的衝突。[37]

35　"M. A. Chungking to the War Office," 13 October 1944, *Yunnan: relation with the Central Government*, WO 208/209, TNA. WO 208/209「雲南：與中央政府關係」（Yunnan: relation with the Central Government）卷宗收入有關雲南與中央政府衝突的資料，時間為 1934 至 1945 年。

36　L. T. (Lindsay Tasman) Ride, "Report on the Activities of a M. I. 9 Organization Operating in South China." Australian War Memorial Collection, MSS0840, pp. 65-66.

37　"War Office to M. A. Chungking," 20 October 1944, *Yunnan: relation with the Central Government*, WO 208/209, TNA; "Extract from: Chungking Report Dated 22 March 1945, Ref: F 1761/186/10," 22 March 1945, *Personalities: Lung Yun*, WO 208/200, TNA. WO 208/200「人物資料：龍雲」（Personalities: Lung Yun）卷宗收入有關龍雲的資料，時間為 1932 至 1945 年，但實際內容不多。

檔案 19：英國駐華大使館武官致陸軍部電（1944 年 10 月 13 日）

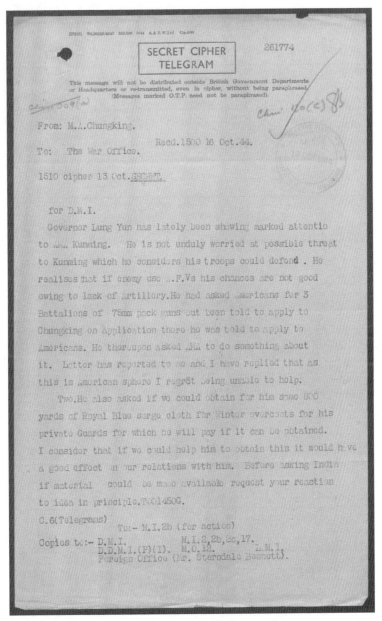

資料來源："M. A. Chungking to the War Office," 13 October 1944, *Yunnan: relation with the Central Government*, WO 208/209, TNA.

檔案 20：英國陸軍部致駐華大使館武官電（1944 年 10 月 20 日）

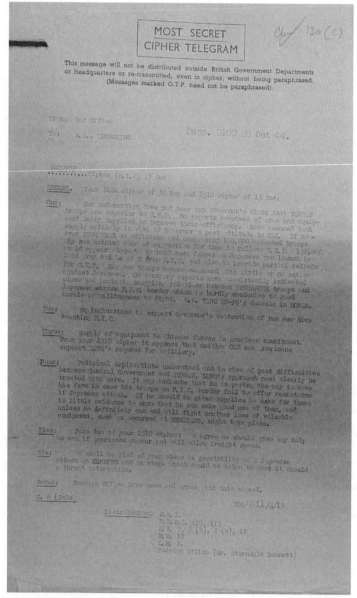

資料來源："War Office to M. A. Chungking," 20 October 1944, *Yunnan: relation with the Central Government*, WO 208/209, TNA.

檔案 21：重慶方面報告節錄（1945 年 3 月 22 日）

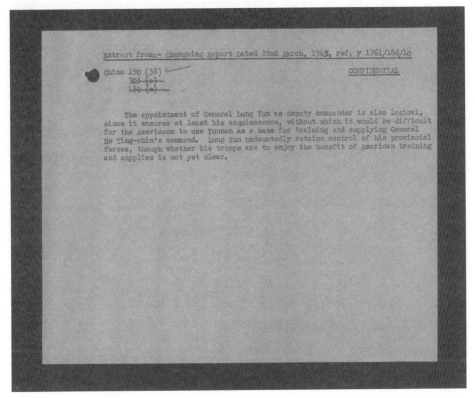

資料來源："Extract from: Chungking Report Dated 22 March 1945, Ref: F 1761/186/10," 22 March 1945, *Personalities: Lung Yun*, WO 208/200, TNA.

另一方面，邱吉爾擔心國民政府崩潰，將使日軍可以抽調大量兵力面對英軍，因此亦同意國府把部隊從緬甸前線調回，特別是曾於印度蘭伽（Ramgarh）受訓的部隊。他回應蔣中正希望把部分在緬兵力調回國內的要求，指出：「他開口要求的話，必須給他」。[38] 可是，危機尚未解除，英、美、中三國已開始就緬甸戰役的論述明爭暗鬥。1944 年 9 月 28 日，邱吉爾於下院討論時提到緬甸戰區，強調英軍的功績，但未有提及國民政府的貢獻，使中方頗為不滿。[39] 蒙巴頓得悉後即嘗試提醒外交部，但後者向蒙氏指出中美兩國有意見，認為緬甸戰役全為中美負責的作戰，因此英國政府有意糾正英國對緬甸戰役毫無貢獻的觀念，並反對作出清澄以安撫中方。[40] 12 月，外交部向英國駐美大使哈利法克斯（Edward Wood, 1st Earl of Halifax, 1881-1959）子爵草擬了一份電報，希望他向美國政治領袖解說英國支持國民政府把國軍調回的決定，並向他們解釋英國在緬甸戰區的貢獻。草稿提到如果國軍調回在緬部隊後，英軍在緬甸無力前進，或魏德邁因此在中國獲得顯著進展時，哈利法克斯該如何解釋。[41] 可是，參謀長委員反對發出此信，認為應該由即將到華盛頓赴任的英國三軍參謀團（British Joint Staff Mission）團長威爾遜（Henry M. Wilson, 1881-1964）元帥負責召開記者會，解釋緬甸戰區的中、英、美三國貢獻。[42] 邱吉爾對英軍在中國戰區參與

---

[38] "Withdrawal of Chinese Divisions from Burma," 3 December 1944, C.O.S.(44)1008(O), *War Cabinet and Cabinet: Chiefs of Staff Committee: Memoranda*, CAB 80/89/72, TNA.

[39] "War and International Situation," HC Deb, 28 September 1944, Vol. 403, cc421-604, https://api.parliament.uk/historic-hansard/commons/1944/sep/28/war-and-international-situation#S5CV0403P0_19440928_HOC_275 (accessed 23 June 2020).

[40] "Chinese Contribution to Operations in Burma," 12 October 1944, C.O.S.(44)898(O), *War Cabinet and Cabinet: Chiefs of Staff Committee: Memoranda*, CAB 80/88/24, TNA.

[41] "British War Effort in Burma," 27 December 1944, C.O.S.(44)1052(O), *War Cabinet and Cabinet: Chiefs of Staff Committee: Memoranda*, CAB 80/89/115, TNA.

[42] "Minutes of Meeting held of Friday 29th December, 1944," C.O.S.(44)1052(O), *War Cabinet and Cabinet: Chiefs of Staff Committee: Minutes. Minutes of Meetings*, CAB 79/84/23, TNA; "Copy of a Letter (Ref. C.O.S. 2100/4) dated 29th December, 1944, from the Secretary, Chiefs of Staff Committee to the Foreign Office," C.O.S.(44)1052(O), *War Cabinet and Cabinet:*

有限似乎耿耿於懷。1945 年 2 月 3 日，邱吉爾和羅斯福在馬爾他（兩人前往雅爾達〔Yalta〕和史達林〔Joseph V. Stalin, 1878-1953〕會面前夕），於美國巡洋艦昆西號（USS *Quincy*）參與英美參謀長聯席會議時，邱吉爾提出派英印軍到中國作戰，但英美參謀長們均表示在後勤上並不可行，美國陸軍參謀長馬歇爾（George C. Marshall, 1880-1959）甚至直言並無需要。[43] 由此可見，不但中、美兩國為「劍拔弩張的盟友」，實則中、英、美三方均處於充滿張力的關係。

Chiefs of Staff Committee: Minutes. Minutes of Meetings, CAB 79/84/23, TNA.

43　"Meeting of the Combined Chiefs of Staff with Roosevelt and Churchill, February 2 1945, 6 p.m., on board the U.S.S. "Quincy" in Grand Harbour," *Foreign Relations of the United States: Diplomatic Papers, Conferences at Malta and Yalta, 1945* (Washington: United States Government Printing Office, 1955), pp. 544-545.

檔案 22：英國參謀首長委員會紀錄，「中國軍隊撤出緬甸」（1944 年 12 月 3 日）

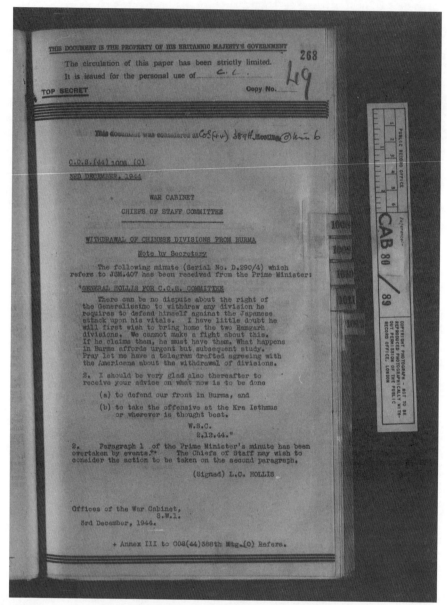

資料來源："Withdrawal of Chinese Divisions from Burma," 3 December 1944, C.O.S.(44)1008(O), *War Cabinet and Cabinet: Chiefs of Staff Committee: Memoranda*, CAB 80/89/72, TNA.

檔案 23：英國參謀首長委員會紀錄，「中國在緬甸戰役的貢獻」(1944 年 10 月 12 日)

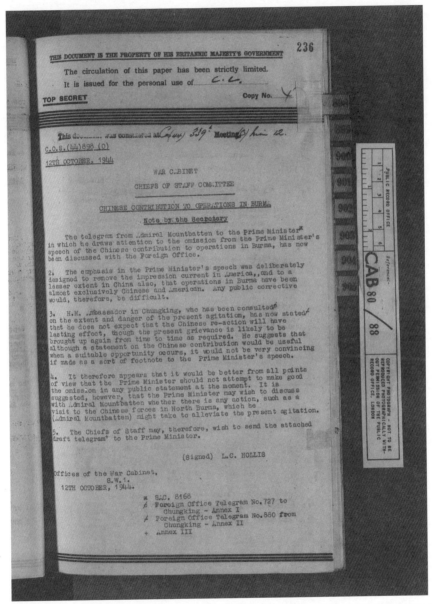

資料來源："Chinese Contribution to Operations in Burma," 12 October 1944, C.O.S.(44)898(O), *War Cabinet and Cabinet: Chiefs of Staff Committee: Memoranda*, CAB 80/88/24, TNA.

237

ANNEX I

Copy of a telegram dated 5th October, 1944
from Foreign Office to Chungking.

Repeated to Supreme Allied Command S.E. Asia.

IMMEDIATE

S.N.A.C. telegram to Foreign Office No.174 [of
October 6th]

You will appreciate the difficulty of issuing any
public corrective when the Prime Minister's speech of
September 28th was clearly designed to remove the
impression which had been spread mainly in America, but
also in China, that operations in Burma had been almost
exclusively Chinese and American.

2. Do you think that Chinese reaction can safely be
left to die down or do you consider it so serious that on
political grounds it is necessary to take some action to
allay it? If so, have you any suggestions? Has General
Carton de Wiart spoken to the Generalissimo, and if so
with what results?

3. So far as morale of Chinese troops in Burma may be
affected, one suggestion which occurs to us is that
Admiral Mountbatten should visit them if this is practic-
able and take the occasion to issue a special order which
could be published and in which the exploits of the
Chinese forces up to date could be described.

4. Please reply urgently.

O.T.P.

ANNEX II

Copy of a telegram No.880 dated 11th October, 1944
from Chungking to Foreign Office

Repeated to SACSEA for Dening.

IMMEDIATE

Your telegram No. 727.

It is no doubt realised that Chinese are not much
interested in fighting in Burma except in so far as by
fighting there, they can hope to restore communications with
China. They understand their own direct interest in the
campaign in North Burma but are inclined to regret use of

-1-

238

Chinese troops on Salween Front at a time when Japanese are
advancing elsewhere. They regard British campaign in Burma
as a defeat of a Japanese offensive but not so far as an
offensive against the Japanese. It is against this back-
ground that recent press agitation must be judged.

2.　On the whole I think that Chinese, though annoyed at
omission of any mention of their efforts, have probably
not been sorry for this opportunity of drawing attention to
the fact that they have received only very small amount of
supplies for their forces in East China. A first-rate
authority puts it at 500 tons since 1941.

3.　I do not expect Chinese reaction will have lasting
effect though present grievance is likely to be brought up
again from time to time as required as has been the case
consistently with the Burma Road. A statement on Chinese
contribution in Burma would be useful when suitable opportunity
occurs, but I do not think it would be very convincing if
made as a sort of footnote to Prime Minister's speech. Admiral
Mountbatten will be best able to judge whether a visit by him
to Chinese in North Burma would be opportune. It will be
easier to judge after General Carton de Wiart has seen Chiang
Kai-Shek which he expects to do shortly. I will then telegraph
again.

O.T.P.

ANNEX III

Copy of a draft telegram (DRASTIC) from A.M.S.S.O.
to TOLSTOY

For Prime Minister from Chiefs of Staff.

We have considered Mountbatten's Telegram to you
(SAC.8168) in consultation with the Foreign Office.

2.　H.M. Ambassador, Chungking, advises that Chinese re-action
to omission of specific praise of their achievements in Burma
from your speech is unlikely to have lasting effect though
grievance might be brought up again from time to time.

3.　We assume that emphasis in your speech was deliberately
designed to remove impression current in America, and to a
lesser extent in China also, that operations in Burma have
been almost exclusively Chinese and American.

4.　We therefore suggest that it would be difficult and
probably unnecessary for you to make any public statement
as an addition to your speech. You might, however, think
it worth while discussing with Admiral Mountbatten whether
there is any action he might take to alleviate the agitation,
such as a visit to Chinese forces in Burma when he might
issue a special order drawing public attention to the exploits
of the Chinese forces to date.

-11-

檔案 24：英國參謀首長委員會紀錄，「英國在緬甸戰役的貢獻」(1944 年 12 月 27 日)

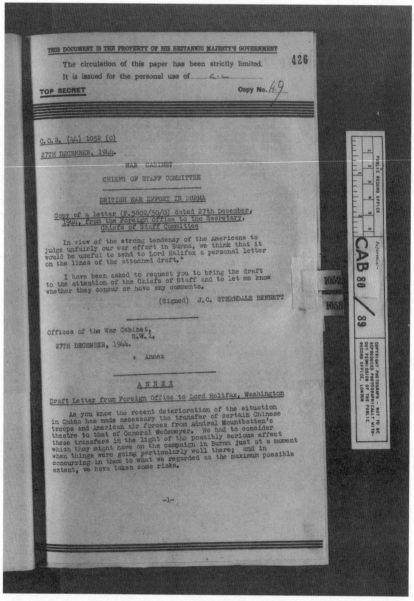

THIS DOCUMENT IS THE PROPERTY OF HIS BRITANNIC MAJESTY'S GOVERNMENT

The circulation of this paper has been strictly limited.

It is issued for the personal use of .... C.L.

TOP SECRET　　　　　　　　　　Copy No. 49

426

C.O.S. (44) 1052 (O)

27TH DECEMBER, 1944.

WAR CABINET

CHIEFS OF STAFF COMMITTEE

BRITISH WAR EFFORT IN BURMA

Copy of a letter (F.5802/59/g) dated 27th December,
1944, from the Foreign Office to the Secretary,
Chiefs of Staff Committee

In view of the strong tendency of the Americans to
judge unfairly our war effort in Burma, we think that it
would be useful to send to Lord Halifax a personal letter
on the lines of the attached draft.+

I have been asked to request you to bring the draft
to the attention of the Chiefs of Staff and to let me know
whether they concur or have any comments.

(Signed) J.C. STERNDALE BENNETT

Offices of the War Cabinet,
S.W.1.
27TH DECEMBER, 1944.

+ Annex

ANNEX

Draft Letter from Foreign Office to Lord Halifax, Washington

As you know the recent deterioration of the situation
in China has made necessary the transfer of certain Chinese
troops and American air forces from Admiral Mountbatten's
theatre to that of General Wedemeyer. We had to consider
these transfers in the light of the possibly serious effect
which they might have on the campaign in Burma just at a moment
when things were going particularly well there; and in
concurring in them to what we regarded as the maximum possible
extent, we have taken some risks.

-1-

資料來源："British War Effort in Burma," 27 December 1944, C.O.S.(44)1052(O), *War Cabinet and Cabinet: Chiefs of Staff Committee: Memoranda*, CAB 80/89/115, TNA.

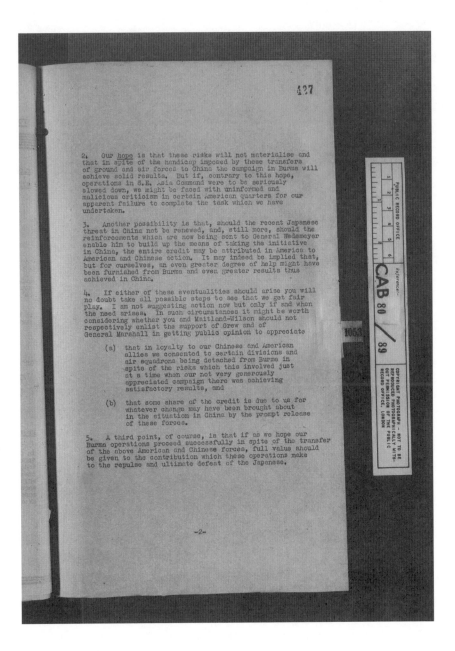

427

2. Our hope is that these risks will not materialise and that in spite of the handicap imposed by these transfers of ground and air forces to China the campaign in Burma will achieve solid results. But if, contrary to this hope, operations in S.E. Asia Command were to be seriously slowed down, we might be faced with uninformed and malicious criticism in certain American quarters for our apparent failure to complete the task which we have undertaken.

3. Another possibility is that, should the recent Japanese threat in China not be renewed, and, still more, should the reinforcements which are now being sent to General Wedemeyer enable him to build up the means of taking the initiative in China, the entire credit may be attributed in America to American and Chinese action. It may indeed be implied that, but for ourselves, an even greater degree of help might have been furnished from Burma and even greater results thus achieved in China.

4. If either of these eventualities should arise you will no doubt take all possible steps to see that we get fair play. I am not suggesting action now but only if and when the need arises. In such circumstances it might be worth considering whether you and Maitland-Wilson should not respectively enlist the support of Grew and of General Marshall in getting public opinion to appreciate

(a) that in loyalty to our Chinese and American allies we consented to certain divisions and air squadrons being detached from Burma in spite of the risks which this involved just at a time when our not very generously appreciated campaign there was achieving satisfactory results, and

(b) that some share of the credit is due to us for whatever change may have been brought about in the situation in China by the prompt release of these forces.

5. A third point, of course, is that if as we hope our Burma operations proceed successfully in spite of the transfer of the above American and Chinese forces, full value should be given to the contribution which these operations make to the repulse and ultimate defeat of the Japanese.

-2-

檔案 25：英國參謀首長委員會會議紀錄（1944 年 12 月 29 日）

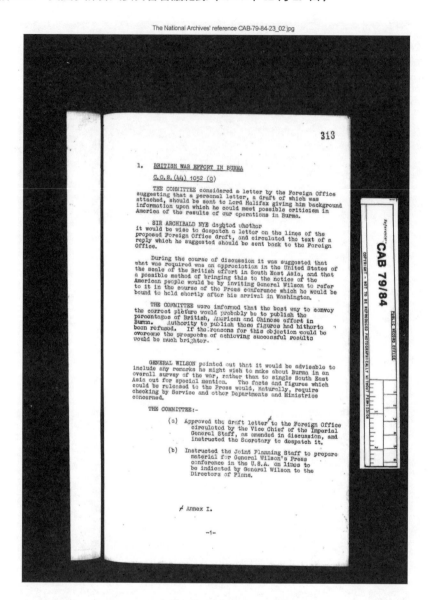

The National Archives' reference CAB-79-84-23_02.jpg

資料來源："Minutes of Meeting held of Friday 29th December, 1944," C.O.S.(44)1052(O), *War Cabinet and Cabinet: Chiefs of Staff Committee: Minutes. Minutes of Meetings*, CAB 79/84/23, TNA.

檔案 26：英國參謀首長委員會秘書代行致外交部信（1944 年 12 月 29 日）

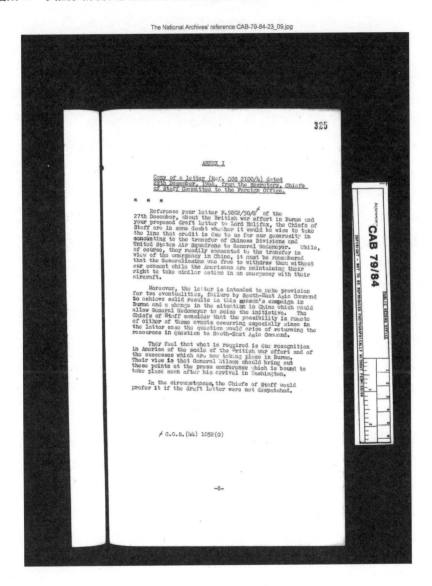

資料來源："Copy of a Letter (Ref. C.O.S. 2100/4) dated 29th December, 1944, from the Secretary, Chiefs of Staff Committee to the Foreign Office," C.O.S.(44)1052(O), *War Cabinet and Cabinet: Chiefs of Staff Committee: Minutes. Minutes of Meetings*, CAB 79/84/23, TNA.

四、結語

　　本文收錄討論的檔案，只是英國國家檔案局收藏中，關於中緬印戰區的極少部分，而且未有引用部分重要檔案，例如各部隊的戰時日誌（WO 208系列），以及英軍服務團和204使團在華活動的檔案[44]。可是，它們足以顯示英國檔案在研究中緬印戰區的戰略以至戰術問題的參考價值。從英國檔案，特別是參謀首長委員會檔案（CAB 79、CAB 80系列），可見英國的戰爭指導者，的確與中方對中緬印戰區有不盡相同的理解。對國民政府而言，其主要戰區當然是中國大陸，緬甸則是其後方交通的關鍵之地，但國府對兩地以外的戰區則無太大興趣。至於美國，其主攻方向是中太平洋，南太平洋和亞太地區只是次要戰區，雖然兩地的政治重要性不可置疑。即使美國在第二次世界大戰，擁有幾乎無窮的物量優勢，但中國戰區處於其交通線的終端，而且在太平洋戰爭的大部分時間中只能依賴空運，因此亦有鞭長莫及之感，不能同時全面裝備國軍，並在中國大陸維持大規模的對日空中攻勢。至於英國，「中緬印戰區」則有特殊意義。英國的目標，正如邱吉爾所言，是「奪回我們在此地區的重要據點」。英國決策當局思考或制訂亞太地區的戰略時，均會將整個東南亞戰區視作一個整體，並重視它與中東、非洲、澳紐—南太平洋等戰區的聯繫。決策者不但要在有限資源和人力的情況下，考慮其他地區（特別是歐洲）的戰局，更要兼顧美、中兩國觀感、各兵種的需要和能力（例如缺乏登陸艦艇一事，使英軍一直不能以海路反攻仰光），以及戰後世界的規劃（例如規復殖民地並處理和中、美、蘇等國的關係）。

　　在實際運作層面，中、英、美三方的合作亦衍生了不少問題。不但各方最高層對這個戰區的理解不盡相同，戰區指揮官們亦對戰略目標、部隊能力、作戰策略，以及後勤安排等問題均有不同意見。英國政府和英軍內部，

44　收藏於澳洲戰爭紀念館（Australian War Memorial）、倫敦帝國戰爭博物館（Imperial War Museum London）、英國國家陸軍博物館（National Army Museum），以及英國國家檔案局等地。

亦有各種想法。在太平洋戰爭爆發前後，倫敦的陸軍計劃者，對國軍能力不抱太大期望，但空軍出身的遠東三軍司令樸芳，卻對中英軍事合作頗為期待。開戰後，接替樸芳的魏菲爾是陸軍將領，對如何和國軍共同防衛緬甸又有另一套看法，他對國軍入緬的後勤問題有其見解，而且並非毫無道理，但他的態度卻被視為拒絕國軍增援。至於邱吉爾，從檔案中可見他與蔣中正一樣，對軍事操作的實際困難不太感興趣，而是從同盟戰爭的角度處理中緬印戰區，既希望保住國民政府並維持中、美、英的關係，更希望在軍事行動上，使英國繼續在東南亞以至中國發揮影響力。英國與中國在中緬印戰區的合作，實為合而兩利，分則俱傷的關係。英軍在戰爭初期雖然屢受慘敗，但在 1942 年中卻成功保住印度和印度洋，使中緬印戰區得以繼續運作。若英國在印地位崩潰，其對國民政府的影響將難以想像；反之，若國民政府崩潰，則英國能否保住印度亦成疑問。由於緬甸戰區的地理特殊性及後勤困難，英國最終只能從陸路緩慢地反攻緬甸。在此過程中，英國亦要承受中、美兩國在不同層面對其戰爭貢獻的指控，當中確有不無道理之處（例如 1942 年緬甸戰役時部分英軍表現拙劣），但從三國對此戰區在資源和人力方面的投入，以及印度作為反攻大後方觀之，英國在此戰區的角色實屬不可或缺。職是之故，深入研究英國相關檔案實有其必要。

檔案原件

檔案 8：英國參謀首長委員會紀錄，「緬甸防務」（1941 年 12 月 16 日）

The National Archives' reference CAB 80/60

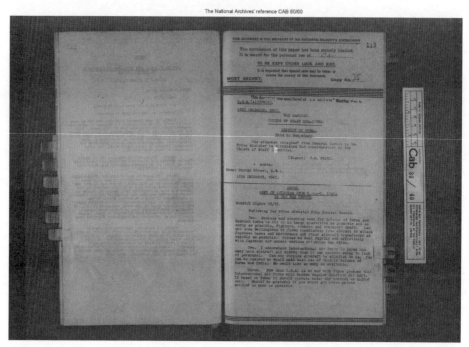

© Crown Copyright

資料來源："Defence of Burma," 16 December 1941, C.O.S.(41)279(O), *Defence of Burma. Note by Secretary*, CAB 80/60/49, TNA.

檔案 15：英國參謀首長委員會紀錄，「中國對盟國戰略貢獻及日本的意圖」報告（1943 年 7 月 16 日）

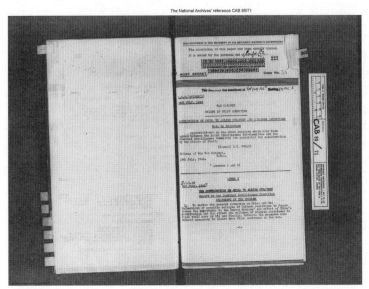

© Crown Copyright

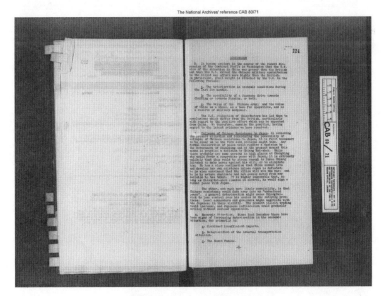

© Crown Copyright

資料來源："Contribution of China to Allied Strategy and Japanese Intentions," 16 July 1943, C.O.S.(43)382(O), *War Cabinet and Cabinet: Chiefs of Staff Committee: Memoranda*, CAB 80/71/52, TNA.

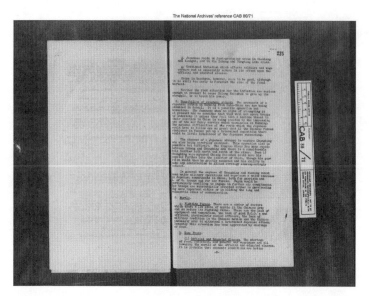

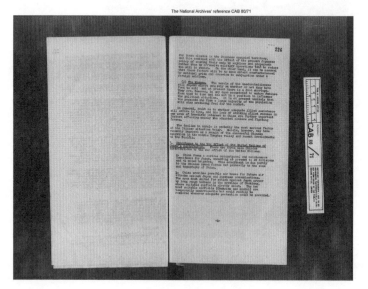

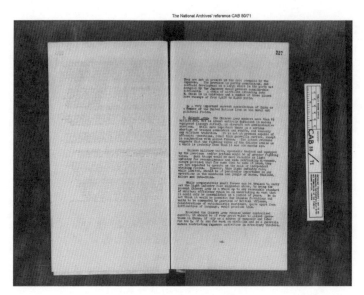

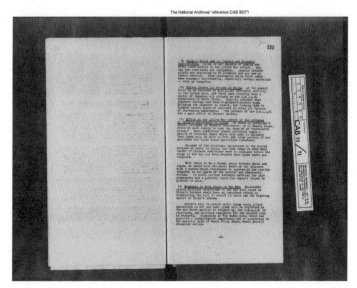

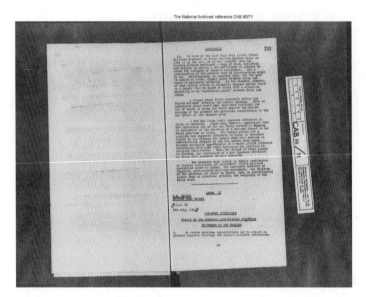

檔案 16：英國參謀首長委員會紀錄，「與將來於緬甸可能之作戰相關的指揮架構」備忘錄（1944 年 6 月 3 日）

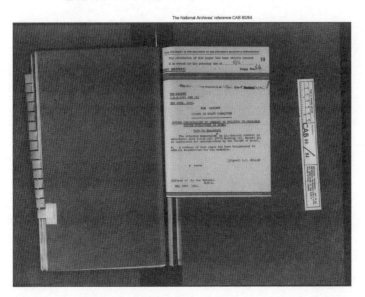

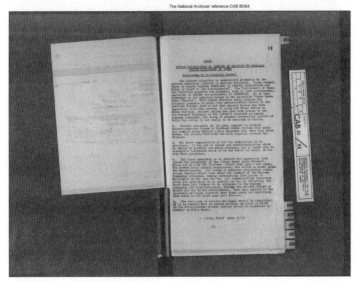

資料來源："Future Organization of Command in Relation to Probable Future Operations in Burma," 3 June 1944, C.O.S.(44)488(O), *War Cabinet and Cabinet: Chiefs of Staff Committee: Memoranda*, CAB 80/84/17, TNA.

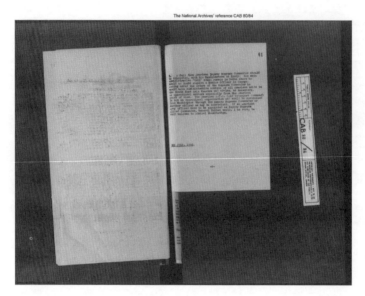

檔案 22：英國參謀首長委員會紀錄，「中國軍隊撤出緬甸」（1944 年 12 月 3 日）

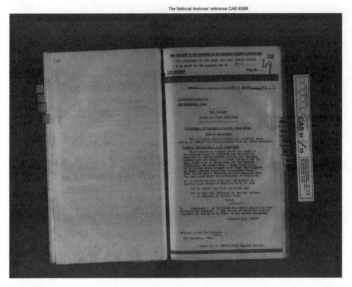

資料來源："Withdrawal of Chinese Divisions from Burma," 3 December 1944, C.O.S.(44)1008(O), *War Cabinet and Cabinet: Chiefs of Staff Committee: Memoranda*, CAB 80/89/72, TNA.

檔案 23：英國參謀首長委員會紀錄，「中國在緬甸戰役的貢獻」（1944 年 10 月 12 日）

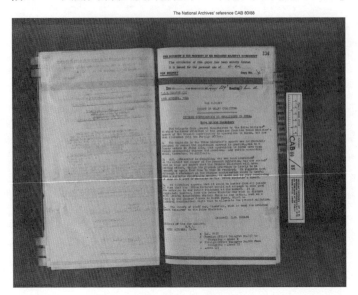

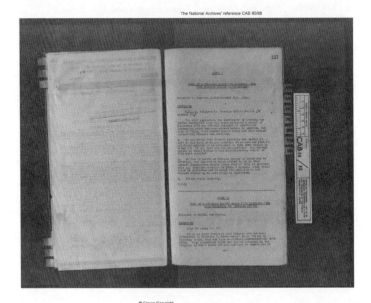

資料來源："Chinese Contribution to Operations in Burma," 12 October 1944, C.O.S.(44)898(O), *War Cabinet and Cabinet: Chiefs of Staff Committee: Memoranda,* CAB 80/88/24, TNA.

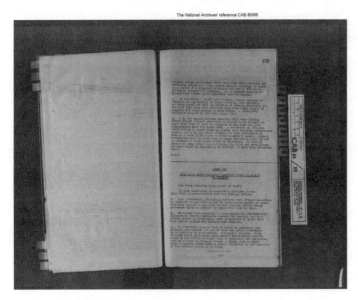

檔案 24：英國參謀首長委員會紀錄，「英國在緬甸戰役的貢獻」（1944 年 12 月 27 日）

The National Archives' reference CAB 80/89

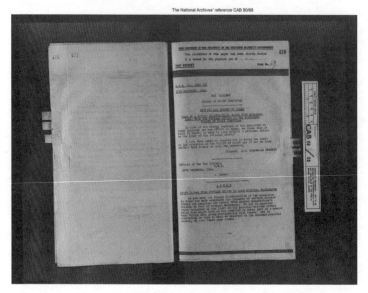

© Crown Copyright

The National Archives' reference CAB 80/89

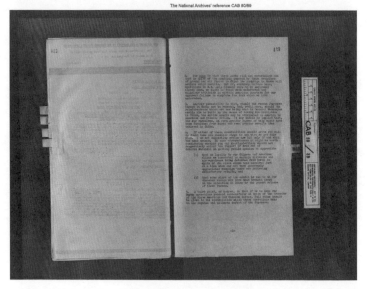

© Crown Copyright

資料來源："British War Effort in Burma," 27 December 1944, C.O.S.(44)1052(O), *War Cabinet and Cabinet: Chiefs of Staff Committee: Memoranda*, CAB 80/89/115, TNA.

從英國檔案探究中國遠征軍與中緬印補給路線

應俊豪
國立臺灣海洋大學海洋文化研究所教授

一、前言

　　關於第二次世界大戰期間，中國在緬印戰區的扮演的角色，已有許多研究成果，特別是在 1942 年入緬作戰與 1943 年起的反攻作戰等方面。[1]但關於中國遠征軍的籌建始末、中緬印補給路線的規劃，以及其衍生出的諸多爭議，仍有一些尚待深入探討的空間。事實上，無論是中國遠征軍或其後的駐印軍、中緬印補給路線規劃等問題，均與英國關係密切。但以往有關兩者的研究，多半均側重從中、美兩國視角來分析其在對日作戰上的軍事地位，忽略了英國在前述作戰與爭議中所居的關鍵地位。中國遠征軍的成立，起初主要為了支援英軍在緬甸的防衛作戰，而中國駐印軍的成立，則是在緬甸作戰失敗後，由撤往印度的遠征軍部分部隊所組成。究其實際，前者的出現，很大程度上，可謂中國應英國之請而派出援軍，而後者的組成，雖與美軍指揮

---

[1]　此類成果大致可以分為三類，其一是戰史研究，其二則是親歷者的回憶或口述歷史，其三是相關史料彙編等，相關成果非常豐碩。舉其要者，如：國防部史政編譯局編，《抗日戰史：緬北及滇西之作戰》（臺北：國防部史政編譯局，1981 年）；國防部史政編譯局編，《抗日戰史：滇緬路之作戰》（臺北：國防部史政編譯局，1982 年）；時廣東、冀伯祥，《中國遠征軍史》（重慶：重慶出版社，1994 年）；羅學蓬、舒鶯，《中國遠征軍》（重慶：重慶出版社，2007 年）；袁梅芳、呂牧昀編著，《中國遠征軍：滇緬戰爭拼圖與老戰士口述歷史》（香港：紅出版、青森文化，2015 年）；國防部史政編譯局，《抗戰時期滇印緬作戰（一）：參戰官兵訪問暨回憶記錄》，上下冊（臺北：國防部史政編譯局，1999 年）；周琇環、吳淑鳳、蕭李居編，《中華民國抗日戰爭史料彙編：中國遠征軍》（臺北：國史館，2015 年）等。

官史迪威（Joseph W. Stilwell, 1883-1946）的大力推動有關，但也需要英國同意，方能讓中國軍隊長期駐紮於印度，進行組訓與換裝。再者，關乎到中國戰區與未來反攻作戰甚鉅的的中緬印補給路線，從路線的劃定與調整、人力的安排，到經費資源的調度等，同樣也必須獲得英國的大力支持與協助，方能順利完成此一偉大公路的修築。因此，本文將從許多關鍵的英國檔案，來介紹並省思中國遠征軍的來由與脈絡、中緬印補給路線在早期規劃過程中曾引發的爭議，進而論述戰時盟邦間互動上的某些有趣面向。

最後，必須強調的，本文將不再重複累述中國遠征軍或駐印軍在滇緬作戰的詳細過程與歷史意義，畢竟此類議題已有不少研究與成果。本文主要的研究目的，乃是試圖透過英國檔案中，有關上述問題的史料記載，從中發掘出一些有趣且前人較少關注到的議題，從而對於二戰期間的中國與緬印戰區，有更豐富的理解與認知。其次，因本文主要使用英國檔案，故研究途徑，乃偏向以英國的視角與觀點，切入緬印戰區，如此或許適足以跟素來以中文檔案與資料為重心的中國抗戰史研究，進行某種程度的對話與比較。再者，因檔案文件內容較為繁雜，為使行文順暢與論述聚焦，本文中所附之檔案擷圖，僅為局部關鍵段落。至於完整的檔案內容，則另外放在文末附件，以供必要時作進一步參考。

二、關於中國遠征軍的籌組及其爭議

關於中國遠征軍的成立，無論是當時的參與者或是後世的研究者，一般都指向 1941 年 12 月 23 日的《中英共同防禦滇緬路協定》。[2] 但是考察中、英相關檔案，均未見該協定。探究歷史脈絡，中國遠征軍的出現，到底應該

2　例如曾任中國遠征軍副司令長官兼第 5 軍軍長的杜聿明（1904-1981）在其回憶中，即稱自該協定簽署，中、英兩國即處於軍事同盟的狀態。參見杜聿明，〈中國遠征軍入緬對日作戰述略〉，收入中國人民政治協商會議全國委員會文史資料研究委員會《遠征印緬抗戰》編審組編，《原國民黨將領抗日戰爭親歷記：遠征印緬抗戰》（北京：中國文史出版社，1990 年），頁 1-39。

歸諸何時、何事？

（一）中國遠征軍的提議

　　根據英國外交部遠東司（Far Eastern Department, Foreign Office）的內部備忘錄資料，蔣中正（1887-1975）早在日本偷襲珍珠港（Pearl Harbor）、太平洋戰爭爆發前，即已經就派兵協防緬甸問題，與英國有所交涉。1941年7、8月間，蔣中正向英國駐華大使館武官提出一項建議，那就是由中國派遣一支10萬人的部隊離開中國作戰，主要是為了協防緬甸，並由英國負責該批部隊的武器裝備與部署調度。[3]

is to an offer made by General Chiang Kai-shek during discussions between our Military Attaché in China in July and August 1941 to make available up to ~~1,000~~/Chinese troops for service /100,000 outside China, Burma being particularly mentioned, provided we could equip and employ them; our principal reasons for showing no particular enthusiasm for this offer were our desire not to provoke the Japanese and our inability to fulfil the condition attached, namely the equipping of ~~1,000~~/Chinese soldiers. /100,000

檔案1：英國外交部遠東司的內部備忘錄（1942年6月）
資料來源："Employment of Chinese Troops in Burma," Minutes of the Far Eastern Department, Foreign Office, June 1942, *Employment of Chinese Troops in Burma*, FO 371/31621, TNA.
資料說明：此份文件是英國外交部遠東司內部在檢討1942年緬甸作戰功過時，由幕僚官員撰寫的備忘錄（Minutes），以回顧中國遠征軍入緬作戰的來龍去脈。

　　但是當時英國對於蔣中正的提案，顯得並不熱衷，此乃基於兩項因素：其一，英國並不想觸怒日本，其二，英國並不具備能夠裝備10萬人部隊的條件與能力。因此，蔣中正派軍協防緬甸的計畫，未獲實現。一直要到美國參戰後，情況有了很大的變化，英國也才同意接受中國派軍增援緬甸。[4]

3　"Employment of Chinese Troops in Burma," Minutes of the Far Eastern Department, Foreign Office, June 1942, *Employment of Chinese Troops in Burma*, FO 371/31621, TNA.
4　"Employment of Chinese Troops in Burma," Minutes of the Far Eastern Department, Foreign Office, June 1942, *Employment of Chinese Troops in Burma*, FO 371/31621, TNA.

（二）蔣中正倡言共組軍事同盟

　　珍珠港事變爆發後，中國除了同時對日、德、義三國宣戰外，也呼籲中、美、英、蘇等國應共組同盟，以便協調對軸心國的軍事作戰事宜。[5] 為表慎重，1941 年 12 月 8 日，蔣中正以中國軍事領導者的身分，親自召見了美、英、蘇三國駐華使節，要求將上述請求，送交給羅斯福（Franklin D. Roosevelt, 1882-1945）、邱吉爾（Winston Churchill, 1874-1965），以及史達林（Joseph V. Stalin, 1878-1953）。[6] 蔣中正提議由英國、美國、蘇聯、澳洲、紐西蘭、加拿大、荷蘭與中國，共組「軍事同盟」（military alliance），「在美國的領導下，隸屬於統一指揮的聯盟軍隊」。英國駐華大使卡爾（Archibald C. Kerr, 1882-1951）隨即將蔣中正的建議，送交英國政府。

檔案 2：英國駐華大使館給英國外交部關於蔣中正提案共組軍事同盟的報告【1941 年 12 月 8 日】[7]

資料來源："War Cabinet Distribution: From China; From Chungking to Foreign Office," 9 December 1941, *Anglo-United States-Chinese Co-operation against Japan*, FO 371/27753, TNA.

資料說明：此份文件，乃是由英國駐華大使館撰寫，詳細報告蔣中正所提軍事同盟的提案內容。因茲事體大，故英國外交部收到該份報告，送交「戰時內閣」進行討論。

5　"Sir A. Clark Kerr, Chungking to the Foreign Office, London," 9 December 1941, *Anglo-United States-Chinese Co-operation against Japan*, FO 371/27753, TNA.

6　蔣中正同時召見美、英、俄三國大使，但因當時英國駐華大使當時不在重慶，故只有美、俄兩國大使出席。之後再由中國外交部將相同的通告，轉交給英國大使館。參見 "Telegram from Ministry of Foreign Affairs to the British Embassy," 9 December 1941, *Anglo-United States-Chinese Co-operation against Japan*, FO 371/27753, TNA.

7　本件檔案依其內容判讀，英國駐華大使館簽署文件的日期為 1942 年 12 月 8 日，文件以電報形式發出與收到的日期則是 1942 年 12 月 9 日，此處乃從其文件署名的日期標示。以下討論的檔案如有發生類似狀況，即經判讀所推知的事發日期，與資料來源所載日期不符者，其檔名處的日期註記改以【　】標示，以茲區別，謹此敘明。

在收到蔣中正的提議後，首相邱吉爾於 1941 年 12 月 11 日，即在英國
下議院（House of Commons）進行報告。國會報告中，邱吉爾聲稱已收到
來自中國軍事委員長蔣中正的訊息，中國不但將決定對日本宣戰，也將同時
對日本的罪惡伙伴德國與義大利宣戰。蔣中正並「進一步向他保證，中國所
有的資源，將為英國與美國之用」，因此，邱吉爾強調：

> 此後，中國的事，就是我們的事。在過去的四年裡，這個國家以
> 無畏的勇氣對抗日本，確實值得成為同盟國。而作為同盟國，從
> 現在開始，我們將一起邁向勝利，不只是對付日本，還包括軸心
> 國。8

IMMEDIATE
　　Following statement about China was included in Prime
Minister's review in the House of Commons yesterday.

　　[Begins].　　The Generalissimo, Chiang Kai-shek, has
sent me a message announcing his decision to declare war
against Japan and also against Japan's partners in guilt,
Germany and Italy.　　He has further assured me that the whole
of the resources of China are at the disposal of Great Britain
and the United States.　　China's cause is henceforth our
cause.　　The country which has faced the Japanese assault for
over four years with undaunted courage is indeed a worthy ally
and it is as allies that, from now on, we will go forward
together to victory not only over Japan alone but over the
Axis and all its works.　　[Ends].

檔案 3：英國首相邱吉爾在英國下議院關於中國的報告【1941 年 12 月 11 日】
資料來源："Telegram from Foreign Office, London to Sir A. Clark Kerr, Chungking," 12 December
1941, *Anglo-United States-Chinese Co-operation against Japan*, FO 371/27753, TNA.
資料說明：在收到蔣中正共組軍事同盟的提案後，英國首相邱吉爾乃正式向國會下議院報告此
事，並做出善意的回應。

　　英國外交部 12 月 12 日在給駐華大使卡爾的電報中，訓令其向蔣中正，
正式表達英國的回應。其一，英國由衷歡迎中國作為同盟國，加入對抗軸心
國的共同陣營。其二，對於中國願意慷慨提供人力與資源等軍事合作之事，
表達感謝，同時也承諾英國將投桃報李，在未來的軍事作戰中，盡其可能地
提供所有幫助。不過，對於中國提議正式簽訂條約，以共組軍事同盟之事，
英國雖表示同情，但仍須詳加審慎考量，並有待與其他相關國家討論後，方

8　"Telegram from Foreign Office, London to Sir A. Clark Kerr, Chungking," 12 December 1941,
　　Anglo-United States-Chinese Co-operation against Japan, FO 371/27753, TNA.

能決定。[9]

　　由邱吉爾在國會上的報告，以及外交部給駐華大使的電報內容，不難看出英國雖然歡迎中國加入共同對抗軸心國的陣營，但對於是否要簽署正式軍事同盟條約，仍有很大的疑慮。事實上，在前述外交部給駐華大使卡爾的電報中，還附帶有兩條祕密的指令，其中即清楚揭露英國的擔憂所在。首先，一旦中、英簽署正式的軍事同盟條約，簽署國雙方均不得再私下與軸心國議和，等於變相使得中國有權介入與阻礙未來和議的進行。因此，英國外交部特別叮嚀卡爾，在與中國交涉軍事同盟等事宜時，必須特別注意，避免讓英國在戰與和的議題上因此受制於中國。其次，英國外交部也向卡爾坦承，就現階段戰況而言，英國應避免向日本宣戰，畢竟集中全力對抗德國，才符合英國當前的利益考量。[10] 換言之，英國的立場，或許乃是在精神道義與口頭上支持中國對抗日本，但在實際的軍事作戰上，仍是以擊敗德國為第一優先；至於對日本，則依然保留政策上的妥協與彈性，不願因與中國的軍事同盟而綁死。

（三）英國請求中國派軍協防緬甸

　　另外一方面，與此同時，由於英軍在馬來亞的作戰失利，以及顧慮到緬甸的防禦力量相對薄弱，恐無力阻擋日軍的進攻，故英國駐華大使與武官乃於 12 月 16 日進見蔣中正，請求中國給予軍事援助。在此次晤談中，英國武官向蔣中正提出了三項請求，其中第二項便是關於中國軍隊協防緬甸問題。英國要求中國提高協防緬甸的軍隊，派遣一個陸軍師，並準備另外一個師當作後備兵力，以便必要時可以馳援。蔣中正則認為防禦緬甸就是防禦中國，遂同意派遣為數達 50,000 人的軍隊進入緬甸地區，由英屬緬甸軍總指揮官

9　"War Cabinet Distribution: To China; From Foreign Office to Chungking," 12 December 1941, *Anglo-United States-Chinese Co-operation against Japan*, FO 371/27753, TNA.

10　"War Cabinet Distribution: To China; From Foreign Office to Chungking," 12 December 1941, *Anglo-United States-Chinese Co-operation against Japan*, FO 371/27753, TNA.

統率，但應指定固定駐防區域，不應與其他緬甸部隊混和在一起，以免發生不必要的麻煩。在會談中，蔣中正並一再重申聯合作戰計畫的重要性，希望中、美、英等能夠在新加坡、緬甸、印度等東南亞地區作戰上，攜手合作共同擬定作戰計畫與步驟。[11] 此次中英會談紀錄中，所提及的出兵緬甸之事，應該就是後來中國遠征軍的前身與濫觴。

檔案 4：蔣中正與英國駐華大使、武官的晤談紀錄（1941 年 12 月 16 日）

資料來源："Military Attaché, Chungking to the War Office," 16 December 1941, *Anglo-United States-Chinese Co-operation against Japan*, FO 371/27753, TNA.

資料說明：戰時英國駐華官員透過兩種途徑向英國政府進行匯報，其一由大使館向外交部報告，其二則是由使館武官向陸軍部回報。因為戰時的關係，凡是與作戰相關事務，牽涉到機密與時效性，往往先由武官向軍方進行匯報。此份報告即英國駐華大使館武官陪同大使薛穆（Horace J. Seymour, 1885-1978）面會蔣中正後，將相關軍事合作事宜，向英國陸軍部回報。

在上述晤談結束後，英國駐華大使館武官給英國陸軍部（War Office）的報告，強調在現階段作戰中，中國的軍事援助至關重要，但是中英軍事合作的關鍵，在於英國能否獲得蔣中正的信任。英國武官並建議，英屬印度軍總司令應盡早派遣軍事官員來重慶，與中國直接商討軍事合作的細節。[12]

為了挽救英國在緬甸可能面臨的危急情勢，同時也為了回應前述蔣中正軍事同盟的提議，英國參謀首長委員會（Chiefs of Staff Committee）在 1941 年 12 月 17 日召開會議，商討與中國軍事合作之事。在會議中，決議派遣英屬印度軍總司令魏菲爾（Archibald P. Wavell, 1883-1950）作為正式代表，前往重慶與蔣中正討論軍事合作細節。參謀首長委員會並決定以英國總參謀長的個人名義，給蔣中正本人的電報一封，由魏菲爾帶去面交蔣中正。在該

11 "Military Attaché, Chungking to the War Office," 16 December 1941, *Anglo-United States-Chinese Co-operation against Japan*, FO 371/27753, TNA.

12 "Military Attaché, Chungking to the War Office," 16 December 1941, *Anglo-United States-Chinese Co-operation against Japan*, FO 371/27753, TNA.

電報中，英國總參謀長對於蔣中正提案出兵緬甸協助防禦等，表示極大的感
謝之意。[13]

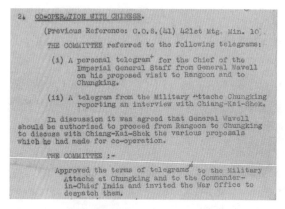

檔案 5：英國參謀首長委員會會議紀錄（1941 年 12 月 17 日）
資料來源："Minute of Chiefs of Staff Committee, War Cabinet," 17 December 1941, *Anglo-United States-Chinese Co-operation against Japan*, FO 371/27753, TNA.
資料說明：英國參謀首長委員會，為英國戰時內閣下，最重要的軍事幕僚會議，由各軍種高階將官組成，除商討有關作戰的大方向外，並提供軍事的專業建言。故有關作戰事宜，參謀首長委員會扮演著極其重要的角色。

（四）中國遠征軍的商定

　　太平洋戰爭爆發後，根據英國陸軍部針對中國遠征軍一事所做的備忘紀錄，很明顯中英雙方並未真正簽署有正式的協定。嚴格來說，應該只是中英軍事會談上所做成的一項作戰計畫。而敲定此項作戰計畫的，則是蔣中正本人與英屬印軍度總司令魏菲爾。但是，英屬印度軍總司令魏菲爾為何會在1941 年底突然訪問重慶，並與蔣中正進行會談，最終商妥中國派遣遠征軍至緬甸作戰之事呢？事實上，誠如前述所言，他正是接到英國參謀首長委員會的命令，在該年 12 月下旬，專程經仰光（Rangoon）前往重慶，以商討中英軍事合作事宜。

---

[13] "Minute of Chiefs of Staff Committee, War Cabinet," 17 December 1941, *Anglo-United States-Chinese Co-operation against Japan*, FO 371/27753, TNA.

12 月 23 日，魏菲爾與蔣中正及其軍事幕僚們，正式就緬甸以及滇緬路線的防禦問題進行討論。在該次會談上，蔣中正提出要派遣「兩個軍的中國遠征武力，用於緬甸作戰」（a Chinese Expedition force of two Armies for service in Burma），魏菲爾則表示同意，雙方並決定：應立即調動其中一個軍，並在 1942 年 1 月中前，部署在泰國與緬甸邊界上，而另外一個軍，則視補給、運輸與聯繫情況，以備支援滇緬路線的防禦工作。此次蔣中正與魏菲爾的軍事會談內容及其決議事項，應該就是中國遠征軍最早的由來。

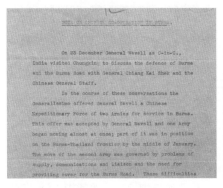

檔案 6：英國陸軍部關於中英在緬甸軍事合作的備忘錄（1942 年 6 月 23 日）
資料來源：War Office, "Note on Chinese Cooperation in Burma," 23 June 1942, *Employment of Chinese Troops in Burma*, FO 371/31621, TNA.
資料說明：此份文件為英國陸軍部針對中國遠征軍入緬作戰一事所做的內部摘要報告，詳細交代其始末。

（五）中國遠征軍引起的中、英嫌隙

雖然透過英屬印度軍總司令魏菲爾的訪問重慶，與蔣中正本人當面敲定由中國派軍協防緬甸與滇緬路線，但事實上，中、英雙方於中國軍隊進入緬甸，在細節安排與時程上，依舊還是有不少的矛盾。特別是英國方面認為中國顯然在刻意在操弄中國遠征軍議題，甚至不惜在美國發動反英輿論宣傳攻勢，一方面致力於美化或「神話化」中國遠征軍作用與重要性，另外一方面則將中英之間種種嫌隙與不合，以及作戰的失利，均歸咎於英國的抗拒與故意阻礙，從而間接導致美國人對於英國的不諒解。[14] 英國外交部遠東司即曾援引 1942 年 5 月 31 日美國《紐約時報》（*The New York Times*）一篇名為

---

14 "Employment of Chinese Troops in Burma," Minutes of the Far Eastern Department, Foreign Office, June 1942, *Employment of Chinese Troops in Burma*, FO 371/31621, TNA.

〈美國的調查：特別〉（American Survey: Special）的報導，痛批是中國刻意
發動的反英輿論宣傳策略。該報導顯然將中國遠征軍在調度上的延遲，歸因
於英國方面的從中阻礙，而英國抗拒的動機，則牽涉到東、西之間的矛盾，
尤其是英國向來帶有歧視觀點的遠東政策，處處掣肘，導致中國遠征軍無
法在軍事上發揮積極的作用，從而造成緬甸作戰的失敗。報導中，主要引據
諾貝爾文學獎得主、素來親華的知名美國作家賽珍珠（Pearl S. Buck, 1892-
1973）的觀點，[15]來印證英國對於中國的偏見，呼籲英國應該盡快改弦易轍，
擺脫過去的成見盡快接受中國的軍事援助，同時也諷刺英國應該及早摒棄傳
統過時的帝國主義思維，不該再將緬甸、印度當作是英國的禁臠，而拒絕中
國，甚至是阻礙美國的介入與援助。[16]

**檔案 7：英國外交部遠東司引據《紐約時報》有關賽珍珠評論的一篇報導：〈美國的
調查：特別〉【1942 年 5 月 31 日】**

資料來源："American Survey: Special," *The New York Times*, 31 May 1942, cited from "Employment
of Chinese Troops in Burma," June 1942, *Employment of Chinese Troops in Burma*, FO 371/31621, TNA.
資料說明：此份文件為英國外交部收到之《紐約時報》剪報打字稿。上文左上角的豎線，乃是
英國外交部遠東司官員所劃，亦即英國所著重之處。該段文字引述賽珍珠的說法，指控英國阻
礙中國遠征軍進入緬甸，影響到後續作戰，又因嫉妒遠征軍指揮官史迪威，故意任命一位同樣
位階的英軍將領，意圖干涉軍事指揮權。

　　究其實際，根據英國外交部內部備忘錄的分析，中國遠征軍入緬作戰
一事，確實有所延遲。1941 年 12 月魏菲爾訪華，雖然與蔣中正迅速議妥中
國派出兩個軍出境作戰，但後續的軍事調動情況卻不如原先預期。首先，

15　賽珍珠雖出生於美國，但因為長期生活在中國，對於中國有著非常濃厚的鄉土情懷，其
　　立場也相當同情中國。關於賽珍珠的中國情結，可參見陳敬，《賽珍珠與中國：中西文
　　化衝突與共融》（天津：南開大學出版社，2006 年）。

16　"American Survey: Special," *The New York Times*, 31 May 1942.

第 6 軍的 2 個師雖然很快就進入緬甸協防，但該軍的第 3 個師卻遭到種種阻礙，延宕至 1942 年 1 月下旬，方始獲得同意進入緬甸。至於另一個軍（即第 5 軍），則更是拖到 2 月初，才開拔前往緬甸。而中國遠征軍在調動上的延遲，英國外交部遠東司分析，很大程度上，可能肇因於兩點：其一可能出自英軍部隊的阻礙，其二則來自於蔣中正本人，因為他要求中國遠征軍的軍事調動，均必須再獲得他的正式批准與授權，以致於程序拖延費時。[17]

　　事實上，英國外交部亦坦承中英軍事合作，可能帶來不小的政治風險，那就是在印緬戰區的英軍部隊指揮當局，對於中國軍隊入緬作戰一事，或多或少還是抱持著抗拒心理，也不太願意動用中國軍隊。而這種情況的出現，很有可能讓英國進一步坐實前述新聞輿論上對於英國的惡意攻訐。也因此，英國外交部早先多次向英國軍方示警，請其多加注意，並希望陸軍部能夠提出強而有力的證據，以駁斥報紙上的不實指控。英國外交部甚至還曾透過情報部（Ministry of Information）輾轉向陸軍部疏通，但是結果卻收效甚微。英國陸軍部對於前述指控的態度，似乎並不太放在心上，他們認為在遠東軍事上的失利就是失利，無須為此再多加解釋。[18]

explanatory. I mentioned the matter to
Mr. Stevens yesterday and he said that his
Ministry had made repeated and unsuccessful
efforts to induce the War Office to do something.
The W.O. took the line that when we lost a part
of the Empire the subject was then closed.
Unfortunately this is not the line taken by
people in the U.S. Mr. Stevens said that it
would be a great help if he could have a letter
from us indicating that he had our support.

檔案 8：英國外交部與情報部官員的內部溝通紀錄：關於英國陸軍部對於報紙指控英軍在遠東地區作戰不力的態度（1942 年 6 月）

資料來源："Employment of Chinese Troops in Burma," Minutes of the Far Eastern Department, Foreign Office, June 1942, *Employment of Chinese Troops in Burma*, FO 371/31621, TNA.
資料說明：此份文件為英國外交部遠東司的內部備忘錄，詳述外交部官員與情報部協調，試圖遊說陸軍部出面，以駁斥外界對於英軍在緬甸作戰不力的指控。

---

17 "Employment of Chinese Troops in Burma," Minutes of the Far Eastern Department, Foreign Office, June 1942, *Employment of Chinese Troops in Burma*, FO 371/31621, TNA.

18 "Employment of Chinese Troops in Burma," Minutes of the Far Eastern Department, Foreign Office, June 1942, *Employment of Chinese Troops in Burma*, FO 371/31621, TNA.

在英國陸軍部的消極態度下，外交部始終無法找到有力的證據，來駁斥前述報導的指控。特別是當此類宣傳口吻，一旦找到某些可供藉題發揮與炒作的素材時，將造成不小的影響。而在報紙輿論有意的推波助瀾下，對於英國在遠東地區作戰不力的指控，也就逐漸成為揮之不去的夢魘。英國外交部認為，如果放任不理，長此以往下來，可能會導致英國在美國的形象急遽惡化，影響到美英關係。英國外交部也坦承，雖然他們一直致力於對抗那些過於貶抑英軍表現與刻意美化中國軍隊作戰能力的輿論宣傳，但卻總是有心無力。他們相當擔心，未來盟軍只要在遠東地區軍事作戰上稍有不順，一些有心人士很有可能會舊調重彈，將軍事失利的責任往英國身上丟，使其成為代罪羔羊。所以，為了亡羊補牢，英國外交部建議與情報部攜手，在美國進行輿論宣傳，盡可能地公開對英國有利的資訊，化被動為主動。畢竟一再的否認指控，只是會讓外界誤以為英國心虛，反而顯得有些欲蓋彌彰，所以與其被動防禦澄清指控，倒不如主動出擊，甚至可以考慮「禮尚往來」，反過來指控中國軍隊的作戰不力，以抗衡與中國方面的輿論宣傳攻勢。[19]

and Dr. T.V. Soong. What appears to be required is that adequate publicity should be given in the United States of America to the British version of our operations in the Far East and in other theatres of war. Steps to this end are, I understand, already being taken by the Far Eastern Section of your Ministry so far as China is concerned, and some improvement in the tone of the Chinese press has latterly resulted. In this way, we should actually achieve more than by standing on the defensive (for as you will remember "Qui s'excuse s'accuse") or by engaging in an exchange of "pleasantries" with the Chinese. But of course if you can get the War Office to produce a convincing case, so much the better.

檔案 9：英國外交部給情報部的建議（1942 年 6 月 10 日）
資料來源："Philip Broad, Foreign Office to R. B. Stevens, Ministry of Information," 10 June 1942, *Employment of Chinese Troops in Burma*, FO 371/31621, TNA.
資料說明：此份文件為英國外交部遠東司官員給情報部官員的書信，希望能夠主動多加宣揚英國版本的戰事經過，讓美國人知道英國在遠東以及各戰區作戰的貢獻，以防止被中國媒體主導了美國觀感。由此可知，英國情報部除負責情報蒐集外，也肩負著宣傳任務。

---

19 "Philip Broad, Foreign Office to R. B. Stevens, Ministry of Information," 10 June 1942, *Employment of Chinese Troops in Burma*, FO 371/31621, TNA.

三、關於中緬印補給路線的早期規劃及其爭議

　　自太平洋戰爭爆發後不久，中、英之間即開始就中緬印補給路線的規劃與修築問題，進行磋商。當時英國稱之為「阿薩密—中國公路」（Assam-China Road）。原先規劃的路線，相較於後來的中印公路，有很大的差異，往北偏了非常遠的距離，起迄點亦非雷多（Ledo）到昆明。當時預計印度端的起點為印度阿薩密省的薩地亞（Sadiya），中國端的起點則是四川的西昌，中間橫跨怒江（薩爾溫江）、眉公河（瀾滄江）、長江（金沙江）的上游地區。不過，當時中、英雙方對於中緬印補給路線的安排，就存有不小的歧見。[20]

（一）南北路線之爭

　　依據 1942 年 1 月的英國外交部的文件來看，最早擬議中的路線有兩條，一條被稱為北方線（Northern Route），另外一條則為南方線（Southern Route）。基本上，蔣中正個人比較傾向於北方線，而英國則比較屬意於南方線。北方線，西起撒地亞、力馬（Rima）、蒙康、鹽井、德欽、永寧，一直到西昌。至於南方線，則是路線稍微南偏，可以繼續往南與緬甸密支那（Myitkyina）接連，但主路線轉向東北方，依然連接到四川的西昌。[21]

20　"Proposed Assam-China Road," Minutes of Foreign Office, January 1942, *Proposed Assam-China Road*, FO 371/31635, TNA.

21　"Proposed Assam-China Road," Minutes of Foreign Office, January 1942, *Proposed Assam-China Road*, FO 371/31635, TNA.

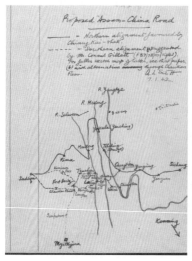

檔案 10：英國外交部繪製的中緬印補給路線規劃圖（1942 年 1 月）

資料來源："Proposed Assam-China Road," Minutes of Foreign Office, January 1942, *Proposed Assam-China Road*, FO 371/31635, TNA.

資料說明：此份地圖為英國外交部遠東司官員在內部備忘錄中，親手繪製的中緬印補給路線示意圖。其中北方線為實線、南方線為虛線。藍色線則為河川，從左至右，分別為薩爾溫江、眉公河與長江。（顏色標示請參見文後檔案原件）

不過，要修築上述規劃的路線，無論北方線或南方線，最大的挑戰，乃是該線必須橫跨地勢甚高的川藏高原，還必須穿越險峻的三條河川，工程難度極大。因此，上述路線最終並未獲得採納。其次，由於北方線由於必須經過西藏地區，故可能挑起中、英（印）、藏三者之間的敏感關係，爭議性始終很大。

所幸最後中國政府還是讓步，同意接受以南方線為主要的規劃方向。[22]

Proposed Assam China Road.
Refers to Foreign Office telegram No.120 of 21st January (F 73/73/10).
Gives substance of memoranda of 28th January and 5th February issued by Chinese Ministry of Communications, regarding construction on the southerly road and contemplated building of internal highway from Myitkyina via Tengyueh to Lungling on the Burma Road. It is implied that construction of northerly route has been abandoned.
Requests instructions regarding reply to these memoranda.

檔案 11：英國外交部內部備忘錄【1942 年 2 月】

資料來源："Proposed Assam China Road," Minutes of Foreign Office, 9 February 1942, *Proposed Assam-China Road*, FO 371/31635, TNA.

資料說明：英國外交部根據中國運輸部在 1 月 28 日與 2 月 5 日發布的兩則通告，判斷中國方面已經決定採取南方線（從密支那、經騰越至龍陵），至於北方線則被放棄。不過，此條路線與上述的最原始的南方線，明顯還是略有調整。

---

22 "Proposed Assam China Road," Minutes of Foreign Office, 9 February 1942, *Proposed Assam-China Road*, FO 371/31635, TNA.

（二）早期路線的初步確定與優先順序

　　根據英國外交部的檔案，中緬印補給路線的大致確定，則可以追溯到1942年2月，在重慶軍事聯席會議（Military Joint Council）上，建議應立即著手建築一條從印度雷多，經緬甸密支那，到雲南騰越的公路。中國方面並允諾將提供人力協助，緬甸部分的建築工程。在路線大致確定之後，中緬印間運輸幹道的相關工程也即將展開。但是英國內部，尤其是緬甸當局，對於哪個工程段應該由優先施工與完工，還是有不同的立場。

檔案 12：重慶軍事聯席會議關於中緬印補給路線的討論【1942年2月】
資料來源：" Military Mission, Chungking to Commander-in-Chief, India," 5 February 1942, *Proposed Assam-China Road*, FO 371/31635, TNA.
資料說明：此份文件為英國駐重慶軍事團給英屬印度軍總司令的電報，內容乃是說明軍事聯席會議上關於中緬印補給路線規劃的討論事項。

　　軍事聯席會議結束後，英國駐重慶軍事代表團也立即請示英屬印度軍總司令、緬甸總指揮官，以及英國陸軍部，對於修築此條公路的看法。[23]整體來說，英國方面對於修築中緬印補給路線一案，多持贊同態度。[24]不過，英國印度緬甸部部長卻對中英之間，能否通力合作修築前述中緬印公路一事抱持疑慮。此乃因緬甸政府方面，當時正忙於兩項重大工程，其一是滇緬鐵路，其二則是從印度阿薩密省英帕爾（Imphal, Assam, India）至緬甸中部曼德勒（Mandalay）的公路，因此並無餘力支援雷多至密支那段公路的修築。所以如要修築雷多密支那線公路，可能需要由中國方面承擔較大的工

23　"Military Mission, Chungking to Commander-in-Chief, India," 5 February 1942, *Proposed Assam-China Road*, FO 371/31635, TNA.

24　"Commander-in-Chief, India to British Military Mission, Chungking," 21 February 1942, *Proposed Assam-China Road*, FO 371/31365, TNA.

作與責任。英國印度緬甸部部長對於英國駐華大使卡爾（Archibald C. Kerr, 1882-1951）究竟是否能從蔣中正那邊獲得充分的合作，不無懷疑。[25] 事實上，根據英國陸軍部繪製的中緬印公路地圖，當時擬修築從印度至緬甸的公路有兩條，一條較為偏北，乃是從印度雷多至緬北密支納，另外一條則在較為偏南，則是從印度的英帕爾至緬甸中部的曼德勒。[26] 不難理解，雷多密支那線將關係到西方物資能否順利運補至中國，而英帕爾曼德勒線則關係到英屬印度軍（英帕爾為英軍重要據點）能否在必要時馳援緬甸。換言之，前者攸關中國，而後者較與印度、緬甸利益相關。因此，就英國而言，為確保印度與緬甸之間的聯繫，自然優先致力於修築自印度英帕爾至曼德勒間的公路，至於雷多密支那線則顯得較為次要。

檔案 13：英國陸軍部繪製的中緬印補給路線地圖（1942 年 2 至 3 月）

資料來源："Routes to China from the West," Enclosure Map of "Road Communications between China, Burma and India," Minutes of Foreign Office, February & March, 1942, FO 371/31635.

資料說明：此份地圖由英國陸軍部繪製。原圖較大，西起阿拉伯半島，東至中國西南地區。本圖為其局部擷圖。其中，紅色實線部分註明為既有道路，紅色虛線部分則為擬議修築的路段。虛線的部分，主要分為兩段，其中北邊的一段即是後來的雷多公路（從印度雷多、經緬北密支那、騰越到龍陵），而南邊的一段則是從印度英帕爾至緬甸中部的曼德勒。（顏色標示請參見文後檔案原件）

---

25 "Telegram from Secretary of State, India Office to the Government of India and Burma Governor," 6 February 1942, *Proposed Assam-China Road*, FO 371/31365, TNA.

26 "Routes to China from the West," Enclosure Map of "Road Communications between China, Burma and India," Minutes of Foreign Office, February & March, 1942, *Proposed Assam-China Road*, FO 371/31635, TNA.

　　事實上，根據英國駐緬甸總指揮官給陸軍部的報告，主張印度英帕爾至緬甸曼德勒的相關工程，其優先性應該要高於北邊的滇緬段。其理由有二：其一，因為防衛緬甸安全的重要性，高於防衛中國，畢竟只有緬甸安全無虞，才能確保補給物資持續運送進中國；其二，受到日本威脅與封鎖的影響，不易從更南邊的仰光港運補物資到緬北地區，而必須透印度阿薩密地區運補，因此勢必得盡快強化印度阿薩密與緬甸中部的運輸幹道。故只要此路線完工，即可以透過印度本身的鐵路系統，快速運輸物資，再透過公路運輸，從英帕爾連接至曼德勒。至於滇緬之間的鐵道交通問題，則可以放在次要位置。[27]

> Consider measures for the defence Burma must have
> priority over those of future offensive from China. Rail
> connection with India is essential to the former and may be
> essential to secure continuation lease lend supplies to China
> which it may not be possible to handle at Rangoon. Recommend
> Yunnan railway should proceed but that 1st. priority be given
> to Assam Burma link. Chinese should be asked to agree temporary
> diversion subject to replacement later of materials now lying in
> Burma for Yunnan railway.

檔案 14：英屬緬甸總指揮官給陸軍部的報告【1942 年 1 月】
資料來源："GOC, Burma to the War Office," 27 January 1942, *Proposed Assam-China Road*, FO 371/31635, TNA.
資料說明：英屬緬甸總指揮官，為英軍在緬甸地區的最高軍事指揮官，其立場自然著眼於緬甸的軍事防務，故大力主張維持印度阿薩密地區與緬甸曼德勒之間的運補暢通，其重要性要高於緬甸與雲南之間的聯繫（滇緬鐵路）。

　　另外一方面，相較於英國印度緬甸部的消極態度，英國駐重慶軍事團卻認為雷多密支那線公路的修築不容延緩。在軍事團給英屬印度軍總司令的電報中，一再強調及時援助中國的急迫性，否則一旦中國無力繼續作戰，將對整體戰局構成嚴重威脅。雖然英帕爾至曼德勒公路也能夠用於輸送支援中國

27　"GOC, Burma to the War Office," 27 January 1942, *Proposed Assam-China Road*, FO 371/31635, TNA.

的物資，但是很大程度上取決於仰光是否能夠維持海運暢通。換言之，一旦
仰光遭到封鎖或是遭到日軍攻擊無法持續輸運物資，則曼德勒北上的補給路
線則告中斷，屆時中國恐怕無法繼續組織有力的對日作戰。相較於英帕爾曼
德勒線的脆弱性，雷多密支那線對於運補中國的功用，則可靠多了，不易遭
到日軍的封鎖與威脅，一旦修築完成，將可以持續且穩定地運補物資。英國
駐重慶軍事團在給英屬印度軍總司令的電報中，重申正是基於上述考量，他
們才會同意接受雷多密支那線修築的提案，也認為印度與緬甸將會全力支援
此路線的修築。畢竟唯有在充分軍事物資的支援下，中國軍隊才能夠發揮戰
力，並持續發揮著牽制日軍的作用。這也是當時英國能夠給予中國最重要的
道德激勵與援助。[28] 簡言之，英國駐重慶軍事團認為，無論如何必須儘速確
保戰略物資運補中國戰區路線的順暢，使中國能夠有效開展對日作戰，從而
減緩英國方面的壓力，所以雷多密支那線的修築，自然是目前的首要考量。

檔案 15：英國駐重慶軍事團給英屬印
度軍總司令的電報（1942 年 2 月 7 日）
資料來源："Military Mission, Chungking to
Commander-in-Chief, India," 7 February 1942,
Proposed Assam-China Road, FO 371/31635,
TNA.
資料說明：中緬印補給路線的規劃與修築，
均與印度密切相關。故英國駐重慶軍事團希
望英屬印度軍總司令能夠支持並大力促成此
案。

（三）關於建築分配與經費部分

　　根據英國駐華大使館給英國外交部的報告，中國政府運輸部提案，將
中印公路的修築，分成西部段與東部段。其中，東部段位於中國境內，而西

---

28 "Military Mission, Chungking to Commander-in-Chief, India," 7 February 1942, *Proposed
Assam-China Road*, FO 371/31635, TNA.

部段則位於印度與緬甸境內。中國將負責東部段的施工，但希望英國政府協助，聯繫印度與緬甸當局，分別負責西部段雷多至密支那的部分。其次，根據重慶軍事聯席會議的決議，如果印度與緬甸方面無法募集到足夠的工人從事修築工作，中國方面可以代為進行建築工程，並在密支那成立建築辦公室。此外，也將由中、美、英、印、緬共同籌組一個「聯合委員會」（a Joint Commission），來一起負責監管中緬印補給路線的行政與交通事宜。[29]

至於此路線的分段距離與預計的建築經費，根據重慶軍事聯席會的決議，分別為中國段長 190 公里（預計費用 950 萬中國法幣），緬甸段長 465 公里（預計費用 2,635 萬印度盧布），印度段 225 公里（預計費用 1,575 萬印度盧布）。各區段的費用原則上由各相關國自行負責，但緬甸段的部分，先期兩個月的工程將由中國方面負責。[30]

檔案 16：重慶軍事聯席會議有關中緬印補給路線建築段與經費的決議【1942 年 2 月】
資料來源："Resolution by the Joint War Council," 3 February 1942, cited from "Mr. Allen, Chungking to the Foreign Office, London," 9 February 1942, *Proposed Assam-China Road*, FO 371/31635, TNA.
資料說明：根據英國駐華大使館給英國外交部的報告，關於中緬印補給路線的建築分段與經費事宜，乃先由重慶軍事聯席會議在 1942 年 2 月 3 日做成決議。中國運輸部則再於 2 月 5 日，依據上述決議，發出相關備忘錄通知。

29　"Memorandum by the Ministry of Communication, China," 28 January & 5 February 1942, cited from "Mr. Allen, Chungking to the Foreign Office, London," 9 February 1942, *Proposed Assam-China Road*, FO 371/31635, TNA.

30　"Resolution by the Joint War Council," 3 February 1942, cited from "Mr. Allen, Chungking to the Foreign Office, London," 9 February 1942, *Proposed Assam-China Road*, FO 371/31635, TNA.

四、結語

　　關於中國遠征軍的出現，中國方面的相關回憶與資料，往往將其歸諸於 1941 年底的《中英共同防禦滇緬路協定》，但是遍查英國外交部的相關檔案，均無發現有此協定。這或許跟中、英雙方對於中國軍隊入緬作戰一事的不同理解而造成。不過，另一方面，如果從英國軍方與外交部門的檔案，去研究中國遠征軍，倒是可以對其有更為清楚的了解。原來早在珍珠港事變之前，蔣中正即曾對英國提議願意出兵協防緬甸，但當時英國因顧忌日本態度，始終並未認真思考此議。之後，太平洋戰爭爆發，歐洲與亞洲戰區合一，中、美、英等開始籌劃協同作戰，這也使得中國入緬作戰一事再度成為重要議題。在蔣中正倡議諸國共商軍事同盟大計，以及英國面對日軍在遠東戰區的咄咄進逼，確實也需要中國軍隊協防緬甸等兩大前提要素的刺激下，英國軍方授意英屬印度軍總司令魏菲爾專程來華，出席重慶的軍事聯席會議，直接與蔣中正面商中英軍事合作之事。也是在此次會議上，中、美、英等盟邦將領，最終敲定了中國遠征軍入緬作戰計畫。不過，從英國檔案來看，英國政府並沒有把此事提高到兩國外交上的正式「協定」層次，相反地，在英國軍方與外交官員眼中，此事或許充其量只是共同商妥的一次祕密軍事作戰計畫罷了。後來隨著緬甸作戰失利，盟邦間又陷入相互指責，中國遠征軍議題，更是成為中、英齟齬與彼此卸責的重要談資。

　　其次，滇緬印運補路線的規劃，同樣也在中英之間惹出不少風波。主要是蔣中正堅持新規劃的運補路線應盡量往北偏，以便途經川藏地區，也比較不易受到日軍兵鋒的切斷與威脅。而英國則比較傾向較為偏南的路線，希望經由緬北密支那，連結滇緬印三地，以顧及英國在緬印地區的整體防禦作戰的規劃，必要時英屬印度軍主力部隊也能夠就近馳援緬甸戰區。究其實際，川藏地區地勢崎嶇、海拔甚高，此類高山公路的修築難度極大，故英國研判蔣中正堅持偏北路線應是別有居心，那就是藉由此路線的規劃與建築，從而強化對於西藏地區的控制力。因此，關於運補路線的規劃問題，自然又在中、英間爭執不斷，所幸後來雙方勉強達成共識。然而，另外一方面，依照重慶軍事聯席會議的決議，中緬印補給路線分成三個區段，分別由印度、緬甸以及中國三方，各自負責其境內的修築與開支。換言之，印度段與緬甸段部分，均將由英國及其轄下的印度與緬甸當局負責。英國內部本身則對於該優先致力於修築印緬段還是中緬段之間，也有歧見。基於防衛作戰的需要，緬甸方面自然希望能先確保印緬之間的聯繫，不但方便英屬印度軍在必要時，可以盡快由印度英帕爾馳援緬甸中部（反之亦然，一旦作戰失利危急時，緬甸軍也可從此路迅速往印度西撤），還可以利用印度本身的鐵路系統強化對緬甸的物資補給。但是英國駐重慶軍事團則認為確保中國物資補給路線的安全與順暢至關重要，否則一旦中國戰區因物資斷絕而陷入危殆局面，恐將影響到整個對日作戰，因此希望英國政府能夠大力支持並優先確保對於中國的運補路線。

檔案原件

檔案 1：英國外交部遠東司的內部備忘錄（1942 年 6 月）
檔案 8：英國外交部與情報部官員的內部溝通紀錄：關於英國陸軍部對於報紙指控英
　　　軍在遠東地區作戰不力的態度（1942 年 6 月）

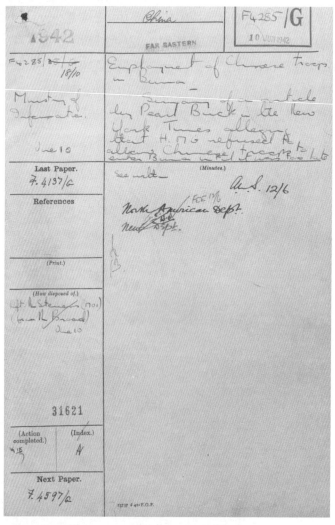

資料來源："Employment of Chinese Troops in Burma," Minutes of the Far Eastern Department, Foreign Office, June 1942, *Employment of Chinese Troops in Burma*, FO 371/31621, TNA.

Minutes.

The attached draft letter is, I think, self-explanatory. I mentioned the matter to Mr. Stevens yesterday and he said that his Ministry had made repeated and unsuccessful efforts to induce the War Office to do something. The W.O. took the line that when we lost a part of the Empire the subject was then closed. Unfortunately this is not the line taken by people in the U.S. Mr. Stevens said that it would be a great help if he could have a letter from us indicating that he had our support.

F.E. Dept.

6th June 1942.

The charge that we refused Chinese offers of military assistance or delayed in accepting them is a "King Charles' Head" which I fear will always be raised in convenient moments, since on the facts available there seems unfortunately to be sufficient basis for the charge to make it difficult for us to issue *a* convincing denial. In fact, Far Eastern Department made representations at the time about political reactions which it was feared might result from the reluctance of our local military authorities to use Chinese troops in Burma.

The facts are given by General Wavell in his telegram of 7th February (F1330/G) - incidentally it is interesting to compare this telegram with the cancelled telegram of 6th February (F1329/G). Roughly they are that it was arranged by General Wavell when he visited Chungking on the 25th December that two divisions of the Chinese Sixth Army should move into Burma forthwith, and a third later. but ~~owing~~ *because of* a variety of reasons it was not until the third week in January that General Wavell authorised the G.O.C. Burma to accept further Chinese assistance, and owing to the necessity of getting General Chiang Kai-shek's approval,

the/

Minutes.

2.

the orders for the Chinese Fifth Army to move
into Burma were not agreed upon until the 4th
February.　It should perhaps be added that the
reference in the penultimate sentence of the
(cancelled) telegram of 6th February (F1329/3)
is to an offer made by General Chiang Kai-shek
during discussions between our Military Attaché
in China in July and August 1941 to make
available up to 1,000 Chinese troops for service　　/100,000
outside China, Burma being particularly mentioned,
provided we could equip and employ them;　our
principal reasons for showing no particular
enthusiasm for this offer were our desire not
to provoke the Japanese and our inability to
fulfil the condition attached, namely the
equipping of 1,000 Chinese soldiers.　　　　　　/100,000

　　　　Far Eastern Department have for some
time been trying to combat the efforts of Chinese
propagandists to boost the often mythological
achievements of Chinese troops and their
depreciation of the achievements of the British
forces.　If the War Office can make out a
convincing and presentable case in our defence
in answer to the allegations made by Mrs.
Pearl Buck and other Chinese propagandists that
would of course be very welcome.　Nevertheless
I feel that the better course may be that
outlined in the alternative draft letter to
Mr. Stevens which I attach.

　　　　As previous papers on this subject are
Far Eastern, perhaps the present correspondence
should also be entered with Far Eastern
Department.

Sir J. Brenan 8/6　　　　An Scott 9/6

N⁰ American Dept

initialled on
jacket by M⁺ Evans
A.S.

5/6.

**檔案 2：英國駐華大使館給英國外交部關於蔣中正提案共組軍事同盟的報告
【1941 年 12 月 8 日】**

[This telegram is of particular secrecy and should be
retained by the authorised recipient and not passed on.]

[CYPHER]　　　　　WAR CABINET DISTRIBUTION.

FROM: CHINA.

FROM CHUNGKING TO FOREIGN OFFICE.

Sir A. Clark Kerr　　　D.　9.00 a.m.　9th December, 1941.
No. 633　　　　　　　　R.　5.20 p.m.　9th December, 1941.
8th December, 1941.

kkkkk

IMMEDIATE.

　　Chiang Kai-shek asks me to send you the following message.

　　[Begins].　Despite sincere efforts made by United States
Government in their recent conversations with Japan to settle by
peaceful means the various questions bearing on the Pacific,
Japan has suddenly launched an attack on the United States and
Great Britain.　This latest act of international brigandage on
the part of Japan has taken even us by surprise.　The fact that
this attack was made while Japan's envoys were continuing their
talks in Washington, shows her plan of aggression was premeditated.

　　2.　Chinese Government now hold itself in full readiness
to collaborate, regardless of all further sacrifices, in any
concerted military plan, which Great Britain and the United
States, Australia, New Zealand, Canada, Netherlands, and the
Union of Soviet Socialist Republics may adopt against Japan and
her Axis partners.

　　3.　Chinese Government has decided to declare war
against Japan, and also her partners Germany and Italy.

　　4.　In order to make possible the full concerted action,
Chinese Government deems it imperative that every member of the
[2 groups undec.] bloc should consider, as a common enemy, every
member of the Axis group.　We therefore suggest that a simultaneous
declaration of war by the United States against Germany and Italy
and by the Union of Soviet Socialist Republics against Japan should
be made.

　　5.　For effective and successful prosecution of the war
Chinese Government consider essential the conclusion of a military
alliance between Great Britain, the United States, Union of Soviet
Socialist Republics, Australia, New Zealand, Canada, Netherlands
and China with a unified command of Allied forces under American
leadership.

　　6.　Chinese Government propose that an agreement be con-
cluded between Great Britain, United States, Union of Soviet
Socialist Republics, Australia, New Zealand, Canada, Netherlands and
China, not to sign any separate peace.　[Ends].
　　Similar messages will be handed to American and Soviet
Ambassadors, Australian Minister and the Netherlands Minister.

(INDIV.)

資料來源："War Cabinet Distribution: From China; From Chungking to Foreign Office," 9 December
1941, *Anglo-United States-Chinese Co-operation against Japan*, FO 371/27753, TNA.

檔案 3：英國首相邱吉爾在英國下議院關中國的報告【1941 年 12 月 11 日】

F. FI3469/13469/10.

[Code] (R)　　　POLITICAL DISTRIBUTION

To:　CHINA

FROM FOREIGN OFFICE TO CHUNGKING

No. 840
December 12th, 1941.　　　D. 12.40. p.m. 12th December, 1941.

Repeated to Washington No.6880.
　　　C.O.I.S. Singapore (for Mr. Duff Cooper and
　　　　Commander-in-Chief Far East) No.448.

b b b b b b

IMMEDIATE

　　Following statement about China was included in Prime
Minister's review in the House of Commons yesterday.

　　[Begins].　　The Generalissimo, Chiang Kai-shek, has
sent me a message announcing his decision to declare war
against Japan and also against Japan's partners in guilt,
Germany and Italy.　He has further assured me that the whole
of the resources of China are at the disposal of Great Britain
and the United States.　China's cause is henceforth our
cause.　The country which has faced the Japanese assault for
over four years with undaunted courage is indeed a worthy ally
and it is as allies that, from now on, we will go forward
together to victory not only over Japan alone but over the
Axis and all its works.　　[Ends].

資料來源："Telegram from Foreign Office, London to Sir A. Clark Kerr, Chungking," 12 December 1941, *Anglo-United States-Chinese Co-operation against Japan*, FO 371/27753, TNA.

檔案 4：蔣中正與英國駐華大使、武官的晤談紀錄（1941 年 12 月 16 日）

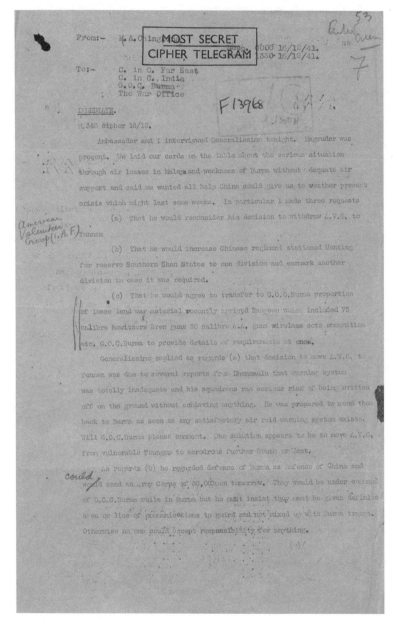

資料來源："Military Attaché, Chungking to the War Office," 16 December 1941, *Anglo-United States-Chinese Co-operation against Japan*, FO 371/27753, TNA.

(c) He would have to consult Minister of War as he was not fully briefed.

:-

                    PART TWO

                                    Desd. 0800 16/12/41.
                                    Recd. 1330 16/12/41.
IMMEDIATE.

M.348 Cipher 16/12.

   He then reverted forcibly to joint planning. Leaving Philippines out of argument absolute essential was to hold Singapore. Next came defence of Burma. What Britain America and China must do was first to decide what is necessary to hold Singapore. Nothing must stand in the way of this absolute essential. Apart from air forces India and Burma must provide all ground troops required to make it absolutely secure. Next step was to decide what troops situation needed from China to make her secure. Thirdly what appeal to China could do to assist. At present everything was haphazard. For nstance Burma asked for division and regiment there. Regiment had been moved to MONGOAWNG but had little idea of its task and this was bad for morale. He had never been taken into our councils for fighting this war.

   Comment.   It is quite obvious that Chinese help is now essential to us to see us through present crisis and we have not right to expect Chinese co-operation unless we take Generalissimo fully into our confidence. The sooner the Officers from India can arrive for joint discussions the better. C. in C. India please wire their names and date of arrival. W.O. telegram 57779(M.O.1)refers.

C.4.(Tels)   To:- M.O.12.(for action)
   Copies to:- S. of S.
   (C.I.G.S.   Foreign Office
                V.C.I.G.S.   (Mr. Sterndale Bennett)
                D.M.O.&.P.   Head of War Registry (Admiralty.
                D.D.M.O.(O)(H)   C.N.S.(Admiralty)
                D.P.   D. of Plans (Admiralty).
                M.O.1.2.10.12.   C.A.S. (Air Ministry)
                D.M.I.   D. of Plans (Air Ministry)
                D.D.M.I.(I)(O)   Col. Jacob (Cabinet Offices)
                M.I.2.(3 copies) Secy. J.P.S. (Cabinet Offices)
                D.S.D.   India Office (Col. McCay)
                                  Burma Office (Major Upson)

檔案 5：英國參謀首長委員會會議紀錄（1941 年 12 月 17 日）

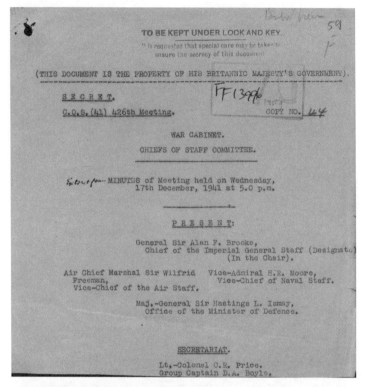

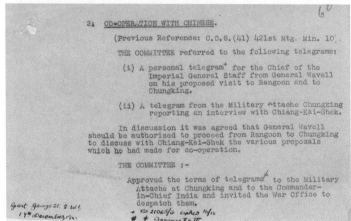

資料來源："Minute of Chiefs of Staff Committee, War Cabinet," 17 December 1941, *Anglo-United States-Chinese Co-operation against Japan*, FO 371/27753, TNA.

檔案 6：英國陸軍部關於中英在緬甸軍事合作的備忘錄（1942 年 6 月 23 日）

SECRET

IC

NOTE ON CHINESE CO-OPERATION IN BURMA.

On 23 December General Wavell as C-in-C.,
India visited Chungking to discuss the defence of Burma
and the Burma Road with General Chiang Kai Shek and the
Chinese General Staff.

In the course of these conversations the
Generalissimo offered General Wavell a Chinese
Expeditionary Force of two Armies for service in Burma.
This offer was accepted by General Wavell and one Army
began moving almost at once; part of it was in position
on the Burma-Thailand frontier by the middle of January.
The move of the second Army was governed by problems of
supply, communications and liaison and the need for
providing cover for the Burma Road.   These difficulties
were overcome, however, and the second Army moved south
towards the middle of February.   By the middle of March
both Armies were in action under the command of General
Stilwell.

Early in April a third Army began moving down
to the Irrawaddy Front.   One division of this Army,
which distinguished itself with General Alexander's
troops in the action round YENANGYAUNG, has accompanied
the British forces in their withdrawal up the valley
of the Chindwin into Assam.

資料來源：War Office, "Note on Chinese Cooperation in Burma," 23 June 1942, *Employment of Chinese Troops in Burma*, FO 371/31621, TNA.

檔案 7：英國外交部遠東司引據《紐約時報》有關賽珍珠評論的一篇報導：〈美國的調查：特別〉【1942 年 5 月 31 日】

AMERICAN SURVEY: SPECIAL

NEW YORK TIMES　May 31:

　　The following three items appeared, unfavourable to Western - and particularly British - policy in the Far East: in a feature article, Pearl BUCK, warns of the possibility that this war may develop into a war between the East and West. "The greatest danger is not only that to-day Japan is in a position of unprecedented power /because Japan is an Asiatic power and whatever her despotism to millions of Asiatics she stands for freedom, at least from the white man's despotism. Can the white and coloured man ever come together in any sort of cooperation? That is the crux of the future. In answer to that question is the answer as to where and when the war will end." She goes on to say that the main barrier between the East and West to-day is that the white man is not willing to give up his superiority and the coloured man is no longer willing to endure his inferiority. She deplores the fact that the United Nations are signally failing t make the most of their greatest asset in this war of peoples, namely, that the Chinese are on their side, saying that the continued exclusion of Chinese from the United States and from citizenship, as well as other instances, is insulting treatment. She continues: "And our British Allies ought to know the ways in which they too are not using this asset. I will mention only two which already have had a serious effect on the war in Burma. Chinese soldiers for a long time were massed on the Chinese border impatient to fight in Burma but they were not allowed to cross over and take part until Rangoon fell and it became obvious that the British alone could not hold the ground. Again, as soon as General STILWELL was appointed head of the Chinese armies, a British general was advanced to a superior rank. I do not pretend to know anything about the military reasons for this, but I do know that the effect on our Chinese Allies was unfortunate. Much will be told one day of the treatment of the Chinese and others in the Allied retreats from China, Malay and Burma but it here may be said certainly that the asset of China is not being used as it might be in our Pacific war. To remove our ignorance of such facts would be one of the first steps towards using to the full our great asset at this moment in China. It is China alone who is contradicting by her very presence at our side the Japanese propaganda that Britain and America will never cooperate with the coloured races. We ought to give China every advantage. She is worth far more to us at this moment than her weight in the future in trade and gold. She may be the one country some day which will prevent a war of the East against the West. But China needs reassurance, and quick reassurance, of her complete human equality in the mind of the white man." Pearl BUCK goes on to show Americans how they are wasting another asset, namely, India, not regarding the latter as their business. "The truth is that India has become the business of the Allies and is no longer the possession of any country. Our American soldiers are being sent there in unknown numbers. They can go as soldiers of the Empire or as soldiers of freedom - those are the two alternatives. If we cannot prove to India that our soldiers are there for freedom, then India will believe that they are there for the Empire.... We are losing our best chances when we encourage an attitude which has given full attention only to an imperial point of view in India, modified and enlightened even as it was in CRIPPS, and when we deny equal attention to the statements of Indian leaders giving the point of view of India. We are losing our chances with India when we allow the slighting comments of ignorant broadcasters and news columnists to go unchallenged - comments for instance which lump together all the Moslems, as though the All-India Congress did not also represent Moslems too and as though the president of Congress were not himself a Moslem, or comments which decry the so-called pacifism of India which is not pacifism at all, but brave determination of the people to resist Japan in the way they know best since arms have not been allowed to them."

　　A leading editorial quoting Pearl BUCK'S views approvingly says that the only way we can successfully deal with the new Oriental attitude is to concede the equality of Eastern and Western races: not their present equality in education, industrial power or standards of living, but equality in rights and responsibilities so that individual for individual is given the same freedom and opportunity. Eastern peoples owe much to the benevolent aspect of Western imperialism.... But benevolence as a quality shown by a superior to an inferior is obsolete. We can henceforth be of real use to people like the Indians and the Chinese only if we let them be equally useful to us as fellow citizens in the civilisation of the democratic world.

資料來源："American Survey: Special," *The New York Times*, 31 May 1942, cited from "Employment of Chinese Troops in Burma," June 1942, *Employment of Chinese Troops in Burma*, FO 371/31621, TAN.

LIN YU-TANG (Lin is the surname) Recd 8/6/42

Lin YUTAN, in a letter, says that Chungking is bitterly dissatisfied with the whole conduct of the war in the Far East. "Wholly unintentionally, and through neglect, China has been shamefully and disgracefully sold by her Allies. I say unintentionally because I know what is at fault is not intention or lack of appreciation of China's services, but the old psychology prevailing between the bureaucrats in Burma and in the councils of the United Nations in the West. It is this psychology that must be changed." Lin YUTAN states that the Chinese soldiers were ready at the Burma frontier in December and that plans for the Chinese defence of Burma had been submitted to the British Government in February, 1941 but had been side-tracked by political chicanery. "When Moulmein fell at the beginning of February, the Chinese soldiers were still not permitted to cross the border. These soldiers were permitted to cross in March when Rangoon fell. And then there were the ridiculous bureaucrats standing at the border with pencil and paper to check the number that got into Burma, to be sure that not too many came in and that the same number would leave when the war was over. On April 24th, when the Chinese had saved the British troops on the Irrawaddy, it was fully six weeks afterwards that the news at last came - 'now there was no limit to the entrance of Chinese troops into Burma'. It was assumed, of course, that there was the intention to defend Burma and save it as a spring-board for a future offensive. It was assumed that there were a million troops in India right across the border and, of course, if the Chinese were not needed then the Indian troops must be coming over the border to relieve the tired troops. Yet we heard only sympathy for the tired troops without reinforcements during the whole three months from February to April inclusive. And then to hear from Major ATTLEE, speaking for the British Cabinet and replying to questions in Parliament of the miserable conduct of the war in the Far East, the bland statement that 'of course, we cannot have adequate forces at every point'. That, of course, irritates me extremely. For what is Burma? Insignificant, like any point for which they could not provide adequate forces and unimportant for the defeat of HITLER: it was nevertheless the jugular vein of China. Furthermore it was the strategic springboard for an Allied offensive. That is the psychology which I say must be changed and without delay." Dr. Lin goes on: "it is not America and England that need assurance from China that she will fight Japan to the end. The presence of that psychology and the record of Britain in the Burmese campaign, make it imperative that America and England reassure China of their unbending and all-out efforts to defeat Japan without politicians' tricks to appease Japan to save her in order to maintain the politicians' theory of balance of power in the Far East after the war. Chungking desperately needs that assurance and reassurance. The written pledge of twenty-six united nations for no separate peace is there, but the Chinese have had reasons during the last few months to think that this pledge is not enough."

From New York
Telegram No. 1070 of June 2nd 1942.

檔案 9：英國外交部給情報部的建議（1942 年 6 月 10 日）

FOREIGN OFFICE, S.W.1.

(F 4285/38/G)　　　　　　　　　　　　　　　　10th June, 1942.

Dear Stevens,

　　　　I understand that Hohler spoke to you recently about the allegations made in the United States' press by Pearl Buck and others that we refused to allow Chinese troops to enter Burma until it was too late.

　　　　Unfortunately there appears to be sufficient substance in these allegations to make it difficult for us to refute them convincingly.　Delays undoubtedly occurred in accepting Chinese military assistance, and it was for instance not until the 4th February that arrangements for the Chinese Fifth Army to enter Burma were finally agreed.　We have been doing our best to combat anti-British Chinese propaganda in the United States of which this appears to be a symptom, and on our instructions Lord Halifax has taken the matter up with Mr. Sumner Welles and Dr. T.V. Soong.　What appears to be required is that adequate publicity should be given in the United States of America to the British version of our operations in the Far East and in other theatres of war.　Steps to this end are, I understand, already being taken by the Far Eastern Section of your Ministry so far as China is concerned, and some improvement in the tone of the Chinese press has latterly resulted.　In this way, we should actually achieve more than by standing on the defensive (for as you will remember "Qui s'excuse s'accuse") or by engaging in an exchange of "pleasantries" with the Chinese. But of course if you can get the War Office to produce a convincing case, so much the better.

Yours sincerely

(sgd) Philip Broad.

R.B. Stevens Esq.,
　Ministry of Information.

資料來源："Philip Broad, Foreign Office to R. B. Stevens, Ministry of Information," 10 June 1942, *Employment of Chinese Troops in Burma*, FO 371/31621, TNA.

檔案 10：英國外交部繪製的中緬印補給路線規劃圖（1942 年 1 月）

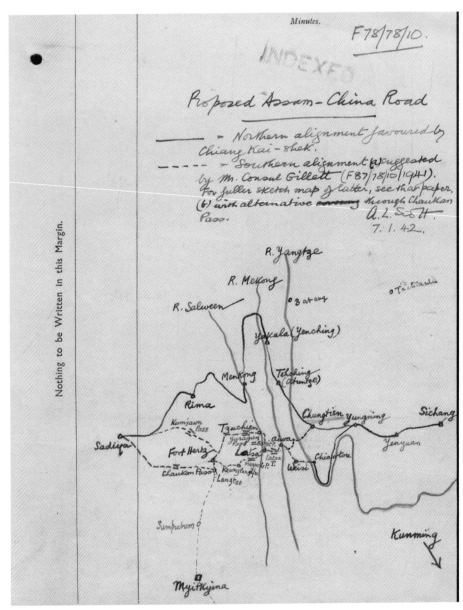

資料來源："Proposed Assam-China Road," Minutes of Foreign Office, January 1942, *Proposed Assam-China Road*, FO 371/31635, TNA.

檔案 11：英國外交部內部備忘錄【1942 年 2 月】

資料來源："Proposed Assam China Road," Minutes of Foreign Office, 9 February 1942, *Proposed Assam-China Road*, FO 371/31635, TNA.

檔案 12：重慶軍事聯席會議關於中緬印補給路線的討論【1942 年 2 月】

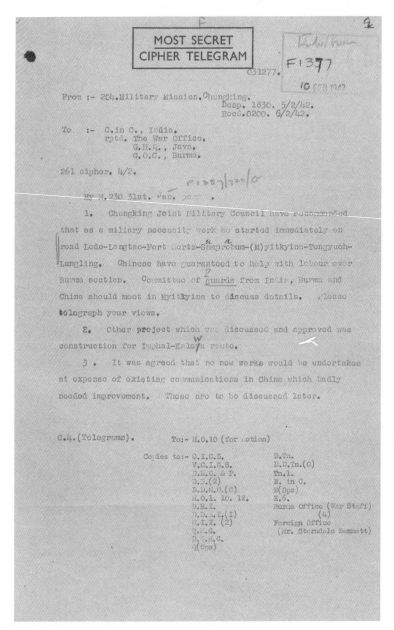

資料來源："Military Mission, Chungking to Commander-in-Chief, India," 5 February 1942, *Proposed Assam-China Road*, FO 371/31635, TNA.

檔案 14：英屬緬甸總指揮官給陸軍部的報告【1942 年 1 月】

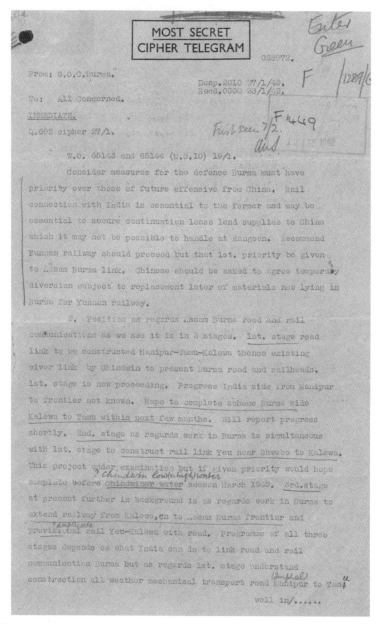

資料來源："GOC, Burma to the War Office," 27 January 1942, *Proposed Assam-China Road*, FO 371/31635, TNA.

well in hand but we have no report of progress.

3. Government Burma are prepared proceed forthwith
with rail connection Yeu-Kalewa with extension to frontier
if India agree to complete section in Assam. Sir John Rowland
can be made immediately available to undertake this work and a
suitable successor can be made available for Yunnan railway.

4. Immediate decision necessary to enable work to be
pushed on as far as possible before monsoon. Survey of line
exists and road should be built as far as possible along same
alignment to facilitate essential conversion.

5. Will telegraph details separately reply para 4
Troopers 65144 (M.O.10) but Rowland states there is sufficient
material here or on the way for Yunnan railway to enable work
to begin at once on Assam-Burma railway if Chinese will agree.
There are also certain tracks in Burma which might be taken up.

C.W.(Telegrams)   To:- M.O.10. (for action).
                   Copies to:- C.I.G.S.
                               V.C.I.G.S.
                               D.M.O.& P.
                               D.D.M.O.(O).
                               M.O.1.10.12.
                               D.M.I.
                               D.D.M.I.(I).
                               M.I.2c.
                               Q.M.G.
                               D.Q.M.G.
                               Q(Ops).
                               D.Tn.
                               D.D.Tn.
                               Tn.1.
                               E.in C.
                               E(Ops).
                               E.S.
                               Burma Office (War Staff).

檔案 15：英國駐重慶軍事團給英屬印度軍總司令的電報（1942 年 2 月 7 日）

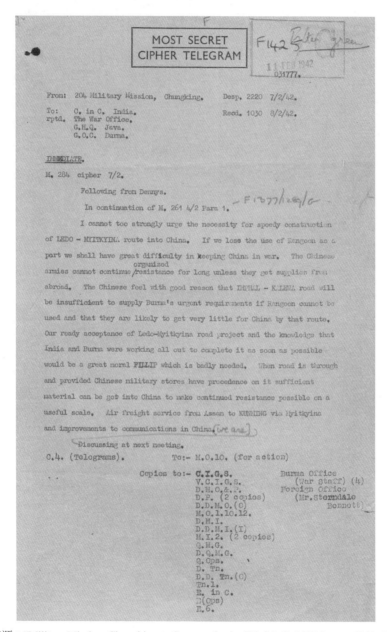

資料來源："Military Mission, Chungking to Commander-in-Chief, India" 7 February 1942, *Proposed Assam-China Road*, FO 371/31635, TNA.

檔案 16：重慶軍事聯席會議有關中緬印補給路線建築段與經費的決議【1942 年 2 月】

AMENDED COPY

[Cypher]   DEPARTMENTAL NO.2.

FROM CHUNGKING TO FOREIGN OFFICE.

Mr. Allen.   D. 7.15 p.m. 9th February, 1942.
No. 174.   R. 3.25 a.m. 10th February, 1942.

9th February, 1942.

Repeated to Burma No. 73)
            India No. 70) via Foreign Office.

                        uuuu

            Your telegram No. 120.

            In memorandum of January 28th Ministry of
Communications state that "Chinese Government have decided
to adopt Western section of the south route for proposed
highway" and request me to approach His Majesty's Government in the United Kingdom to give such assistance and
instructions to the *Governments* of India *and* Burma
as would enable quick construction of a road *between
Ledo* and Myitkyina via Langtao and Sumprabum. Simultaneously the Chinese Government will undertake construction
of the eastern section of the proposed highway between
Sichang and Chungtien. While construction of the
eastern section is going on, comparison will be made between
the north and south routes from Chungtien to India. If the
south route is feasible, construction will be in fact
between Chungtien and Langtao. If Burma and India are
short of labour, Ministry of Communications will undertake
construction for their account. Memorandum adds "as for
remaining un-demarcated frontiers between Northern Burma
and China, question will be taken up by Ministry of Foreign
Affairs".

            2.   Further memorandum of February 5th states that
in connexion with the above scheme the Chinese Government
contemplate building internal highway from Myitkyina via
Tengyueh to Lungling on the Burma Road. As the entire highway will pass through India, Burma, and China the Chinese
Government think it will be best to start construction
simultaneously in the three different sections. The Chinese
Government are aware of the shortage of labour in Burma,
and being anxious to see early completion of project are
ready to send Engineer Corps in sufficient numbers to undertake construction in Burma. Ministry of Communications
request me to obtain permission of Government of Burma for this
corps to carry on the work for account of the Government
of Burma and say that a construction office will be set up
in Myitkyina to this end. Memorandum adds that Ministry
proposes a joint commission with one representative of each
of the interested countries (United States, Great Britain,
China, India and Burma) to have unified control of the entire
highway in matters relating to traffic and administration.

                                        /But

資料來源："Mr. Allen, Chungking to the Foreign Office, London," 9 February 1942, *Proposed Assam-China Road*, FO 371/31635, TNA.

2.

But construction should be undertaken without delay
while Commission is being organised. I am informed
orally that labour for Engineers Corps will be from
Yunan Burma railway and engineer in charge of construction on the railway is being sent to Burma
immediately to make arrangements.

3.　This memorandum is based on resolution
of Joint *War* Council of February 3rd details of
which were telegraphed by Military Mission to
appropriate military authorities in telegram No. M261
February 4th.

4.　It gives the following estimates of expenses.

(1)　India *Ledo* to Chouhan Pass 225 kilos
rupees 15,750,000.

(2)　Burma *Section i.e. Chouhan pass*, Langtao
Sumprabum via Myitkyina to *China frontier, total length*
465 kilometres, *estimated cost* rupees 26,550,000.

(3)　China frontier to Lungling 190 kilos Chinese
National dollars 95,000,000.

Construction expenses of each section to be borne
by respective governments but China is prepared to advance
the needed construction expenses for the first two months
on the Burma section.

5.　Memoranda nowhere definitely state that the
northern route has been abandoned but they rather imply it.
This impression was strengthened in conversation with the
head of recent survey party who is definitely in favour
of southern line. Minister of Communications assured His
Majesty's Ambassador orally that in effect the Chinese
Government had chosen the southern route, but it would be
unwise to place too much reliance on this.

6.　Copies of memoranda follow by safe opportunity.

7.　I should be grateful for instructions as to reply
I should give.

[Copies sent to Telegraph Branch India Office].

[Amendments received from Chungking].

(INDIV)

德軍太平洋戰爭情報地圖分析

周惠民
國立政治大學歷史學系教授兼人文中心主任

一、前言

　　中德兩國的軍事合作關係起源甚早，李鴻章（1823-1901）曾向德國大量購買船艦、武器與軍火，並派遣官兵前往德國學習軍事。民國以後，德國軍事顧問在各處服務，國民黨北伐之際，還積極尋求引進德國軍事技術，1927年11月，德國上校鮑爾（Max Bauer, 1869-1929）於廣州面見蔣中正（1887-1975），又展開另一階段的中德軍事合作，直到1938年7月，希特勒（Adolf Hitler, 1889-1945）下令所有在華軍事顧問立即撤出。這10多年間，德國軍事顧問深入中國軍隊，清楚中國的武器配備，也了解軍事發展進度。他們定期向德方報告，這些檔案文件，多數藏於德國聯邦檔案館的軍事檔案館（Das Bundesarchiv-Militärarchiv, BArch-MA）。

　　德國聯邦檔案館的軍事檔案館位於德國西南部的弗萊堡（Freiburg），是第二次世界大戰之後才建立的新機構，但庋藏的內容卻包括自1867年以後的普魯士與德意志帝國時期、第三帝國時期檔案，也包括德意志聯邦共和國乃至原德意志民主共和國（東德）的許多軍事相關檔案。其前身為德意志聯邦共和國建立後的軍事檔案處，1955年成立於柯布倫茲（Koblenz），1968年後擴大為軍事檔案館，歸於德國聯邦檔案館管理。德國原設有「軍事史研究館」（Militärgeschichtliches Forschungsamt），館內保存軍事相關檔案。德國聯邦檔案館的軍事檔案館成立後，接收這一部分資料，1990年以後，更接收設於波茨坦（Potsdam）的各種前東德時期的軍事檔案。

　　德國近代軍事組織有過幾次變化：德意志帝國成立後，其負責陸地的國防軍力稱為帝國陸軍（Reichsheer），並建立帝國海軍（Kaiserliche Marine）負責海上防禦，以及帝國保衛軍（Schutztruppe）保護海外殖民地區的安全；第一次世界大戰後，威瑪政府成立國家防衛軍（Reichswehr），下轄陸軍（Reichsheer），以及海軍（Reichsmarine），其軍隊的規模與軍備都受到《凡爾賽條約》的限制；希特勒執政後，逐漸擴充軍事力量並實施普遍徵兵制，將國家防衛軍改稱為納粹國防軍（Wehrmacht）[1]，下轄陸軍（Heer）、作戰海軍（Kriegsmarine）與正式新建的空軍（Luftwaffe）。三軍各有其指揮系統，各稱為總司令部（Oberkommando），包括陸軍總司令部（Oberkommando des Heeres, OKH）、海軍總司令部（Oberkommando der Kriegsmarine, OKM）及空軍總司令部（Oberkommando der Luftwaffe, OKL），均設於柏林（Berlin）。這些機構，除了負責軍事發展之外，也蒐集各種情報，建立國防安全。第二次世界大戰後期，因德國戰事失利，許多資料毀於轟炸，尤以陸軍及空軍部分損失最為嚴重。但是海軍檔案與 1943 年以前陸軍的「作戰日記」（Kriegstagebücher），相對保存的較為完整。

　　1936 年以前，德國軍事顧問團在中國的工作成效良好，相當獲得蔣中正信任，德國與列強關係仍維持表面和諧的狀況，所以其對華的外交平穩。1938 年 7 月下令撤出駐華軍事顧問團，駐華大使陶德曼（Oskar P. Trautmann, 1877-1950）也奉命不得返回武漢任所，駐華使館業務交德國駐日大使迪克森（Herbert von Dirksen, 1882-1955）代管，兩國雖未宣布正式斷交，但兩國的關係似乎已經全面斷絕。

　　我國原駐德大使程天放（1899-1967），在 1938 年 6 月初辭去駐德大使職，蔣乃於 6 月 15 日指派外交部次長陳介（1885-1951）繼任，顯示我方仍重視中德邦交。但陳介抵達德國之後，希特勒拒絕接受陳介呈遞到任國書。

1　德國威瑪時期或希特勒執政時期，其國防軍隊的正式名稱在德語中並未冠上威瑪時期或納粹政權執政等字樣。然為使中文讀者能快速了解其中差異，在中文翻譯上將威瑪時期的 Reichswehr 譯為「國家防衛軍」，希特勒執政時期的 Wehrmacht 譯為「納粹國防軍」，謹此敘明。

蔣基於戰略物資的考慮，未採取任何舉動，而德國也並未與中國斷交。1940年 11 月 30 日，日本與南京汪精衛（1883-1944）政權達成協議，雙方建立正式關係，企圖以此壓迫蔣，卻仍屬無效。1941 年 7 月 1 日，德、義等國，同時承認南京政權，我國隨即於次日宣布與德、義兩國斷交。1941 年 12 月，日本突襲珍珠港（Pearl Harbor），美國對日宣戰，歐洲戰事的規模隨之擴大，我國也與美國同步，對日、德等國宣戰。此時德國與日本相當友善，其駐華人員也未離境，繼續向柏林提交工作報告。當時這些報告，軍事部分，陸軍與空軍對東亞局勢的定期報告，分別藏於陸軍總司令部與空軍總司令部。這種局勢分析報告多以地圖方式呈現，本文特地找出 16 幅地圖解析，可看出 1941 年以後德國描繪的戰爭進度，也呈現出太平洋戰區的形勢變化。

　　中國遠征軍是中華民國在戰時與盟軍最重要的一次聯合作戰。1941 年 12 月，太平洋戰爭爆發，中華民國在單獨對日抗戰 4 年半之後，美國終於對日宣戰，並開始與中國並肩作戰，英軍也因實際需求，願意與中國為盟友。但在此時，日本一直企圖切斷中國對外交通線，政府只能經由陸路通往東南亞，以尋求補給戰略物資。如何修建並維持滇緬公路成為當務之急。1938 年春，政府耗費大量人力物力，開始修建滇緬公路，以昆明為起點，至雲南瑞麗出境，抵達緬甸臘戍（Lashio），再以鐵路經臘戍、曼德勒（Mandalay），至仰光（Rangoon）出海。1938 年底，公路大致完成，海外物資也能順利抵達。日本政府為此不斷壓迫英國政府，1940 年 7 月，邱吉爾（Winston Churchill, 1874-1965）內閣同意封閉滇緬公路。3 個月後，英國因日本與德、義建立同盟，才重新開放滇緬公路。1941 年底，太平洋戰爭爆發，日軍迅速占領香港、菲律賓、馬來亞、新加坡、婆羅洲等地，並直逼緬甸，企圖封鎖中國。蔣中正乃向英國提議：由中國派軍協防緬甸，此即為遠征軍之濫觴。

　　1942 年 3 月，由精銳的第 5 軍、第 6 軍、第 66 軍組成，總數約 10 萬人的「中國遠征軍」正式入緬，提供英國適當的協助，保衛緬甸，以確保中國抗戰能夠繼續獲得必要的戰略物資。但 3 月 8 日時，日軍已經占領緬甸首府仰光，滇緬公路出海口失陷。遠征軍則在同古（Taungoo）抵禦日軍，並在仁安羌（Yenangyaung）協助英軍突圍，不過仍不敵日軍猛攻，最終被迫退出緬甸。遠征軍一部隨英軍赴印度，另一部則返回國內。

1943 年 10 月，在印度新編成的中國駐印軍為打通中印公路，開始反攻緬甸。在加邁（Kamaing）、孟拱（Mogaung）、密支那（Myitkyina）等地取得勝利。1944 年 4 月，雲南方面的中國遠征軍也渡過怒江策應，並相繼占領龍陵、松山、騰衝等地。1945 年 1 月 27 日，遠征軍與駐印軍在芒友（Mong Yu）會師，完成了打通中印公路的戰略目標。

二、說明

本系列地圖為德國聯邦檔案館的軍事檔案館中第三帝國的陸軍與空軍，對於太平洋戰爭的形勢研判圖，包含各國陸軍兵力、航空機配置、海戰結果、空襲次數等資料，應為德國自日本取得相關資料再繪製成圖。

若參照日本戰後官方戰史《大東亞戰爭全史》（為日軍參謀服部卓四郎〔1901-1960〕運用日本參謀本部、軍令部資料，在盟軍總部授命下進行撰寫之戰史）記載，日軍與盟軍在索羅門群島海域交戰中，日方戰報出現嚴重誤差。日方稱盟軍戰損 46 艘各類型軍艦，實際上盟軍僅戰損 1 艘。然而此項錯誤的情報卻也記錄在德軍地圖上，顯現出德軍應是透過日方所提供之戰情，製作亞洲戰場的戰爭情勢地圖。這些地圖極可能是日軍情報的再呈現，但亦可看出軸心國的情報交換體系與戰情判斷等之合作情況，作為德國軍事高層戰略規劃時的參考。

從地圖顯示的東亞戰爭形勢，可以看出日軍在中國戰區及太平洋東部地區的兵力配置與戰事進度，認識當時日軍東西兩線作戰時的窘迫，這與德國的東西線同時作戰的情況相當類似。當日本國力不足，軍火工業無法提供有效後勤支援時時，其在滇緬戰區的空中作戰能力就受到極大的影響。在德國空軍繪製的地圖中，清楚呈現出這一趨勢。

三、系列地圖

（一）RH 2/753-K

〔按：本件為該檔號的第一件地圖〕

時間：1942 年 3 月 16 日。

地圖類型：陸軍兵力配置圖。

地圖描述：

1. 日軍兵力

（1）中國派遣軍（畑俊六〔1879-1962〕將軍指揮）：20 至 25 個步兵師、21 個混成旅、3 個騎兵旅。

（2）飯田軍（第 15 軍）：第 50 師團、第 53 師團、2 個山地師、1 個摩托化師（快速部隊）。

（3）法屬印度支那：北部 1 個師（？）；南部 1 個師（？）〔按：問號見於檔案原件，應表德軍對情報內容不確定，下同〕。

（4）泰國：第 2、第 3、第 4 泰國師位於泰緬邊境；1 個山地師位於曼谷（Bangkok）；第 5、第 6 泰國師位於泰馬邊境。

（5）馬來亞：1 個軍與 3 至 4 個師（近衛師團、第 2 師團、第 5 師團、1 個師）。

（6）婆羅洲：薄弱占領軍。

（7）荷屬婆羅洲：3 個加強營。

（8）3 月 12 日、3 月 13 日對爪哇登陸。

2. 盟軍兵力

（1）國軍第 5、第 6 軍（遠征軍）。

（2）印度：2 至 3 個步兵師、1 個獨立旅、1 萬至 1 萬 5 千人。

小結：

本圖為 1942 年 3 月 16 日德軍針對太平洋戰區繪製之日軍與盟軍兵力配置（以梯形投影呈現），顯示了第一次緬甸作戰（1942 年 3 月）日軍的部署以及前進路線、中國遠征軍（5. u. 6. chinesische Armee）入緬等情形。緬甸方面日軍軍長為飯田祥二郎，正式番號為第 15 軍，本地圖稱之為「飯田軍」。可以看到日軍取道泰國進攻緬甸，計畫先攻擊仰光再向北進攻。國軍則已部署在泰緬邊境，同時預測有南下的行動。

（二）RH 2/754-K

時間：1942 年 3 月 1 日。

地圖類型：日本陸軍兵力配置圖（含飛行機數量）。

地圖描述：

　　1. 個別說明

（1）　滿洲：24 個步兵師、10 個鐵路守備隊（Bahnschutz-Abt.）、1 個獨立步兵團、2 個騎兵旅、2 個摩托化機械化旅、2 個裝甲旅、4 個獨立裝甲團、1,300 架航空機。

（2）　華北：8 個步兵師、11 個獨立旅、2 個騎兵旅、2 個裝甲團、1 個獨立裝甲營。

（3）　華中：9 個步兵師、8 個獨立旅、1 個裝甲團。

（4）　廣東：3 個步兵師、1 個獨立旅、2 個獨立裝甲營。

（5）　海南：1 個步兵師（？）。

（6）　中國派遣軍總計：20 個步兵師、20 個獨立旅、2 個裝甲旅、3 個裝甲團、3 個獨立裝甲營、850 架航空機。

（7）　朝鮮：3 個步兵師。

（8）　日本：11 個步兵師、2 個騎兵旅、1 個裝甲團、1,150 架航空機。

（9）　菲律賓：3 個步兵師、1 個獨立旅（？）、1 個裝甲團（？）、1 個獨立裝甲營（？）。

（10）法屬印度支那：1 個步兵師。

（11）南洋增援：3 個海軍陸戰隊旅、1,200 架航空機。

檔案 2【RH 2/754-K】：日軍推定軍力及分布（1942 年 3 月 1 日）

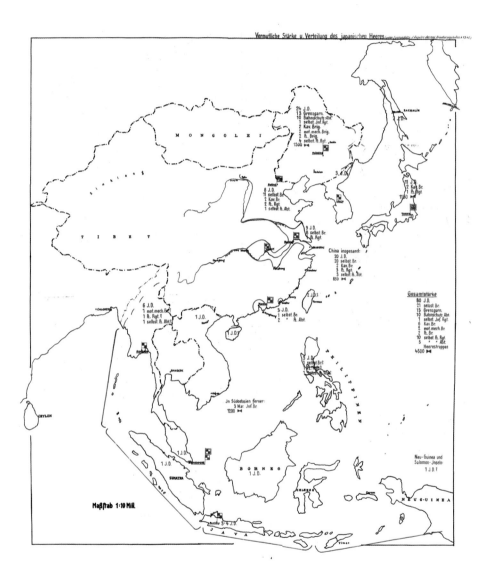

資料來源："Vermutete Stärke und Verteilung des japanischen Heeres (unter Zugrundeleg. d. Angaben des russ Orientierungsheftes v.1.3.42)," *Militärische Lage in Fernost, Austausch militärischer Erfahrungen mit Japan u.ä.*, Bd. 2, BArch, RH 2/754-K, BArch-MA.

（12）緬甸：6 個步兵師、1 個摩托化機械化旅（？）、1 個裝甲團
　　　　（？）、1 個獨立裝甲營（？）。

（13）馬來亞：1 個步兵師。

（14）婆羅洲：1 個步兵師。

（15）蘇門達臘：1 個步兵師。

（16）爪哇：3 至 4 個步兵師。

（17）新幾內亞與索羅門群島：1 個步兵師（？）。

2. 整體說明：80 個步兵師、21 個獨立旅、13 個邊防軍（Grenzgarn.）、
　　10 個鐵路守備隊、1 個獨立步兵團、6 個騎兵旅、2 個摩托化機械化
　　旅、2 個裝甲旅、10 個獨立裝甲團、5 個獨立裝甲營、陸軍 4,500 架
　　航空機。

小結：

　　本地圖為德軍繪製的日軍東亞兵力配置之地圖。與其他地圖不同，並未
繪出盟軍兵力。因此僅能看到日軍方面的部屬。在緬甸方面則以虛線表示為
占領圈之未定界。由此圖可看出緬甸戰區在日軍總兵力比約占 7.5%，在南
洋日軍中則占 42.8%。

（三）RH 2/1812-K（之 1）

〔按：原件無序號，因本件含兩張圖，為利區別而加〕

時間：1943 年 2 月 14 日。

地圖類型：陸軍兵力配置圖。

地圖描述：

1. 日軍兵力

（1）　滿州

　　A.關東軍：3 個軍、9 個師、2 個裝甲師；另外至少 5 個滿洲國師。

　　B.邊防部隊：2 個軍、6 個師。

（2）　中國

A.華北駐屯軍：5 個軍、10 個師、1 個騎兵師、4 個步兵師、1 個獨立摩托化團、6,000 蒙古人。

B.華中：3 個軍、14 個步兵師或步兵旅。

C.國民政府（汪政權）。

D.廣東：4 個師、2 個步兵旅。

（3）　朝鮮：3 個師及訓練部隊。

（4）　日本、臺灣：18 個師。

（5）　菲律賓：至多 2 個師。

（6）　法屬印度支那：小於師級兵力。

（7）　泰國：1 個團（曼谷）。

（8）　緬甸：6 個師。

（9）　馬來亞：1 個師。

（10）蘇門達臘：2 個師及預備部隊。

（11）婆羅洲：1 個加強團。

（12）爪哇：預備部隊（高於師級兵力）。

（13）帝汶：2 至 3 個師。

（14）拉包爾：2 至 3 個師。

（15）基斯卡島：1 個加強團。

2. 盟軍兵力

（1）　印度：8 個英國師、2 個中國師、350 架飛機。

（2）　國軍：150 萬人、350 架飛機。

（3）　新幾內亞：2 個美國師、2 個澳洲師、300 架飛機。

（4）　澳洲：11 個澳洲師、2 個美國師、500 架飛機。

（5）　瓜達康納爾島：5 個美國師、1 個美國陸戰隊師、1 個紐西蘭師、250 架飛機。

（6）　斐濟群島：2 個美國師、1 個紐西蘭師、100 架飛機。

（7）　蘇軍：20 個蘇聯師、4 個蘇聯旅、2 個蒙古騎兵師；5 個裝甲旅、3 個摩托化旅、1,000 架飛機。

小結：

　　本圖為 1943 年 2 月 14 日德軍針對太平洋戰區繪製之日軍與盟軍兵力配置圖。其時已占領仰光，並與英軍、國軍在緬甸交戰中。太平洋部分以虛線大略劃出日軍占領區域。

（四）RH 2/1812-K（之 2）

〔按：原件無序號，惟因本件含兩張圖，為利區別而加〕

時間：1943 年 2 月 14 日。

地圖類型：陸軍兵力配置圖。

地圖描述：

1. 日軍兵力：總兵力約有 71 個步兵師、21 個獨立旅、6 個騎兵旅、4 個裝甲師、2 個裝甲旅、16 個本土預備師。

（1） 滿洲：24 個步兵師、2 個騎兵旅、2 個裝甲師、2 個裝甲旅；另有 16 萬 5 千人滿洲部隊。

（2） 朝鮮：3 個步兵師。

（3） 南庫頁島：2 個步兵師。

（4） 日本：16 個預備師、2 個騎兵旅。

（5） 華北：7 個步兵師、11 個獨立旅、2 個騎兵旅。

（6） 華中：11 個步兵師、8 個獨立旅；另有 20 萬南京（汪政權）部隊。

（7） 臺灣：2 個步兵師。

（8） 華南：2 個步兵師、1 個獨立旅。

（9） 法屬印度支那：1 個步兵師。

（10）緬甸：4 個步兵師、1 個裝甲師；3 個步兵師、1 個裝甲師；另有 5 至 6 萬泰國部隊。

（11）馬來亞：1 個步兵師。

（12）菲律賓：2 個步兵師、1 個獨立旅。

（13）蘇門答臘：2 個步兵師。

（14）爪哇：1 個步兵師。

（15）婆羅洲：薄弱占領軍。

（16）新幾內亞：4 個步兵師。

（17）瓜達康納爾島：2 個步兵師。

2. 盟軍兵力

（1） 紐澳地區兵力約有：

    A.澳洲軍：8 個步兵師、2 個騎兵師（？）、1 個裝甲師、1 個組建中的裝甲師、18 萬 6 千人預備役、民兵、國民防衛隊。

    B.紐西蘭軍：3 個師、4 萬 2 千人預備役與民兵、10 萬人國民防衛隊。

    C.美軍：4 個步兵師、不足 1 個師的裝甲部隊、海軍陸戰隊。

（2） 印度地區兵力約有：

    A.英軍：5 個步兵師、1 個裝甲師、1 個裝甲旅。

    B.印度軍：5 個步兵師、1 個獨立旅、1 個裝甲師、6 個組建中的步兵師、1 個組建中的裝甲師。

    C.錫蘭：1 個印度步兵師、1 個非洲步兵師（？）。

    D.中國：3 百萬中國部隊。

    E. 夏威夷：3 個步兵師。

（3） 蘇聯：10 個步兵師、4 個裝甲旅、1 個空降部隊；15 個步兵師、5 個裝甲旅、3 個步兵旅、1 個空降部隊；7 個步兵師。

小結：

　　本圖與前圖雖歸屬同一檔案，但地圖資訊完全不同。由於日軍占領區域較之前增加聖伊莎貝爾島及新喬治亞島，故其時間應在前圖之後。可以看到日軍已取得第一次緬甸作戰勝利，並占領緬甸全境、截斷滇緬公路。日軍在緬甸之兵力約占全體 9.86%、南洋之 40.9%，但裝甲兵力約占全體 40% 至 50%。

（五）RL 2-II/1850

時間：1943 月 10 月 3 日至 10 月 9 日。

地圖類型：日軍、盟軍空襲對方占領區、海戰損失圖。

地圖描述：

1. 東南亞戰區：地圖標示盟軍從英屬印度的達卡（Dhaka）進攻，一路經曼德勒往土瓦（Tavoy），一路則從阿恰布（Akyab）往仰光。但此次攻擊應僅是情勢預判，並無實際作戰行動。當時日軍方面執行「烏號作戰」（ウ号作戰），由第 56 師團在 10 月 3 日對中國遠征軍第 36 師展開怒江作戰，試圖驅離在怒江西岸的國軍。

2. 中國戰區：盟軍空襲河內（Hanoi）與九江。日軍方面則進攻重慶、桂林、泉州、建寧。但此次攻擊亦僅為情勢預判，並無實際作戰行動。雙方於此時也並無執行大規模作戰。

3. 太平洋戰區：索羅門群島海域上，日、美海軍爆發維拉拉維拉海戰（Battle of Vella Lavella）。根據日方戰報，日方損失 1 艘軍艦，美方在日方戰報上損失 5 艘軍艦，實際上日方損失 1 艘軍艦、美軍則是重傷 2 艘軍艦。在新幾內亞島方面，澳軍登陸新幾內亞的芬什港（Finschhafen），並建立機場開始空襲俾斯麥海域日軍。日軍地面部隊則試圖從新幾內亞的馬丹（Madang）奪回芬什港。另外盟軍也開始空襲威克島與班達海海域島嶼。

（六）RL 2-II/1851

時間：1943 年 10 月 10 日至 10 月 16 日。

地圖類型：日軍、盟軍空襲對方占領區、海戰損失圖。

地圖描述：

1. 東南亞戰區：盟軍地面作戰行動為中國遠征軍與日軍在怒江西岸交戰，而與地圖上盟軍從達卡往緬甸各地進攻的情勢較無關聯，故該情勢可能為日軍研判盟軍的進攻路線。至於日軍從占領的安達曼群島進

攻印度的馬德拉斯（Madras）與錫蘭島，因確認當時並無實際之作戰
行動，僅能研判其為日軍之作戰規劃。

2. 中國戰區：時值常德會戰（1943 年 11 月）前夕，在此之前雙方並無
大規模作戰。另外地圖顯示盟軍有空襲海防。

3. 太平洋戰區：盟軍從新幾內亞島的摩斯比港（Port Moresby）空襲日
軍的拉包爾（Rabaul）基地，而日軍試圖在新幾內亞發動對芬什港、
摩斯比港等地的進攻。而在索羅門群島海域上，盟軍損失 7 艘軍艦。
另外盟軍以澳洲為基地，往班達海方向進攻。至於在北太平洋部分，
地圖顯示日軍進攻阿留申群島的阿圖島，惟日軍在當地最後之攻勢為
當年 5 月底，故此處攻擊可能僅為規劃。

（七）RL 2-II/1854 [2]

時間：1943 年 11 月。

地圖類型：日軍、盟軍空襲對方占領區、海戰損失圖。

地圖描述：

1. 東南亞戰區：地圖顯示盟軍針對緬甸地區諸如曼德勒、仰光、密支那
等地展開總計 208 次空襲。日軍方面則對加爾各答（Kolkata）、英帕
爾（Imphal）等地執行總計 6 次空襲。而在地面作戰中，中國遠征軍
雖然在與日軍第 56 師團交戰中被迫撤離怒江西岸據點，但另一方面
國軍新編第 38 師從雷多（Ledo）出發，在 10 月底時與駐防胡康河谷
的日軍第 18 師團展開激戰。

2. 中國戰區：首先是越南方向，盟軍對河內、海防等地執行總計 8 次
空襲。然後是華南地區部分，盟軍從桂林對廣州、香港等地執行 6 次

2　此系列地圖均標有「大東亞地區」（Großostasiatischer Raum），日本在第二次世界大戰時
提倡「大東亞共榮圈」，範圍包括現今東亞、東北亞、南亞和大洋洲等地，德國聯邦檔
案館的軍事檔案館歸檔時，將其歸入「東南亞與太平洋地區」（Südostasien / Pazifik），
因而並列，謹此敘明。

空襲。日軍則從廣州執行 7 次空襲。至於正在進行常德會戰的華中地區，盟軍從重慶對常德、漢口、九江執行總計 8 次空襲。日軍則從漢口對重慶、常德等地執行總計 5 次空襲。另外一項特殊的作戰則是盟軍執行對新竹的空襲任務。

3. 太平洋戰區：盟軍從達爾文（Darwin）對班達海海域日軍占領島嶼展開總計 48 次空襲，日軍則從帝汶島對澳洲展開 2 次空襲。而新幾內亞方面，盟軍從摩斯比港對新幾內亞、拉包爾等地展開 115 次空襲。日軍從馬丹對新幾內亞展開 38 次空襲。而在索羅門群島戰役（Solomon Islands campaign）中，美日雙方分別對雙方展開 92 次與 42 次空襲。日方合計損失 4 艘，日方戰報顯示美方損失總計 46 艘軍艦，然而實際損失 1 艘。另外，盟軍在吉爾伯特群島海域發起對馬紹爾群島總計 29 次空襲，並執行馬金（Makin）、塔拉瓦（Tarawa）登陸作戰，日方則從馬紹爾群島對塔拉瓦執行 4 次空襲。

（八）RL 2-II/1855

時間：1944 年 1 月。

地圖類型：日軍、盟軍空襲對方占領區、海戰損失圖。

地圖描述：

1. 東南亞戰區：盟軍從英帕爾對曼德勒、密支那等地執行 18 次空襲。日軍則從密支那對印度境內與中緬邊境空襲合計 2 次。另外盟軍從吉大港（Chittagong）出發，對緬甸的阿恰布、仰光、曼德勒以及泰國的南奔（Lamphum）、曼谷等地進行合計 47 次空襲，日軍則從曼德勒對吉大港展開 3 次空襲。而此時東南亞地面戰線並無顯著變化，經判斷應為英帕爾作戰（Battle of Imphal）前夕（日軍於 1944 年 3 月發動作戰）。

2. 中國戰區：盟軍從南寧對海南島、河內展開 3 次空襲，日軍則從河內對雲南展開 1 次空襲。另外盟軍也從桂林對廣州展開 3 次空襲，日軍則從廣東對桂林、建寧等地展開 6 次空襲。另需指出盟軍也從建寧對高雄展開空襲。而此時中國戰區地面部分，從地面戰線判斷日軍已從常德會戰中撤離，而尚未爆發豫湘桂作戰（日軍於 1944 年 4 月展開一號作戰第一期的豫中作戰）。

3. 太平洋戰區：盟軍從達爾文對班達海海域日軍占領島嶼展開總計 35 次空襲。另外盟軍也從新幾內亞對卡維恩（Kavieng）、拉包爾等日軍駐地展開總計 77 次空襲。日軍則從新幾內亞的馬丹對芬什港等地展開 6 次空襲。除了新幾內亞外，盟軍也從新喬治亞島及周邊海域對拉包爾等地展開 42 次空襲，日軍則從拉包爾對新不列顛島等地展開 14 次空襲。根據日方戰報，盟軍總計在索羅門群島損失 21 艘各類型軍艦。至於在吉爾伯特群島海域方面，盟軍發起對馬紹爾群島總計 18 次空襲，日軍則從賈盧伊特（Jaluit）對塔拉瓦、布塔里塔里（Butaritari）執行 7 次空襲。

（九）RL 2-II/1857

時間：1944 年 2 月。

地圖類型：日軍、盟軍空襲對方占領區、海戰損失圖。

地圖描述：

1. 東南亞戰區：盟軍從英帕爾出發，轟炸密支那、曼德勒、泰國曼谷等地，總計 29 次。以及從吉大港出發，轟炸仁安羌、仰光等地，總計 19 次。至於日軍則是以曼德勒為基地，空襲中印邊境、加爾各答等地，總計 7 次。地面戰線方面並無變化，經判斷應為英帕爾作戰前夕（日軍於 1944 年 3 月發動作戰）；另外日軍也從安達曼群島基地，空襲錫蘭 1 次。

2. 中國戰區：盟軍以桂林為基地，轟炸越南河內、海防、海南島、東沙島等地，共 10 次。地面戰線則沒有變化，經判斷尚未進行豫湘桂作戰。

3. 太平洋戰區：盟軍從達爾文對班達海海域日軍占領島嶼展開總計 31
次空襲。新幾內亞方面則從芬什港往馬丹、海軍上將群島、卡維恩、
拉包爾等日軍據點空襲總計 58 次。日軍方面也從拉包爾空襲新幾內
亞東部及其周邊海域和布干維爾島。盟軍也在特雷熱里群島周邊海域
對拉包爾、布干維爾（Bougainville）、布卡（Buka）等地展開 57 次
空襲。另外盟軍也繼續從吉爾伯特群島海域對馬紹爾群島展開 24 次
空襲，以及從馬紹爾北方海域對威克島和夸加林環礁展開 8 次空襲。

（十）RL 2-II/1859

時間：1944 年 4 月。
地圖類型：日軍、盟軍空襲對方占領區、海戰損失圖。
地圖描述：

1. 東南亞戰區：1944 年 3 月 5 日英軍發動「星期四作戰」（Operation
Thursday），由欽迪特突擊隊（Chindits）空降戰線後方，進行特種作
戰。同時對密支那、曼德勒、仰光、曼谷等地進行空襲。

2. 太平洋戰區：美軍登陸中部太平洋的埃內韋塔克環礁（1944 年 2 月
17 至 23 日），並發動冰雹作戰（Operation Hailstone），空襲特魯克
群島（1944 年 2 月 17 至 18 日），同時在北部太平洋方面仍持續空襲
幌筵島、占守島、溫禰古丹島等地。

（十一）RL 2-II/1860

時間：1944 年 5 月。
地圖類型：日軍、盟軍空襲對方占領區、海戰損失圖。
地圖描述：

1. 東南亞戰區：日軍開始發動英帕爾作戰，由牟田口廉也（1888-1966）
將軍所指揮的第 15 軍下轄 3 個師團，向印度東部重鎮英帕爾進攻。
此在緬甸戰役中是一次相當大型且重要的作戰。並曾短暫將英軍圍困

於英帕爾,使得盟軍必須抽調駝峰航線的運輸機進行空中運補。同時英美空軍以達卡為基地,空襲進攻的日本陸軍,日本航空隊也針對英帕爾等地進行空襲。

2. 中國戰區:1944 年 3 月,日軍在此發動日本陸軍史上最大的一次作戰計畫:「大陸打通作戰」(日方正式名稱為「一号作戰」),動員 50 萬人、10 數個師團之兵力,作戰目標預計打通平漢線、粵漢線,並占領美軍航空基地。第一階段先從河北、湖北兩方面夾擊河南地區的國軍第一戰區,稱為「京漢作戰」(日方正式名稱為「コ号作戰」),中國方面則稱為「豫中會戰」。日軍同時空襲西安、桂林、南寧等地,以支援陸上作戰。中美空軍則空襲漢口、香港、海南島、法屬印度支那等地。

3. 太平洋戰區:美軍延續此前的作戰行動,在中部太平洋開始登陸,收復日軍占領的環礁。諸如登陸烏傑朗環礁(1944 年 4 月 22 日)、艾塔佩(Aitape)登陸戰(1944 年 4 月 22 日至 5 月 4 日),並空襲關島、特魯克群島、威克島等地。南部盟軍空軍也以澳洲、新幾內亞、俾斯麥群島為基地,持續空襲日軍占領區。

(十二) RL 2-II/1861

時間:1944 年 7 月。
地圖類型:海、空局勢及亞洲戰場敵我占領區。
地圖描述:

1. 東南亞戰區:日軍發動的英帕爾作戰此時已基本宣告失敗,自 6 月起自行退出,南方軍則遲至 7 月 2 日方正式下達終止作戰命令。另一方面,為打通中印公路,以中國遠征軍為首的聯軍亦於此時對密支那展開進攻。聯軍序列包含中國第 30 師、第 50 師、第 14 師,以及美軍麥瑞爾突擊隊(Merrill's Marauders)下轄之 3 個大隊。日軍密支那守軍則以步兵第 114 聯隊、第 18 師團殘部以及第 56 師團一部組成。

2. 中國戰區：此時中國戰區正進行長衡會戰，長沙此時已遭占領，衡陽保衛戰仍在進行中。美軍第 20 航空軍（XX Bomber Command）執行馬特霍恩作戰（Operation Matterhorn），於 6 月 15 日從成都起飛 B-29 空襲位於九州的八幡鋼鐵廠。

3. 太平洋戰區：6 月 19 至 20 日，美日海軍於菲律賓海進行決戰（日方稱作「マリアナ沖海戰」或「あ号作戰」），日軍大敗。盟軍已大致掌握新幾內亞一帶海域，並以達爾文港為基地進行空襲。美軍亦從阿留申群島方向空襲幌筵島、占守島、溫禰古丹島。

（十三）RL 2-II/1862

時間：1944 年 9 月。

地圖類型：海、空局勢及亞洲戰場敵我占領區。

地圖描述：

1. 東南亞戰區：日軍在英帕爾作戰遭遇毀滅性失敗，日軍主力第 15 軍損失過半，原先的 11 萬 5 千兵力最終僅 5 萬人撤出。由地圖判斷，此時參與英帕爾作戰之日軍正逐步向東南撤出，緬甸地區日軍大致轉入防守，英軍則自英帕爾方向緊追在後。日本第 33 軍發動「斷作戰」（斷作戰），試圖確保中印間連結中斷，該軍下轄第 2 師團及第 56 師團，第 33 軍的行動同時亦有支援松山、騰衝一帶日本守軍之目的，然而在作戰發動不久，兩地之日本守軍即於 9 月間遭中國遠征軍陸續殲滅。密支那此時已被盟軍攻克，以中國新 1 軍為主體的聯軍即將開始進攻八莫（Bhamo），八莫日本守軍約 1,180 人。盟軍以吉大港作為該區主要空軍基地，支援地面部隊追擊日軍，對英帕爾和八莫等地發動多次空襲，與之相對，日本空中武力僅能以曼德勒為基地向八莫守軍進行有限支援。

2. 中國戰區：為消滅桂林一帶活躍的美軍機場，日本第 23 軍發動桂柳會戰以期肅清該區機場。

3. 太平洋戰區：美軍正在進攻民答那峨島東方的貝里琉島；同時，美軍以塞班島為基地對周邊各島嶼之日軍展開空襲；美國航空母艦也對小笠原群島進行轟炸，或許是開始為未來登陸琉璜島做準備；新幾內亞一帶的日軍已被分割成數個小群，盟軍的腳步也開始靠近菲律賓一帶。

（十四）RL 2-II/1863

時間：1944 年 11 月，此圖描繪大致為 10 月分之局勢。
地圖類型：海、空局勢及亞洲戰場敵我占領區。
地圖描述：

1. 東南亞戰區：地圖之描繪主要以 10 月分的局勢為準，中國遠征軍正與日軍於龍陵一帶交戰，新 1 軍則對密支那—八莫一線展開攻堅。日軍第 2 師團自第 33 軍中調離，重新配置到緬甸南部，第 53 師團補充進日本第 15 軍。英國第 11 東非師及印度第 5 師繼續自英帕爾方向朝仰光推進。

2. 中國戰區：桂林尚未失陷，顯示桂柳會戰仍在進行當中。美軍以成都等中國境內基地起飛 B-29 戰略轟炸機轟炸滿洲、九州以及高雄等地，但受限於航程，自中國起飛的 B-29 還無法到達本州進行大規模轟炸。

3. 太平洋戰區：菲律賓戰役（Philippines campaign）開始，1944 年 10 月的雷伊泰灣海戰（Battle of Leyte Gulf）是此時太平洋戰區的主軸，值得注意的是地圖中有關雙方艦船損失紀錄與事實有相當大出入，雷伊泰灣海戰中日本海軍最後有生力量損失殆盡，美軍則僅受到輕微損失。

（十五）RL 2-II/1865

時間：1944 年 12 月。

地圖類型：海、空局勢及亞洲戰場敵我占領區。

地圖描述：

1. 東南亞戰區：日軍敗象已現，原先於緬北固守之防線遭陸續擊破，11
月下旬，日本第 15 軍（第 53 師團、第 15 師團）駐防曼德勒，第 33
師團則撤至更的宛河（Chindwin River）以東。12 月中旬，駐防八莫
之日軍向南撤出。日軍整體防線成環狀向南撤退。

2. 中國戰區：豫湘桂作戰結束，日軍基本達成戰略目標。成都的 B-29
活動開始減少，推測是受補給困難且航程受限影響，再者塞班島的
B-29 已開始對本州進行轟炸，成都的 B-29 相形之下重要性下降所
致。

3. 太平洋戰區：菲律賓戰役繼續進行。前述的雷伊泰灣海戰中日本海軍
力量受巨大打擊，但日方對自身戰果有過分樂觀的錯誤估計，開始由
奧爾莫克灣向雷伊泰島輸送支援（日方稱作「多号作戰」）並與美軍
交戰，即奧爾莫克灣作戰（Battle of Ormoc Bay），該戰及民都洛島戰
役（Battle of Mindoro；日軍的反擊稱作「礼号作戰」），最終皆由美
軍獲勝，針對呂宋島的攻堅戰此時也即將展開。

（十六）RL 2-II/1866

時間：1945 年 1 月。

地圖類型：海、空局勢及亞洲戰場敵我占領區。

地圖描述：

1. 東南亞戰區：戰線已向南推進至阿恰布—曼德勒一線，中印公路也已
於 1945 年 1 月 27 日打通，物資開始向昆明輸入。以英軍為主的聯軍
部隊繼續朝仰光方向進軍，中國第 14 師、第 22 師返回中國。

2. 中國戰區：豫湘桂作戰結束後，日本的中國派遣軍基本無力再發動攻

勢作戰，1945 年初之日軍基本採取守勢。

3. 太平洋戰區：菲律賓方面，1945 年 1 月 9 日美軍自呂宋島西部的仁牙因灣（Lingayen Gulf）開始登陸作戰，此時已占領南部的克拉克（Clark）。雷伊泰島已被美軍占領。塞班島上的美軍轟炸機開始針對日本本州進行較高頻率之轟炸，美軍航空母艦也繼續對小笠原群島進行空襲。